COOKING TO HOOK UP

COOKING TO HOOK UP

The Bachelor's Date-Night Cookbook

Ann Marie Michaels
and Drew Campbell

The Globe Pequot Press

GUILFORD, CONNECTICUT

Illustrations by Bunky Hurter
Text design by Nancy Freeborn

Library of Congress Cataloging in Publication Data

Michaels, Ann Marie.

    Cooking to hook up: the bachelor's date-night cookbook / Ann Marie Michaels and Drew Campbell.

        p. cm.

    ISBN 0-7627-2967-8

    1. Cookery for two. 2. Menus. I. Campbell, Drew. II. Title.

  TX652.M495 2004

  641.5'612—dc22

                2004047344

Manufactured in the United States of America

First Edition/First Printing

Acknowledgments

We'd like to thank:

Taylor Ball (Indie Guy); Phyllis Campbell (Progressive Girl); Esther K. Chae (Indie Girl); our project editor, Imee Curiel (Progressive Girl); John "Otter" Davis (Gourmet/Indie Guy); Chris Durmick (Progressive Guy); Catherine Forester (Progressive Girl); Vivi Friedman (Gourmet/Indie Girl); Steve Halasz (Indie Guy); our editor, Megan Hiller (Progressive Girl); our fab illustrator, Bunky Hurter (Uptown then Indie then Party then Career then Girl Next Door then Granola Girl); Kyle Johnson (Gourmet/Indie Guy); Lara Mai Landa (Indie Girl); Amy Michaels (Academic/Gourmet Girl); Dr. Barbara Michaels (Academic/Gourmet Girl); Christopher Mur (Athletic/Guy Next Door); Jennifer Nash (Indie Girl); Chris Nordling (Academic/Indie Guy); Marcello Picone (Gourmet/Indie Guy); Maria Pumilia (Granola Girl); Tina Pumilia (Granola/Indie Girl); Larry Sisson (Academic/Gourmet Guy); Amanda Sutherland (Girl Next Door); Cheryl Sutherland (Party Girl); Kitty Sutherland (Girl Next Door); Stacey Sampo (Career/Indie Girl); and Valerie Campbell (Progressive Girl).

I'd like the chef salad, please, with the oil and vinegar on the side. And the apple pie a la mode. But I'd like the pie heated, and I don't want the ice cream on top, I want it on the side. And I'd like strawberry instead of vanilla if you have it. If not, then no ice cream, just whipped cream, but only if it's real. If it's out of a can, then nothing.

—Sally Albright in **When Harry Met Sally**

I read recipes the same way I read science fiction. I get to the end and I think, "Well, that's not going to happen."

—Jack Handy, **Saturday Night Live**

Contents

Introduction

Why Cook for a Date?

**You had me
at bruschetta.**

—Valerie, Drew's girlfriend (now wife)

Think back five million years. Remember how good it felt to come back to the camp with your kill over your shoulder? Remember the feelings of belonging and community as you watched that antelope being ceremoniously spitted and cooked? How you felt you were playing a part in the eternal movement of the cosmos, just by providing for the culinary needs of others?

Trust us, that's how you felt. Cooking a meal for someone is the equivalent of starting your own little tribe, only without the grass skirt and the bone through your nose. It's all about home and hearth. Cooking is a basic, primal, human activity, and when you do it for someone else, you are speaking to her in a universal language. You are communicating at the level of basic needs and shared struggle against the elements.

Life is simpler in the digital age. What with salad spinners and microwave ovens, cooking is easy in our modern times. Well, most of it is, anyway. Really complicated gourmet cooking is hard. Shopping for exotic, Indonesian spices and marinating chicken livers for three days in a secret sauce made from a recipe brought back from the Crusades is hard. Face it: Julia Child was famous for a reason. She was a genius, every bit as practiced and talented as Rembrandt or Michael Jordan. But cooking—basic, tasty, putting-food-on-the-table cooking—is easy, fast, and rewarding. And, minute-for-minute, cooking

1

someone else a meal is the fastest, most efficient way to give her the message "I care about you," or at least, "I am very interested in having you spend the night."

We can firmly state that any woman will be more impressed with a quality home-cooked meal than with an expensive restaurant one. Women will always choose men with wooden spoons over men with Gold Cards (unless you're in Los Angeles).

Why? Because it's dead sexy. Drew's wife, Valerie, was succinct after their first date. "The flowers were nice," she said, "but you had me at bruschetta."

The bottom line is: You don't need to understand eggplants at the cellular level to make a good meal. You don't have to shop for hours or have a huge stock of ingredients or follow complicated directions. What you need is a small supply of tools (all of which you can score at the discount store of your choice), a dozen mostly nonperishable staples, and a few minutes after work to grab ten items at the express lane.

Of course if you really want to go further, that's wonderful. It would gladden our hearts to see you catch the cooking fever and broaden your knowledge beyond this book. We'll even provide some extra tips, labeled "Bonus Points," should you want to embellish the recipe beyond the basics. But those are extra, optional, and voluntary. Let's get you into the kitchen first.

Every menu in this book is a complete meal, entree to dessert to beverage, using the basic list of utensils that we provide. With the exception of the Gourmet Girl meals, none of them will take more than an hour to prepare, and most of them have a fifteen-minute break built in so you can get the laundry off the couch, make the bed, and otherwise prepare your home for a romantic visitor. Don't skip the "Preparing the House" section, and remember, cleaning the bathroom is *critical*.

If you are still cooking when she arrives, you can even ask her to help. Cooking together is another great way to bond. Make sure that you pay attention to the introduction to each Girl as well. We list suggestions that can make the difference between a washout and the kind of night that makes you want to start keeping a journal. Many men do not understand the importance of detail when it comes to women. Women notice what is on the coffee table, on the stereo, and on your feet. And whether your bathroom is clean. Did we mention that cleaning the bathroom is *critical*?

So head out to the mall and pick up whatever utensils and pans you don't already have. Then put the twelve staple items in your pantry and go find someone who makes you want to write bad checks and be crazy. Invite her over and hit the grocery store express lane. In no time, you'll be gathered around your modern-day hearth, cooking dinner and gettin' busy.

How to Use This Book

Casanova, arguably the most successful seducer in history, had a simple philosophy: Get to know the woman, find out what she lacks, and provide it. If she sought adventure and romance, he would sweep her away to a remote castle. If she needed lofty ideals and friendship, he became her bosom companion, confidant, and philosopher. If her life was too perfect and serene, he would throw a wrench into it.

This sort of approach is time-consuming and mentally challenging but, as Casanova's romantic résumé proves, it is well worth the effort.

So, okay. You're smitten. Admit it. You've seen that one girl in the office, at the Starbucks, in your building, wherever, and you've decided that she's *the one*. You may not be choosing wedding china yet, but you've at least decided that you'd like her to think of you as a solid possibility.

Having reached this stage of infatuation, most guys turn away. Most guys assume that she's not interested, or she's above them, or she needs a guy with more money, or that she is, naturally, already taken. A girl like that? Me? Pass me a beer, bro.

The fact of the matter is that you may not have a bunny's chance in a dog pound. But the other fact of the matter is that you may have much more than a chance. You may be able to write this one up in your memoirs, because right here in these pages, we're going to give you the keys to the castle.

Your grandmother said that the way to a man's heart is through his stomach, but that advice actually crosses genders. Seduction through food is a time-tested technique. However, and this is the big *however,* you must choose the right food, the food that works for her, the particular forkful that makes her sit up in her chair, look at you in an entirely different way, and say, "You know, I never noticed that you have such classic features . . ."

Food—the *right* food—can do that.

And how do we choose the right food? By watching, listening, and paying attention to her. Here's a news flash, guys: Women are different. Women come in every color of the rainbow and every note of the orchestra, so, rule one: Pay attention. Take note of her interests, her politics, her culture, and her conversation. What is she wearing? Saying? Watching? Empirical observation is required, so proceed scientifically. Take notes.

Getting the dope on your girl doesn't just mean watching what she does, though. You also have to delve into her motives. The Progressive Girl may make homemade popcorn balls at Christmas because she wants to avoid crass commercialism. The Indie Girl might make them, too, but for an entirely different reason: She loves '50s kitsch! She may be dyeing them blue for her poodle-skirt-and-Blue-Elvis Christmas party. The Girl Next Door makes them because her mom always did, while the Gourmet Girl special-ordered Hopi Indian popping corn from a gourmet Web site and added dried cranberries and pistachios. Don't just watch what she does—watch *why* she does it.

Use the chapter intros to hone in on which girl you are dealing with, then choose a meal that will knock her stockings off (for starters). Don't stop with the menu, though. The food is one part of an ever-expanding circle of culture, clothes, decor, media, music, and conversation. You have decisions to make and preparation to do if you want to get to our last chapter, "So You Got Lucky." Men sometimes chafe at the notion that they have to put in time on things like these to impress a potential lover, but the rewards are worth it. Haven't had much luck with the ladies lately? Wanna know why?

Many women may object to being pasted into one of ten categories, and some actually fit into more than one. See the section on "Dealing with Hybrids" for tips on handling multicategory dates. Don't be afraid of making mistakes, though. Unlike most other parts of life, in romance, guys get points for trying.

We wrote this book to help you plan and pull off a splendid evening of dining in, which, when followed appropriately, could be the start of something big. Following directions, however, is key. So here are directions on How to Use This Book:

Get to Know the Girl

Use the chapter intros to identify which girl you are planning on hosting.

Stock the House

See "Twelve Staples" in the next section, Part One, for the short list of staple items that you will need to have on hand to make any meal in this book.

Choose the Meal

Once you have identified your date's category, read through the meal intros to find the one that works best for you. Note that some take more time and preparation than others.

When you make the date for dinner, make sure you ask if there's anything she doesn't eat. God forbid you find out about her peanut allergy in the emergency room.

Prepare Your Place

Read "Preparing the House" in Part One for tips on making your home date-friendly. Then, read the appropriate chapter intro for information on decor, music, and coffee-table magazines. This process may take a little time, so we recommend doing it before the day of the date. The whole ditch-it-all-in-the-closet thing was funny in college. Now, not so much.

Shop the Express Lane

Every single meal in this book can be prepared with ten or fewer ingredients (not counting staples), so you can drop through the express lane on the way home from work. Note that the Gourmet and Uptown Girl meals, although they also have ten or fewer ingredients, may require more than one day's preparation.

Hit the Liquor Store

Most meals have a suggestion for a liquid libation. Read the "For the Love of the Grape: A Basic Wine Primer" in Part One beforehand so you will not have your thumb in your mouth at the liquor store. Some Girls drink more than others—the Granola Girl or Athletic Girl, in particular, aren't big boozers—and some may not drink at all. Some Girls will closely watch the brands you pick, while some—the Girl Next Door, for example—may not give a rat's tail. Read your Girl's chapter intro for guidance.

Don't Forget the Flowers

Each chapter intro has a suggestion about which flowers to buy, so stop by the florist on your way home as well. Follow the guidelines in "Preparing the House" in Part One for displaying them.

Before She Arrives

We have given you a specific time for each thing you have to do before she shows up. Do *not* freak out if you are a little ahead or behind. This is dinner, not a missile launch. For most menus (unless you are serving tea, a picnic lunch, or dessert only), these times are based on having dinner at the very civilized time of 8:00 P.M. If you are shooting for a different hour, alter the times accordingly. Note that for the Gourmet Girl, these times sometimes start several days in advance.

Before she arrives, we prepare sauces, chop vegetables, marinate meat, and so on. These are the time-consuming, inglorious parts of the meal that you are better off doing without the added pressure of her presence. Follow the steps in order. You will be switching back and forth between various parts of the meal, but that is necessary. Remember, timing is everything. The biggest trick to throwing a dinner party, whether for two or twenty, is getting everything to the table at the right moment. That's why some things need a head start. Also, make sure you wash your hands and any utensils after handling raw meat. Food poisoning isn't even romantic when you are on vacation.

After She Arrives

We almost always leave a portion of the cooking to be done after she arrives. This isn't just a timing thing—this is part of the overall effect. You want to know what sexy is? Sexy is a guy who gives a woman a glass of wine and listens to her talk about her day while he chops carrots. With a routine like that, you could be a gawky Nintendo nerd with a penchant for saving old *Mad* magazines and still get a nod from a classy gal.

Bonus Points

Every meal has one or more "Bonus Points" listed at the end. These are not essential items, just extra added attractions that will push your meal beyond the one-to-ten scale and take it all the way to eleven. Bonus points generally require buying an extra ingredient or tool, so take note of that before you go shopping.

So You Got Lucky

You are *the man.* You pulled it off. You brought together that blend of personality and preparation that made the magic happen. Don't let the mood slip away, though. The "So You Got Lucky" chapter at the end of Part Two contains ten different recipes for breakfast— one per Girl. If confidence is high, include these items in your shopping list the day before. If the whole thing is a surprise, you can always tell her you are going out to fetch her a latte, then stop at the grocery store on the way back.

part one

Getting
Ready to Cook

Materials: Twelve Staples to Have at All Times

There are twelve staples that you must have in your kitchen all the time. Most are nonperishable and can gather dust on top of the microwave until you are ready. Some need to be renewed every couple of weeks or so.

1. GARLIC
2. ONIONS
3. BUTTER
4. EGGS
5. MILK
6. FLOUR
7. SUGAR
8. SALT
9. PEPPER
10. BALSAMIC VINEGAR
11. OLIVE OIL
12. VEGETABLE OR CHICKEN BROTH

Let's break it down.

1. Garlic

You can buy prepeeled and pressed garlic in a jar, but in general we don't recommend it. For the Gourmet Girl, this is a fatal error. Buy a couple heads of garlic—they last a long time and do not need to be refrigerated. As you break the heads open, they will separate into individual cloves. Peel the cloves before you use them. Then you can chop them up in a food processor, crush them with a chef's knife (just put the flat side of the knife over the clove and give the knife a good whack with your fist), or use a garlic press.

2. Onions

White or yellow, it doesn't really matter. We may occasionally call for another type, but that will be under "To Buy." Keep the onions anywhere that's dry. But don't store the onions with potatoes, like your mother did. The onions will cause the potatoes to sprout.

3. Butter

This will last a long time, provided you keep it covered and in the refrigerator. Don't leave it out on the counter. You can get away with margarine with some of the lower-risk Girls, but why? Buy real, *unsalted* butter. Using anything other than unsalted butter with the Gourmet Girl is a major faux pas.

4. Eggs

Keep a dozen on hand. Eggs last about six weeks in the refrigerator. Egg cartons usually have "sell by" dates stamped on them. If you're dating a Gourmet Girl or lacto-ovo Granola Girl, you'll want to go with the free-range variety (the chickens are not kept in cages and the eggs tend to taste better).

5. Milk

Keep a half gallon of 2 percent milk around—you will need it. It's the most middle-of-the-road variety. Make sure you check the "sell by" date before you head for the grocery store. If there is any doubt about its vintage, get a new one. One tip: Keep a box of powdered milk or a carton of soy milk in the cupboard. Both of these will suffice in an emergency, although your food will taste a little different.

6. Flour

Get "all-purpose" flour, not "self rising" or something else. A five-pound bag is fine. You can get organic flour for the Granola Girl. If you're dating the Gourmet Girl, try to get King Arthur's. It's the best.

7. Sugar

This one is pretty basic. Just remember, when we call for sugar, we are talking about white granulated sugar. If you need brown or powdered sugar, we will call for it in the "To Buy" list. Get a five-pound bag. It will keep until death do you part.

8. Salt

What can we say? Get some salt. Gourmet Girls love kosher salt and sea salt.

9. Pepper

You can get regular pepper and fill up a pepper shaker, but we highly recommend buying a pepper grinder and black peppercorns. Besides the improved taste, you get to do that cool thing where you bring the grinder to the table and ask her if she wants some on her salad.

10. Balsamic Vinegar

Balsamic is the darker, more flavorful variety of vinegar. There are other kinds of vinegar (e.g., red wine, white, or rice vinegar), but we will let you know if that is what we want you to use by listing it as an ingredient "To Buy."

11. Olive Oil

The most staple of the staples. It is more digestible than other oils and can be used in a wider variety of recipes. Olive oils are ranked by acidity, from the least (extra-virgin) through the moderate (virgin or just "olive oil") to the most (refined). This is not a question of quality but of taste. For our purposes, get virgin or plain olive oil.

12. Vegetable or Chicken Broth

Vegetable or chicken broth comes in a can, in a cardboard carton not unlike a milk carton, or as bouillon cubes that have to be dissolved in boiling water. All three options work, so just pick your favorite. Stick with vegetable broth for the Granola Girl.

Tools: Essential Equipment and Utensils

Drew's dad used to say, "Proper tool for the proper job," and it still holds true, whether you are building a set of shelves or making pot roast. Actually, the two tasks are more similar than you might think. You prepare the wood by sanding and drilling, just as you prepare your food by cleaning and chopping. You attach the wood with nails or screws, just as you combine ingredients with mixers and bowls. Your woodworking project needs setup time for the glue to take hold, then oil or stain to bring out the beauty of the grain. Food needs cooking time, then glazing, garnishes, and presentation. In both cases craftsmanship is important, but the right tools are key. Remember, every good job needs lubrication, too, so we've included a few bartender tools.

You won't need everything on this list for every recipe, so don't worry about taking out a second mortgage to equip your kitchen (especially if you don't have a first one). You can accumulate the power tools and cooking tools as you need them. It helps to read the recipe ahead of time to see what you need. Make sure that you have the other categories (especially "Bar" and "Emergency") covered before you start.

Note that the Gourmet Girl menus require special tools beyond what is on this list.

Measuring Tools

1 set of metal mixing bowls: small (approx. 1 quart), medium (approx. 2½ quarts), and large (4–6 quarts)
1 set of measuring spoons
1 set of measuring cups
1 liquid measuring cup (2-cup size is handy)

Cutting Tools

1 vegetable peeler
1 large chef's knife
1 serrated bread knife
1 paring knife
1 cutting board

Power Tools

Small food processor
Electric hand mixer
Toaster or toaster oven
Microwave oven
Coffeemaker

Preparation Tools

1 can opener
1 grater
1 salad spinner
1 rolling pin
1 garlic press
1 metal spatula
1 rubber spatula

Preparation Tools (continued)

1 slotted spoon

1 wooden spoon

1 wire whisk

1 colander (strainer)

1 roll of paper towels

1 box Ziplock bags

1 roll of plastic wrap

Cooking Tools

1 timer (probably on your stove already)

1 roll of aluminum foil

1 oven-safe stockpot with cover

1 small (1-quart) saucepan with cover

1 medium (2- to 3-quart) saucepan
   with cover

1 large (4- to 6-quart) saucepan
   with cover

1 (8- or 10-inch) frying pan

1 (9-inch) square glass baking dish

1 (9x13-inch) glass baking dish

1 loaf pan (approx. 9x4 inches)

1 (9-inch) pie pan

1 baking sheet

1 basket steamer

1 pepper grinder

2 hot pads or oven mitts

Serving Tools

4 dinner plates (sometimes you will need
   extra for preparation)

4 salad plates (ditto)

4 soup bowls (double ditto)

2 sets of silverware (each set should
   include a dinner knife, spoon, soup
   spoon, dinner fork, and salad fork)

2 steak knives

4 cloth napkins

2 candlesticks and candles

1 tablecloth

1 vase for fresh flowers

Bar Tools

1 Melitta coffee filter holder and filters
   for coffeemaker

2 martini glasses

2 coffee mugs

6 wineglasses

2 water glasses

2 (pint) beer mugs

2 old-fashioned glasses (aka "rocks"
   glasses)

2 shot glasses

1 corkscrew/bottle opener

1 martini shaker

4 champagne glasses (for Uptown and
   Gourmet Girls)

2 brandy snifters (for Uptown and
   Gourmet Girls)

Emergency Tools

Basic first-aid kit

Fire extinguisher

Preparing the House

Step One: Remove All Indications of Previous Women

Men do not realize this, but females of every species mark their territory. Tigers do it by spraying musk on trees. Humans do it by "leaving things around." You may have to look closely to see if you have been marked. It is part of the secret language women use to communicate. Indications of female territorialism include:

- Chick rock CDs (i.e., Sarah McLachlan, Tori Amos, anything from Lilith Fair)
- Earrings (check between couch cushions and under the bed)
- Feminine toiletries (blonde highlights shampoo, mud masks, tampons)
- Hair scrunchies
- Pictures of ex-girlfriends
- Teddy bears or other stuffed animals (doesn't matter if it was a gift from your sister; she will assume it is from an ex-girlfriend)

Don't just think you can shove these things into a closet. She will look. Physically remove them from your house or apartment. If you really must keep them, consider a safe-deposit box. (Hide the key.)

Step Two: Get Rid of Anything Else Questionable

In addition to the feminine territorial marks listed above, you will also need to dispense with these other female-repelling items:

- Anything Dungeons & Dragons related
- Pornography (including pseudoporn—see Step Four regarding the bathroom)
- Pinups of supermodels
- Workout equipment in the living room (a weight set in the bedroom says "health conscious," but a weight set in the living room says "hairy back and mullet")

The point is not that you need to "feminize" your apartment. On the contrary, visiting a space that totally reflects your masculine personality is an adventure for her. Don't worry about accommodating her every need. If she moves in, she's going to change everything anyway. In the meantime our mission is just to make it as inoffensive as possible so as not to scare her away. A little clutter is okay—just focus on hygiene.

Step Three: Get Rid of Smells

You *must* get rid of weird smells. We highly advise having a trusted female friend step into your place and give it the "stink test." Trust us: Your nose isn't up to it. These heinous odors are like subatomic particles, invisible even to an electron microscope, yet clearly detectable by female nostrils. Think of your friend as a Geiger counter for smell. It could be rotting gym socks under your bed or an ancient ham sandwich in the closet, but whatever it is, chances are you've gotten used to it and don't even notice. Once your human stench meter gets a signal, locate the offending item and remove it to a Dumpster (not just the trash can). Check for leakage from the item, wipe it with a sponge, then fumigate the entire area with disinfectant spray. Lastly, open all the windows—even if it's snowing outside.

Step Four: Clean the Bathroom

Seven Things You *Must* Do to Your Bathroom Before You Have a Girl Over:

1. *Remove all potentially embarrassing items.* These include: 24-pack of condoms, anti-lice cream, hemorrhoid ointment, or old antibiotic prescriptions (female translation: possible STD).

2. *Remove all improper reading material.* Improper reading material includes any pornography or pseudopornography. Remove any magazine with a seminaked woman on the cover. Period. Also includes tacky bathroom humor books, anything from Spencer Gifts. Come to think of it, remove *all* reading material from the bathroom. She doesn't want to think about your marathon sessions on the throne.

3. *Remove all toiletries from the sink area.* The only things that should be there are a toothbrush holder, a glass, and a soap dish. However, do not go overboard. Putting flowers or candles in the bathroom will not increase your chances. The woman in question will either smell your agenda or think you're gay.

4. *Wipe all surfaces* with Windex, Comet, Formula 409, or some combination thereof. "All surfaces" includes shower and/or bathtub, shower door, sink area (including mirror and medicine cabinet), and the floor.

5. *Clean the toilet thoroughly both inside and outside* using any of the listed cleaners and a toilet brush. We highly recommend pouring toilet bowl cleaner into the bowl and leaving it for at least an hour. Make sure you cover the following areas: bowl, seat and lid, the undercarriage, the outside and top of the tank, and the little space of floor behind the toilet. She will notice. Don't bother cleaning the inside of the tank. If she looks there, she's neurotic and we don't recommend dating her anyway.

6. *Restock toilet paper and hang a set of clean towels.* Remember, toilet paper should feed over the top of the roll, not poke out from underneath. Note on towels: If they are not white, you can't tell if they are dirty by looking, so you need to smell them. This may need to be part of the "stink test" (see Step Three). Fresh towels are important in case she spends the night and wants a shower in the morning. Also, make sure there are hand towels on the rack next to the sink. She'll need towels after she washes her hands, which women do after they use the bathroom.

7. *If your bathroom has a rug and/or shower curtain, run them through the wash beforehand.* (By the way, if your shower curtain is plastic, don't put it through the dryer.) If you're short on time, at least shake the rug out the back door. It could very well be one of the possible offending smells (see Step Three).

Bathroom Bonus Points

If you're dating a Career Girl, put some Aveda products in the bathroom.
If you're dating a Granola Girl, make sure your shampoo isn't tested on animals.
If you're dating an Indie Girl, get a rubber ducky.

Step Five: Put on the Finishing Touches

Music

We've provided you with music suggestions for each type of girl, so a trip to the CD store may be necessary. Be advised, however, that she will scan your music collection and use the contents as an indicator of compatibility. Have something playing when she arrives, preferably on a multi-CD changer with the "random" function on. Music that shifts from artist to artist is preferable, allowing you to capitalize on those magic moments when you get the perfect song choice for whatever topic you are discussing. This phenomenon is completely random, of course, but, if you choose your tunes wisely and talk long enough, you are bound to get at least one good coincidence before the night is out.

Magazines

What is a coffee table for if not to display the fruits of your intellect? Here you can reference your hobbies, lifestyle, or politics with the appropriate magazines and newspapers. In each chapter intro we give suggestions for good magazines to set out, depending on your Girl's interests.

Flowers

It is never wrong to give flowers, but there is a right way and a wrong way. Meeting her at the door with a big bouquet, shouting "My love! My only!" is the *wrong way*. Getting some flowers, putting them in a vase on the dinner table, and *not saying a word about it* until she notices is the *right way*. By the way, if she ever mentions a preference for a particular flower, having that flower on the table when she arrives means *massive points for you, you smoldering hunk of rock star*. If she hasn't mentioned a preference, go with the suggestions we give in each chapter intro. Clip off the last inch of each stem (it makes them last longer) and put them in a vase with a tablespoon of sugar or the contents of the little packet they give you. Put the vase in the center of the table and under no circumstances make any reference to it at all. Nothing, and we're not kidding, no matter what you've had to drink. You'll blow the effect, like Bill Murray in *Groundhog Day* when Andie McDowell finds out he's been cataloging her favorite things, just to seduce her, and slaps him silly about two dozen times.

The Table

Take time to consider the layout and style of the table. Even if you are not hosting the Indie Girl, the dinner table is still the set on which this evening's story will be played out. It's worth the effort to make it right.

Place the two table settings at right angles to one another. (Never across from one another. Having the full width of the table between you creates an emotional distance that runs contrary to the objective of the date.) This creates a connection between you. Sitting at right angles allows you to turn slightly and address her in a relaxed fashion. You can also turn straight ahead and gaze into space for a moment as you consider the deeper implications of that fascinating thing she just said (and compose your witty response). Sitting at right angles also allows you to lean in conspiratorially and share an item in confidence, which is always a good thing, even if there are no prying ears around to avoid. It's the thought that counts. And the leaning.

Place settings may differ slightly from meal to meal, but at a minimum, your table should have the following:

- Tablecloth *or* placemats: Best results come when you make some effort to match the linens to the Girl—plain and simple for the Girl Next Door, offbeat for the Indie Girl, stylish and high quality for the Uptown Girl, etc. Make sure they are freshly laundered.
- Cloth napkins (ditto)
- Wine glasses
- Water glasses
- One set of silverware (knife, fork, and spoon) per place setting
- Centerpiece: the flowers you bought, displayed in a vase.

You will need extra silverware for additional courses called for in the Uptown and Gourmet Girl chapters. Add a second, smaller fork for a salad course, a soup spoon for a soup course and/or a dessert fork, if necessary. All the other Girls can keep the initial place setting and use it throughout the meal.

The arrangement of the silverware is a time-honored tradition, as proven by this childhood rhyme: "The silverware got in a fight. The knife and the spoon were right. So the fork left." (That's a good one to share with the Girl Next Door, by the way.) In any case, in accordance with the rhyme, you put the knife and the spoon to the right of the plate, with the knife closest to the plate. The fork goes to the left of the plate, on top of the folded napkin. If you are cooking for a Gourmet or Uptown Girl, you might want to investigate napkin-folding techniques online so you can put an elegantly folded napkin in the center of the plate instead. Everyone else can find the napkin under the fork. Additional knives, forks, and spoons can be added next to the main ones. The idea is that the Girl will start with the utensils farthest from the plate and work her way in. A salad fork is placed on the outside of the dinner fork (i.e., farther away from the plate), for example, because the salad course comes before the main course and will be eaten first.

The wineglass goes above the knife and the water glass goes above the fork. If you are using a salad plate, it goes above and to the left of the fork.

For the Love of the Grape: A Basic Wine Primer

I would wander up and down the aisle until some bottle shape or label seemed to intimate that its contents were the right stuff. After staring at this bottle for a moment or two, in a state of exquisite hesitation, I would seize it up, assume an expression of casual assurance, and bear it to the cash register.

—John Thorne, from his essay, "Knowing Nothing about Wine"

If you like baseball, you're going to love wine. Beer is more like football—simple, straightforward. Baseball, on the other hand, is more subtle and specialized. With beer you can simply shop by the brand; no need to worry about the year or rating. Guinness and Budweiser are the same, year in, year out. With wine, however, changes in weather can make this year's crop a gold medal delicacy while next year's is a varnish substitute. With its complex rating systems, myriad grape varieties, and detailed vintage charts, choosing a wine is much like comparing batting averages and fielding percentages when choosing a lineup for fantasy baseball. Baseball lovers, like wine connoisseurs, understand the appeal of details. And remember, hitting a home run with a girl is all about the details.

However, those of you die-hard football fans may be saying, "Come on guys, can't I just stick with beer? Is it really worth all this trouble to learn about wine?" Our answer: a resounding yes. And for one very important reason: There are few things more macklicious than a man who knows how to pick out a decent bottle of wine. It says "sophisticated" and "worldly"—in a nutshell, that you know what you're doing.

Oprah Winfrey said once that you can tell how good a man is between the sheets by how well he dances. We could say the same thing about choosing wine. Wine is sensual. As you would appreciate a lover, you can appreciate wine for its visual beauty, its perfumed scent, and, yes, its sumptuous taste. Everybody knows that wine (and a little candlelight) equals romance. It's the liquid equivalent of a dozen long-stemmed red roses.

Consequently, a little education is in order. Since we know you don't have time to read a 700-page tome written by Snobby McSnob Snob, we're gonna topline you. So study up, boys. Know your grapes, then swing away. You'll soon be making your way 'round the horn.

How to Choose a Decent Bottle of Wine

Of course it all comes down to taste. But you can't taste before you buy. So whom do you ask? Winemakers want to make a profit, and wine stores are eager to move inventory. The question is: Whom can you trust?

Answer: Ratings. Magazines like *Wine Spectator* are to wine what *Baseball Digest* is to America's game. Most publications use a 100-point system. Look for bottles with at least 90 points out of 100. Some liquor stores will even have them posted alongside the wines (although many will not; remember, they are in business to sell bottles—not educate you).

Don't want to go to the trouble of reading thousands of wine reviews just to be able to pick a decent chardonnay? We don't blame you. Here's a really great shortcut: Subscribe to Wine Pocket List (www.winepocketlist.com). They cross-reference all the various periodicals so you don't have to, then they list only wines that they rate B+ or above, and they list only bottles that are priced at $30 or less. You can either buy a subscription or the quarterly printed book. Go with the online version if you can, because you can make your own searchable, printable lists.

White vs. Red

In the Bond film *From Russia with Love,* Agent 007 catches the bad guy because the villain commits a faux pas and orders a Chianti (a red wine) with his fish. You know the old rule, "white with fish and chicken, red with meat." Well, things have changed. These days it's not about white vs. red. It's about light vs. heavy. Not how heavy it is to lift the glass off the table, but how it feels in your mouth—in other words, how robust or "big" it is. An entree with a more robust taste, like steak, needs a more robust wine, whether red or white.

According to this logic, you could drink a chardonnay with a filet of beef, because even though it's a white wine, a chardonnay is full-bodied enough to match the strong flavor of beef. Similarly, you could do a pinot noir with salmon. For a red wine, pinot noir is very light and will not overpower the fish. You can search online to find out which wines go with which foods, but if you follow the light-versus-heavy rule, you should be OK.

Incidentally, contrary to popular belief, white wine is not necessarily made from white grapes. All grape juice is colorless, so you can make white wine from white or red grapes. For red wine, the grape skins and seeds are left in the mix during the fermentation process. For white wine, they are left out. Rosé wine, which has been around in France for centuries, is somewhere between the two.

Oh, and one other thing about white versus red: Some people think it is only cool to drink red wine. They think white wine is passé. They are wrong. The only thing that is passé is drinking wine out of a box.

Grapes vs. Regions

In the United States we buy wine by the grape. We go to the store to buy a bottle of chardonnay, cabernet, sauvignon blanc—all names of grapes. In Europe they buy wine by the name of its place of origin—Bordeaux, Burgundy, Champagne, for example. They don't need to put the name of the grape on the label, because the region name already tells them what kinds of grapes they're getting. In France, for example, it is common knowledge that red Bordeaux is a blend of five grapes: cabernet sauvignon, cabernet franc, merlot, malbec, and petite verdot.

It gets a little more complex from here, however. Within each region, there are subsets and subsets within subsets. Some are as small as a single hillside. This is why you see bottles of French Bordeaux with interminably long (not to mention hard to pronounce) names, like Château Le Prieure, Saint Emilion, or Château Haut-Brion Pessac. And it isn't just the French who propagate this complexity. There are thirty-seven wine regions in the tiny little boot of Italy alone.

Why this obnoxious hyperclassification of regions? You can thank Charlemagne, the French monarch crowned in A.D. 771. He passed laws making it illegal to plant anything except certain kinds of grapes in certain areas of France. He wasn't pulling this stuff out of thin air, though; he was drawing on centuries of peasant know-how. The important thing is, at a very early age, French wine making became about maintaining *standards*. But you don't need to know about Charlemagne. You just need to be familiar with some of the important regions and the kinds of wine they are known for (since you can't buy French and Italian wines by the grape like we do here).

So here we go . . . In France, some of the best known are Alsace (produces sweet white wines like Germany's Rieslings and gewürztraminers), Bordeaux (the biggest and most famous wine region in the world), Burgundy, Chablis, Champagne, the Loire Valley (subsets are Sancerre and Vouvray), and Côtes du Rhône. In Italy, you have Emilia-Romagnia, Piedmont, Sardinia (known for dessert wines), Sicily, Tuscany (home of Chianti and the trendy Super Tuscans), Umbria (famous for Orvieto, a white), and Veneto.

There are a number of other parts of the world that also produce some wonderful wines. Here are a few, along with the wines they are famous for: Australia (Shiraz), Germany (sweet whites like Riesling), New Zealand (famous for its fantastic sauvignon blancs), Portugal (port, a dessert wine), Spain (Rioja, sherry, and Cava), and South Africa (known for pinotage, a cross between pinot noir and Cinsault).

Now that you have a grasp of the regions, here is a quick list of some of the wines you will encounter and how to pronounce them. (You'll notice that some are named for grapes and some are named for the region they came from.)

White Wines

1. Chardonnay ("shar-duh-NAY")
Chardonnay wins the popularity contest for whites worldwide. It was introduced to California in the 1930s but was not well known until the 1970s. It tends to be bigger than the sauvignon blancs and other whites. Flavors you may notice: apple, pear, peach, melon, citrus, honey, vanilla, butterscotch, and hazelnut. Chardonnays from California can taste buttery. They can also be very ''oaky'' because they are aged in oak barrels. The oak taste can overwhelm the other flavors.

2. Sauvignon Blanc/Fumé Blanc/Sanscerre ("sew-vin-yon BLAHNK"/"foom-may BLAHNK"/sahn-SARE")
A crisp, refreshing white wine. Tastes citrusy, floral, and grassy. Sancerre is the French region where sauvignon blanc grapes are grown, hence the French name for the wine. In the 1970s American Robert Mondavi came up with the name fumé blanc. New Zealand sauvignon blancs are some of the best in the world.

3. Reisling ("REES-ling")
A sweet German white wine. Flavors you may notice: peach, apricot, spice, floral.

4. Gewürztraminer ("guh-VERTZ-trah-meen-er")
A sweet, zesty, brisk white wine. *Gewürz* is the German word for ''spice.'' *Traminer* comes from the town in Italy, Tramin, where the wine originated. Flavors: roses, floral, lychee, cloves, nutmeg. It goes particularly well with Asian and spicy foods.

5. Pinot Gris/Pinot Grigio ("PEE-noh GREE"/"PEE-noh GREE-geeoh")
Called pinot gris in France and pinot grigio in Italy, it is dry and light as air. The perfect summer white. Tastes flinty, minerely.

6. Chenin Blanc ("SHEH-nihn BLAHNK")
A sweeter, more intense wine. From the French Loire Valley region, it forms the basis of wines such as Vouvray and Saumer. You may taste melon, citrus, peach, and spice.

7. Chablis ("shah-BLEE")

French Chablis wines are made from chardonnay grapes in the Burgundy region. Drier than other white Burgundies, these are some of the most fantastic wines you can imagine. You may taste minerals like flint, limestone, as well as vanilla. Chablis is especially good with oysters. (Note: Chablis is also a generic name for ordinary, inexpensive white wine made outside of France, which is absolutely not the same thing.)

8. Viognier ("vee-oh-NYAY")

Viognier is a difficult-to-grow, hence, rare white grape from the Rhône Valley in France. Very dry and floral. Flavors: peach, apricot, pear.

Red Wines

1. Cabernet Sauvignon ("ca-ber-NAY so-ven-YON")

"The big dog" of reds, and everyone knows it. It's the corollary to chardonnay. Like chardonnay, it's big (meaning "robust") and complex. Best when aged. Classic flavors include black cherry, raspberry, black currant, plum, and spice. You may taste hints of herb, bell pepper, anise, cedar, olive, mint, and even tobacco.

2. Merlot ("mer-LOW")

You can't go wrong with a merlot, that's what everyone says. It's the grilled cheese of wines. In French, the word *merlot* means "young blackbird," probably due to the dark color of the grape. Smoother and not as full-bodied as a cabernet, it doesn't need to age as long. Flavors you may notice: cherry, black currant, and mint.

3. Pinot Noir ("PEE-no NWAHR")

The pinot noir grape is the crème de la crème of grapes grown in the Burgundy and Champagne regions, and it has been grown in France for more than 2,000 years. Pinot noir is lighter-bodied and a bit woodier and earthier than other reds. Younger vintages taste fruitier, with flavors such as cherry, raspberry, plum, and strawberry. As they mature, pinots become more complex, with hints of figs, prunes, smokiness, truffles, chocolate, game, and violets. California and Oregon produce some of the very best.

4. Zinfandel ("ZIN-fen-del")

The quintessential Californian wine, zinfandel is big and spicy, and similar to a Spanish Rioja. Common flavors are cherry, plum, raspberry, pepper, and spice, with more subtle notes of earth, tar, and leather. Note: Zinfandel is not to be confused with "white zinfandel," the sweet blush wine that was so popular in the '80s.

5. French Bordeaux ("bore-DOH")

Bordeaux is the region in France where you find some of the best wines in the world—your Château Lafites and Mouton-Rothschilds. These wines are as good as it gets in the world of wine in terms of status and quality. As a result, they don't come cheap. Mature Bordeaux are an acquired taste, however. With descriptions like "sweet damson nose," "cigar box," and "sweaty saddle," you might feel like you need a master's degree to make sense of them. We're not saying you can't handle it; we're just saying you might want to get through kindergarten before you start working on that dissertation. (Note: There are also white Bordeaux.)

6. Burgundy ("BUR-gun-dee")

While Bordeaux is often called the "intellectual" wine, Burgundy is dubbed the "sensual" one. Made from the pinot noir grape, it is easier to grasp than Bordeaux, yet is still one of the best wines in the world. (Note: There are white Burgundies as well, such as Chablis.)

7. Beaujolais ("boh-zhoh-LAY")

If Bordeaux is the village elder of French wine, rich with complexity and wisdom, Beaujolais is the sassy teenager, fresh and bright but with very little depth. (It's actually a subset of the Bordeaux region.) Very light, sweet, and young, and meant to be drunk right away, it can be described as an explosion of fruit. Beaujolais Nouveau is a subset of Beaujolais that is aged for only seven to nine weeks and then released on the market every year on the third Tuesday of November.

8. Chianti ("kee-YAHN-tee")

There are lots of subsets of Chianti, the popular blend from Tuscany in central Italy. Chianti Classico is the best, and you can identify it by the black rooster on the label. You may taste plum, dried cherry, and a bit of spice. Aged Chianti, called riservas, has more complex flavors including chocolate, leather, smoke, fig, prune, and earth.

9. Barolo ("bah-ROH-lo")

This is the king of Italian wines, comparable to the French Bordeaux. Barolo wines take a while to age (and hence they are more expensive), but when they mature, they are robust and very complex, with characteristics of chocolate, earth, and truffles.

10. Petite Sirah ("peh-TEET sih-RAH")

Very robust and spicy and similar to a Zinfandel, this grape is grown mainly in California.

11. Sangiovese ("san-geeoh-VAY-seh")

A wine so old, it predates the Romans. The name means "blood of Jove." Very zesty and medium to full-bodied, Sangiovese is best known for providing the basis for many excellent Italian red wine blends like Chianti, as well as the Super Tuscans. Flavors include cherry, raspberry, spice, and anise.

12. Syrah/Shiraz ("sih-RAH"/"shih-RAHZ")

Originally from the French Rhône region, syrah is called shiraz in Australia. These wines age slowly. When young they are spicy with hints of tar and pepper. As they mature they develop fruity flavors of plums and black currants, and hints of smokiness.

Sparkling Wines

There are lots of kinds of sparkling wines. Some of the main ones are Champagne (the king of the sparklers, named after the Champagne region of France), Prosecco (from Italy), Spumante (also from Italy), and Cava (from Spain). Some people (OK, the French) feel that "Champagne" is always superior to "sparkling wine," but that isn't necessarily true.

Dessert Wines

Here are some of the dessert wines you need to be aware of: port (from Portugal), muscat (from France), sherry (the Oloroso version, from Spain; the other kinds of sherry, such as amontillado or fino, are actually aperitifs, to be served before dinner), and brandy (from France). Cognac and Armagnac are both brandies named after the French wine regions where they are distilled from wine. Like whisky or port, the longer the brandy is allowed to age in the cask, the smoother and more complex (and, obviously, more expensive) it becomes. From youngest to oldest: VO stands for very old; VSO, very superior old; VSOP, very superior old pale; and XO means extra old.

How to Open a Bottle of Wine (with a Corkscrew)

1. With a knife or other sharp implement (you can purchase a foil cutter), cut and remove the foil from the top of the bottle.

2. Put the tip of the corkscrew in the middle of the cork and hold the corkscrew straight up. Turn the corkscrew, pushing it down through the cork—but don't go all the way through the cork, just put the corkscrew about an inch into the cork.

3. Along the side of the corkscrew should be a metal hook (it might look like a regular screw cap opener). Pull the hook out and attach it against the lip of the bottle so that you can use it as a lever to pull the cork out of the bottle.

How to Open a Bottle of Champagne (or Sparkling Wine)

1. Pull off the foil to reveal the cork.

2. Place your thumb on the cork, and keeping the cork pointed away from you (and your guest), undo the wire cage.

3. Put a towel or dishcloth over the cork.

4. With one hand, hold the cork through the towel. With your other hand, slowly and gently turn the bottle (as opposed to the cork) until the cork is released. The release of the cork should be slow and should sound like a sigh, not a pop.

5. Remove the cork and pour.

One Last Tip

You can open a bottle of wine with any old corkscrew (although some are easier to use than others); however, keeping it fresh is another matter entirely. If you just stick the cork back in, the wine may oxidize and quickly go bad. Pretty depressing, especially if you've had the Gourmet Girl over and sampled a flight of five different vintages. The best tool we've found to remedy this is the Vacu-vin. It's a nifty little low-tech gadget that sucks the air out of wine bottles. Using the Vacu-vin, you can extend the life of reds to three days and whites to five. Very reasonably priced and available at cooking stores, we cannot recommend it highly enough.

 The Vacu-vin doesn't work with Champagne or other sparkling wines. You pretty much have to finish the bottle (we know, *bummer*).

The Risk Continuum

All women appreciate a guy making the effort to cook. Some of them, however, are willing to leave it at that: "A" for effort, and the rest of the evening is graded on a curve. Some women, however, will judge you on both effort *and* achievement. You can seriously damage your romantic chances by blowing it in the kitchen around these Girls.

The first rule of cooking for a date is: Know what you are getting into. If you are comfortable in the kitchen and ready for a challenge, then by all means, jump in and cook for the Uptown or Gourmet Girls. If you are a slacker chef who still eats dinner over the sink, you might want to restrict yourself to the Girls Next Door or the Party Girls. Let's face it: Some Girls are more high-maintenance than others. In order to judge your chances this evening, we put together this Risk Continuum to give you an idea of the difficulty of cooking for various Girls. We've listed them in order of difficulty, from low risk to high-wire act.

Low Risk

Girl Next Door. If you know where the kitchen is, the Girl Next Door is impressed. Go for it.

Party Girl. You can cook anything for the Party Girl, as long it's fun—or you've got plenty of drinks.

Athletic Girl. Keep it low-fat and you've got a good shot. It can get complex, depending on how strictly you adhere to her diet plan (40-30-30, Body for Life, Atkins, Weight Watchers, Carb Loading), but the meals themselves are not challenging. As long as you try to stay healthy, you'll still be in the running.

Medium Risk

Academic Girl. You can't go too far wrong with this Girl as long as you are well-read or can successfully fake it. Making obscure references to scholarly texts can overcome cooking mistakes. The risk comes from the possibility of being found out.

Progressive Girl. You will always get points for effort from the Progressive Girl, but she also wants to see that you know what you are doing. Her small-town values will always prevent her from pointing out that her big-city needs are not being met. She will judge you on the meal but never admit it.

Indie Girl. Like the Academic, the Indie Girl can be wooed by appropriate references, but those references must be artistic rather than scholarly. You can screw things up with the Indie Girl if you are too bland or too normal. The only true meal killer for the Indie Girl is mediocrity.

Granola Girl. More complicated than some others to cook for but not necessarily more expensive, difficult, or time-consuming. Due to her dietary restrictions, you must be cautious about your meal choices. Do your homework and find out what type she is, such as vegan, lacto-ovo, or macro. The meals themselves are not hard to make, but you can get dumped for choosing the wrong one.

High Risk

Career Girl. Career Girl meals are not necessarily more difficult than other Girls' meals; let's just say she has higher standards. To succeed with her, you have to prepare foods that say "success." You also have to have nicer furniture. It's all about appearing upwardly mobile. This Girl requires a higher financial investment than the lower-risk Girls, but there is such a thing as sweat equity with the Career Girl. It's okay if you don't have a lot of money, as long as you're ambitious and incredibly hardworking.

Uptown Girl. With the Uptown Girl, there is no sweat equity. There is no cheap date option here. You might need to save up for a few months. Or take out a loan. Excessive cash does not, however, guarantee entrance onto the Uptown Girl's list of potential suitors. Dating her is like being back in high school and pursuing the head cheerleader. This woman wants to date a member of the aristocracy. And don't think that being nouveau riche will automatically save you; the Uptown Girl may require money, but she also wants breeding and manners. The crystal is Waterford, the entree is filet, and the gift is from Tiffany's. Note that Downtown Boys may date Uptown Girls, but they must have roguish charm or a successful band.

Gourmet Girl. She is not only expensive but also knowledgeable and particular. Not only do you need bucks, you also have to know how to spend them on food. Anyone with a pile of cash can buy some caviar and a bottle of Dom, but it takes skill and knowledge to prepare Italian sbrisalona or caramelize a crème brûlée. When you can snatch the truffle from my hand, then you are ready to cook for the Gourmet Girl.

Dealing with Hybrids

We hate to break it to you, but most Girls will not fall neatly into one type. It can be very gratifying when you pick up the book, read through a few chapters, and zango! There she is, a perfect Academic or Indie or Uptown. What a rush. Off to the grocery store. More often than we like, however, we find women who straddle two categories. She's very politically active (Granola), but she loves Hal Hartley movies (Indie). She's from Old Money (Uptown), but she runs the New York City Marathon every year (Athletic). No matter what you try, you just can't get her to fit into a single category.

Welcome to the human race, bucko. Six billion individuals and no two any more alike than two snowflakes. This may lead you into despair. You thought we were going to solve all those problems, after all. Oh, quit your complaining—if women were easy, every guy would be Casanova. Look at it this way: It's more of an art than a science. Besides, when you are dealing with a hybrid, you are looking at an opportunity. Now you've got not five but ten recipes to choose from and ten chances to impress her.

If you've got a hybrid on your hands, it can be a bit tougher not only to identify her but to please her. Try digging a little deeper, especially if you suspect that she is part Athletic or Granola. These Girls often have dietary restrictions. Get more facts. If you can take her girlfriend into confidence, talk to her about it. A Girl's best girlfriend can figure this stuff out in no time flat. If the girlfriend is not an option and you are still unsure, ask the Girl. Straight up. "Would you rather have chicken in orange sauce or salmon in dill?" What you will lose in surprise, you will gain in peace of mind. If you are truly going in without any information (like you've got a blind date), go with a Progressive Girl meal. She is the most middle-of-the-road option, and her recipes will give you a fighting chance with almost any Girl.

If you think you've got a hybrid, the following list offers some suitable meal options. If your gut tells you to go a different way, however, do that. For one thing, you are probably right. For another, you can't blame us for getting it wrong.

Academic/Athletic
Pub Grub II: Welsh Rabbit vs. Rarebit

Academic/Career
Shakespeare on a Plate: A First Quarto Sampler

Academic/Girl Next Door

Pub Grub I: Pygmalion Bangers and Mash

Academic/Gourmet

A Chaucerian Feast: Chiknes with the Marybones

Papa's Tapas, or *A Moveable Feast*: Hemingway's Picnic of Spanish Tapas

Comfort Food Redux: New American

There's No Taste Like Foam: Spanish Surrealist

Academic/Granola

Papa's Tapas, or *A Moveable Feast*: Hemingway's Picnic of Spanish Tapas (just leave out the Spanish ham)

Pub Grub II: Welsh Rabbit vs. Rarebit

Any of the Granola Girl meals will work—decide based on what kind of vegetarian she is

---

Academic/Indie

Papa's Tapas, or *A Moveable Feast*: Hemingway's Picnic of Spanish Tapas

Like Water for Chocolate: Chiles en Nogada and Chocolate Flan

---

Academic/Party

Papa's Tapas, or *A Moveable Feast*: Hemingway's Picnic of Spanish Tapas

Fun-due: Cheese Fondue and Wine Coolers

Academic/Progressive

Shakespeare on a Plate: A First Quarto Sampler

Academic/Uptown

Afternoon Tea at the Savoy: Finger Sandwiches and Scones

A Meal Fit for a Queen (and a Duke): Beef Wellington and Cherries Jubilee

Shakespeare on a Plate: A First Quarto Sampler

Athletic/Career

Any of the Athletic Girl meals—depending on her diet

Midtown Power Dining: Ahi, Shrimp, Scallops, and Vegetables on a Bed of Baby Greens

Achieving Synergy: Spinach, Raspberry, and Goat Cheese Salad

Maximizing Your ROI: Low-Investment, High-Yield Sushi

Athletic/Girl Next Door

Any of the Athletic Girl meals—depending on her diet

Athletic/Gourmet

Comfort Food Redux: New American (don't serve dessert)

R is for Risotto, Radicchio, and Romance: Classic Italian (don't serve dessert)

Athletic/Granola

Any of the Athletic Girl meals—depending on her diet

Any of the Granola Girl meals—depending on her diet

Athletic/Indie

Tampopo: Spaghetti Western Udon Soup

Eat Drink Man Woman: Shrimp and Fortune Cookies

Any of the Athletic Girl meals—depending on her diet

Athletic/Party

Any of the Athletic Girl meals—depending on her diet

Athletic/Progressive

"Pesto, the Quiche of the '80s": Pesto Swordfish over Capellini

"I'll Have What She's Having": Salmon in Dill Sauce

Any of the Athletic Girl meals—depending on her diet

Athletic/Uptown

Sinatra at the Sands: Martinis, Oysters, and Filet Mignon

Dinner on the Yacht in the French Riviera: Champagne, Caviar, and Lobster

Any of the Athletic Girl meals—depending on her diet

Career/Girl Next Door

Bottom-Line Priorities: Just Dessert

Hot Dish: Midwestern Tuna Casserole

Career/Gourmet

R is for Risotto, Radicchio, and Romance: Classic Italian

Comfort Food Redux: New American

It's a Small World, After All: Pan-Asian Fusion

Midtown Power Dining: Ahi, Shrimp, Scallops, and Vegetables on a Bed of Baby Greens

Getting to the Top: Trump Tower of Polenta and Pork Tenderloin

Career/Granola
Achieving Synergy: Spinach, Raspberry, and Goat Cheese Salad
Bottom-Line Priorities: Just Dessert
Any of the Granola Girl meals—depending on her diet

Career/Indie
Maximizing Your ROI: Low-Investment, High-Yield Sushi
Bottom-Line Priorities: Just Dessert
Eat Drink Man Woman: Shrimp and Fortune Cookies

Career/Party
Bottom-Line Priorities: Just Dessert
Maximizing Your ROI: Low-Investment, High-Yield Sushi
Tex-Mex Fiesta: Fajitas and Spanish Fly Cocktails
Fun-due: Cheese Fondue and Wine Coolers

Career/Progressive
Bottom-Line Priorities: Just Dessert
Midtown Power Dining: Ahi, Shrimp, Scallops, and Vegetables on a Bed of Baby Greens
"What is Tiramisu?": Chicken Piccata and Tiramisu

Career/Uptown
Getting to the Top: Trump Tower of Polenta and Pork Tenderloin
Bottom-Line Priorities: Just Dessert
Afternoon Tea at the Savoy: Finger Sandwiches and Scones
Sinatra at the Sands: Martinis, Oysters, and Filet Mignon

Girl Next Door/Gourmet
Comfort Food Redux: New American
Some Like It Haute: Classic French

Girl Next Door/Granola
Vegan Thanksgiving: Tofurkey Dinner

Girl Next Door/Indie
Amélie: Le Fabuleux Dîner d'Amélie Poulain
Any Girl Next Door meal, but play up the kitsch—serve it on Hello Kitty plates

Girl Next Door/Party

Very Happy Hour: Bar Food and Screaming Orgasms

Spring Break South of the Border: Ultimate Nachos and Body Shots

Girl Next Door/Progressive

"Go to the Mattresses": Chicken and Artichoke Cacciatore

"What is Tiramisu?": Chicken Piccata and Tiramisu

Hot Dish: Midwestern Tuna Casserole

Girl Next Door/Uptown

A Meal Fit for a Queen (and a Duke): Beef Wellington and Cherries Jubilee

Gourmet/Granola

R is for Risotto, Radicchio, and Romance: Classic Italian (replace lobster tail with porcini mushrooms)

Gourmet/Indie

Amélie: Le Fabuleux Dîner d'Amélie Poulain

Like Water for Chocolate: Chiles en Nogada and Chocolate Flan

Eat Drink Man Woman: Shrimp and Fortune Cookies

There's No Taste Like Foam: Spanish Surrealist

It's a Small World, After All: Pan-Asian Fusion

Gourmet/Party

There's No Taste Like Foam: Spanish Surrealist

Gourmet/Progressive

R is for Risotto, Radicchio, and Romance: Classic Italian

Some Like It Haute: Classic French

Gourmet/Uptown

At the Villa in Avignon: Coq au Vin and Tarte Tatin

Some Like It Haute: Classic French

Granola/Indie

Tampopo: Spaghetti Western Udon Soup (replace shrimp with tofu)

Eat Drink Man Woman: Shrimp and Fortune Cookies (replace shrimp with tofu)

Lacto-Ovo: Greekin' Out

Granola/Party
Raw Lust: Sprout Salad and Wheatgrass Shots
Lacto-Ovo: Greekin' Out (be sure to serve the ouzo)
Fun-due: Cheese Fondue and Wine Coolers (substitute veggies or tofu for
   chicken sausages)

Granola/Progressive
Lacto-Ovo: Greekin' Out
"Take Me to Bed or Lose Me Forever": Lemon Shrimp Linguine (take out the shrimp)

Granola/Uptown
Afternoon Tea at the Savoy: Finger Sandwiches and Scones

Indie/Party
Eat Drink Man Woman: Shrimp and Fortune Cookies
Monsoon Wedding: Bollywood Curry Chicken
Like Water for Chocolate: Chiles en Nogada and Chocolate Flan
Fun-due: Cheese Fondue and Wine Coolers
Saucy and Sweet: Pizza, Flaming Dr Peppers, and Banana Splits

Indie/Progressive
Amélie: Le Fabuleux Dîner d'Amélie Poulain
Monsoon Wedding: Bollywood Curry Chicken

Indie/Uptown
Sinatra at the Sands: Martinis, Oysters, and Filet Mignon

Party/Progressive
Tex-Mex Fiesta: Fajitas and Spanish Fly Cocktails

Party/Uptown
Dinner on the Yacht in the French Riviera: Champagne, Caviar, and Lobster
Sinatra at the Sands: Martinis, Oysters, and Filet Mignon

Progressive/Uptown
Dinner on the Yacht in the French Riviera: Champagne, Caviar, and Lobster
Afternoon Tea at the Savoy: Finger Sandwiches and Scones

Bailing Out: Dealing with Disaster

U h-oh. OK, so you blew it. The soufflé fell, the risotto burned, you're making filet mignon and you forgot to buy the meat—whatever it was, let it go. This isn't the time for postmortems or recriminations. This is the time to think fast. She's due any minute, and it's pretty obvious there isn't going to be a suitably impressive dinner waiting for her. You've got to have a fallback option, an exit strategy, a Plan B. Dammit, man, you've got to get the hell out of there.

Think, man, think. Whatever the dating guides or your therapist says, this is not a time to honestly lay the facts on the table and be the caring, communicative future boyfriend that you one day hope to be. She is coming over to your place *any freakin' minute* with high expectations, and she is not going to be amused to find you standing in a smoking kitchen, holding the charred remains of her meal, and suggesting that she just nibble around the burned parts. No, you said dinner, and she has the laughable notion that you meant an edible one. Even the Girl Next Door, the most easygoing of them all, won't want to fall back on TV dinners when Plan A goes south.

The solution, then, is to present a perfectly acceptable explanation, one that quickly explains exactly why you were not able to come through on your earlier promise. Then you provide a wonderful second choice that, while it may not be the fantasy experience she was hoping for, will still salvage the evening and keep you in the running.

Translation: Lie through your teeth and get her to a restaurant.

Ah, but which lie? And which restaurant? As always, it depends on the Girl. Following are ten "slight exaggerations of the truth" and ten suggestions for backup restaurants, all with the Cooking to Hook Up Official Stamp of Bachelor Approval. It is an excellent idea to have the restaurant scoped out in advance. Note: If you are feeding a Gourmet or Uptown Girl, it's a good idea to make a reservation ahead of time, just in case disaster strikes. If everything goes swimmingly, you can cancel the reservation before she arrives. But if the Pan-Asian Fusion ends up fused to the pan, you'll have a contingency plan that'll prevent you from going from the frying pan straight into the fire.

We'd like to state that lying is, in general, not the most positive way to start a relationship. So just this once and that's it, OK guys? OK? Guys?

All right, here's the strategy:

Academic Girl

"I was translating Ovid and I lost track of time."

Take the Academic Girl to a university pub or cafe that serves food, preferably one where people are lounging around talking about Great Thoughts. Look for the one with the bulletin board covered with stapled-up ads for term paper typists and Greek history lectures and the lending library.

Athletic Girl

"I sprained my ankle training for a triathlon and I can't stand up to cook."

Duh. Look for a health food restaurant. Note, however, that many health food restaurants are vegetarian and she may want to have some kind of protein other than tofu. In that case, think Middle Eastern or Japanese. They eat healthy stuff, plus they eat meat.

Career Girl

"I tried to get out of the office, but they needed me on the Hong Kong conference call."

Take her to a restaurant in a hotel, preferably the top floor of the hotel with a panoramic view of the city. Think upscale and downtown.

Girl Next Door

"I spent the whole evening on the phone with my mother, planning my grandparents' anniversary."

The Girl Next Door wants a place that is familiar and not pretentious. Look for a Chili's or an Olive Garden.

Gourmet Girl

"I was going to surprise you with the raw milk Epoisses I smuggled in from Paris, but it was confiscated in customs."

Pick up a copy of the Zagat's restaurant guide. You're going to be needing it anyway, if you keep hanging out with Gourmet Girls. Look for a three- or four-star French place: Le Something or Chez Someone. Be sure you have made reservations well in advance, just in case.

Granola Girl

"We were discussing the agenda for our anti-industrial rally and it took all afternoon to reach consensus."

Look for a vegetarian eatery. The Internet can help you out. Search for "vegetarian" and the name of your city. You'd be surprised how many are out there.

Indie Girl

"I was so inspired after we talked last night that I stayed up all night working on my novel—do you mind if we just go out to dinner?"

Of course now you're going to have to make up a whole novel, because she's going to want to hear all about it over dinner. If you're dating an Indie Girl, however, you're going to have to learn to be creative anyway, so this is good practice.

Think ethnic: Indian, Vietnamese, Greek, Japanese, or Ethiopian. (Do *not* do the standard joke about Ethiopian restaurants—as in "I thought they didn't have any food in Ethiopia." It wasn't funny twenty years ago, and it's still not funny.)

Party Girl

"Check it out! My kitchen is on fire!"

OK, so there is one Girl you can tell the truth to, as long as you keep it light and fun. Mix her a big ol' drink and elaborate at length on all the trials and tribulations of making dinner. Keep her laughing and you can just order pizza for dinner. You only get to do this once per Party Girl, though, so enjoy it.

Progressive Girl

"It's just such a beautiful night, and I don't want to be cooped up indoors. I know a place where we can eat outside."

Progressive Girls love new experiences, especially when they involve encounters with nature and the great outdoors. Look for a restaurant with a patio and a view of the night sky. If you live by the coast, take her to a nice seafood restaurant where she can listen to the surf. Note: If it's 20 below zero, you're screwed.

Uptown Girl

"My cleaning lady had a family emergency and had to take the day off, so I thought it would be better if we went out."

The Uptown Girl understands better than anyone that you can't be expected to keep house without a hired domestic, and she certainly doesn't want to hang around your messy apartment. Pick up the Zagat's Guide and find the most expensive restaurant in the city. Don't complain to us about the price. *You're* the one that wanted to date the Uptown Girl. Note: Last-minute reservations to glitzy restaurants can be hard to come by, so you probably want to make a reservation (as a backup) as soon as you set up the dinner date.

part two

The Menus

The Girl Next Door

I come from a home where gravy is a beverage.

—Erma Bombeck

The Girl Next Door is from a small town, a large family, or both. She still has a healthy dose of what people 'round these parts call "family values." She calls her grandparents every Sunday and she's got her mom on speed dial. The Girl Next Door likes an uncomplicated life filled with the simple pleasures of family, home, kids, and food. She may not actually live on a farm, but she tends to keep a menagerie. Asked to choose between a dog and a cat, she generally won't. What's a good guard dog without a mouser to keep it company? She is caring and warm, welcoming and friendly. Anybody in your office ever bring in chocolate chip cookies? You got yourself a Girl Next Door.

The defining characteristics of the Girl Next Door are simplicity and tradition. Simplicity means that, unlike the Academic Girl, she's really not that interested in the great questions that keep philosophers up at night. When she can sit in the kitchen, drinking coffee, eating shortbread cookies with a friend, and listening to the cat purr on top of the radiator, what else is there to life? What else, indeed.

Tradition means that she enjoys her place in an ongoing history, whether it's family, friends, school, or even the company she works for. She may have gone to the same college as her parents. You can bet she had a "Sweet Sixteen" party, a class ring, and a date to the prom with her high school beau. She actually *comes home* for Homecoming. Girls Next Door love the holidays and the traditions that go along with them. Even dating traditions appeal to them. As far as they are concerned, relationships should move along at a measured pace, with definite landmarks. This date we kiss, this date we undo buttons, this date we do what comes after that. This same approach applies to work as well. The Girls Next Door are the ones who keep track of people's birthdays in the office and bring them cards and cake.

She may also have strong feelings about traditional male-female relationships. It's not that she is going to fade away into the background of a man's life and be happy with having dinner on the table and the kids scrubbed up every night by six. However, she may be very comfortable with divvying up the household chores along gender lines. She concentrates on food and laundry, while the man takes care of car repair, mowing the lawn, and taking out the garbage. She will also appreciate any domestic urges you might have. When you finally visit her place, offer to nail up that board that's coming down over the sink and you may get a job as resident fix-it man and boyfriend.

Her daily diet consists of what the rest of us refer to as "comfort food." This Girl loves the All-American menu. The basics. Meatloaf. Tuna casserole. Pot roast. Ground chuck with a healthy side of baked, broiled, hashed, spitted, or sauced potatoes. Low fat content and organic ingredients are low on her list of priorities. A warm kitchen and an apple pie waiting for ice cream are high.

While it's true that most Girls Next Door originate from suburban and rural areas, they do migrate to cities from time to time. If they do, they are "in" the city, but never "of" it. There are no Girls Next Door on *Sex and the City*. There are nothing but Girls Next Door on the *Prairie Home Companion*. If you find a girl who gets great joy out of walking the dog, making a roast, playing cribbage, or making Easter cards by hand, you have found the Girl Next Door. And in this great big mess of a world, when everything seems to be going to heck in a hand basket, that's a pretty nice thing to find.

She Might Be a Girl Next Door If:

1. **She drives:** a good, solid American car—a Ford Taurus, Chevy Cavalier, or Dodge Stratus.

2. **She can talk for more than ten minutes about:** her family's holiday traditions.

3. **She begins her sentences with:** "My mother says . . ."

4. **She'd never:** go to a rave.

5. **She owns any of the following:** scrapbooks, heirloom quilts, a Bible, family recipes, her grandmother's engagement ring.

Where You'll Find Her

At a high school football game, at the mall, in a quilting class. Shopping at Target. Iowa.

How to Spot Her

The Girl Next Door is pretty unassuming. She won't be wearing anything fancy or expensive. Most of them have one good piece of jewelry that they like to wear a lot, and it was probably a present from someone who means a lot to them. Sensible shoes, mostly, but they will throw on a pair of Keds (white ones) when they want to look cute. And they do.

Famous Girls Next Door

Sally Field, plus most of the parts she has ever played, including her roles in *Gidget*, *Norma Rae, Steel Magnolias, Places in the Heart*, and *The Poseidon Adventure*. Also, Mary Ann on *Gilligan's Island*, Dorothy Gale from *The Wizard of Oz*, and Nia Vardalos's character in *My Big Fat Greek Wedding*.

Your Place

The Girl Next Door is most at home in the suburbs or in small towns. If you do live in a big-city warehouse loft, make sure you pepper it heavily with framed photos of your parents, grandparents, and any kids you are related to. Sports paraphernalia, such as football pennants, work nicely, as do quilts. A dog (especially a Lab, golden retriever, or basset hound) would be a nice touch. La-Z-Boy chairs and furniture from Target are OK. Stay away from anything pretentious, like avant-garde artwork or glass-topped tables. If you have any furniture you inherited from your grandparents, mention it.

The Conversation

Your family. Her family. Families in general. Kids. Sports. Dogs. Steer clear of politics, sex, and religion. Conversations that stray too much into abstract intellectual thinking will probably bore her. "Let's talk about something that matters to real people," she will think.

The Coffee Table

The daily paper. *Life, Sports Illustrated, People, Reader's Digest, Popular Mechanics.*

The Music

Top 40, or even better, country music will win this girl's heart. You can pretty much put on the radio and set it on low. Playing a band that is from her home state is a surefire winner. We know one Hawaiian Girl Next Door who fell head over heels for a guy because he played hula music during dinner. A Girl Next Door from North Carolina was won over by the music of bluegrass singer Mike Cross, a true Blue Ridge Mountain boy.

The Drinks

The Girl Next Door is right at home sipping a Budweiser out of the can at the baseball game. However, if she doesn't like beer, a wine cooler is always a sure bet. For a cocktail, she prefers mainstream drinks—the kind you order in college: rum and Coke, Jack and Coke, gin and tonic. Drinks that involve soft drinks are a good bet. The soft drinks alone will work if she avoids alcohol. No need to spend dough on fancy booze; well liquor is fine. This may be the only Girl you can serve wine out of a box to. It isn't that she's low-class; she just doesn't mind these things.

The Shoes

Pretty much anything. The Girl Next Door is the one type of girl who won't put too much emphasis on footwear. You can wear anything from cowboy boots to sneakers and she'll be OK with it. Really. (We can hear the collective sigh of relief from our readers as we write this sentence.)

The Flowers

The Girl Next Door is one of the lowest-maintenance girls on the planet, so receiving flowers of any kind will thrill her. She'll be happy with roses, carnations, daisies, you name it. If you want to hit a homer, though, send her a floral arrangement with a stuffed animal.

Fourth of July Fireworks: Fried Chicken and French Fries

I know I-talian food when I hear it! It's all them "eenie" foods . . . zucchini . . . and linguini . . . and fettuccine. I want some American food, dammit! I want french fries!"

—Ray Stoller in **Breaking Away**

FRIED CHICKEN STRIPS
FRENCH FRIES
COLESLAW
BUDWEISER LONGNECKS
VANILLA ICE CREAM WITH CHOCOLATE SAUCE

What says "Girl Next Door" more than fried chicken? Fried chicken with french fries, that's what. Add a simple coleslaw and you've got an afternoon picnic from her childhood that'll make her want to open up the photo album. And boy, when a Girl Next Door starts showing you the photo album, you know you're in. Don't laugh at her third-grade photo with the knobby knees, though. Her grandmother loves that picture and keeps it next to the strawberry jam she puts up every fall.

The theme here is small-town America, the kind of place that all Girls Next Door are from, even if they grew up in the big city. Their hearts are with the small-town doctors, the drugstore soda fountains, the three old guys sitting outside the barbershop watching the scuffed-up kids riding their bicycles. Yes, this vision of Norman Rockwell America has slipped away, buried under Nintendo and Web browsing and reality television, but it doesn't matter. To the Girl Next Door, this is how life should be, and darned if she isn't gonna believe in it anyhow. There's no place like *home,* especially when the flag is flying on the Fourth of July, so fry up some chicken and let the neighborhood smell it. Those kids are being called home by their mothers and Grandpa'll be home soon from the barbershop. So just you wash up and set the table.

Note: Pay attention to the instructions about "flash" frying the meat. The last thing you want on her trip down nostalgia lane is dry chicken. We've chosen to make chicken strips as opposed to cut-up chicken parts because it's a little easier to eat, but feel free to substitute a cut-up fryer if you want drumsticks, wings, thighs, and so on.

To Buy

1 head cabbage (3 cups)

1 small jar mayonnaise (½ cup)

Lemon juice, bottled or freshly squeezed from 1 lemon (1 tablespoon)

2 russet potatoes

4 boneless, skinless chicken breasts

1 small bottle corn oil (2 tablespoons plus ½ cup)

1 container Lawry's Seasoned Salt (1 teaspoon)

1 bottle or carton buttermilk (1 cup)

1 tub vanilla ice cream

1 bottle or can Hershey's chocolate syrup

Staples

Flour

½ teaspoon salt

¼ teaspoon pepper

1 tablespoon sugar

From the Liquor Store

Budweiser longnecks (bottled beer)

Before she arrives:

7:00

1. Chill the beer in the refrigerator.

2. Coarsely grate enough cabbage for 3 cups; place into a medium mixing bowl. In a small mixing bowl, combine ½ cup mayonnaise, 1 tablespoon sugar, and 1 tablespoon lemon juice and stir. Pour the mixture over the cabbage and toss until coated. Cover the bowl with plastic wrap and refrigerate.

7:15

3. Don't skin the potatoes! Cut them into ¾-inch slices, then cut the slices into ¾-inch-long strips. Pour 2 tablespoons corn oil, 1 teaspoon seasoned salt, and the potatoes into a plastic bag. Shake until the potatoes are fully covered. Lay them out on a baking sheet and set aside.

4. Preheat the oven to 400 degrees.

5. Lay the chicken breasts flat on a cutting board. With a sharp knife, cut them into 1-inch strips. Pour 1 cup buttermilk into a soup bowl and cover a plate with a thick layer of flour. Add ½ teaspoon salt and ¼ teaspoon pepper to the flour and stir. Take each strip of chicken, dip it in the buttermilk, roll it in the flour, and set aside on a plate.

After she arrives:

8:00

6. Offer her a beer.

7. Put the potatoes in the oven and bake for about 25 minutes. Flip them over about halfway through. They should be golden brown when done.

8. While the potatoes are cooking, put ½ cup of corn oil in a small frying pan over medium-high heat. Let it warm up for a few minutes. To determine if it is hot enough, toss in a pinch of flour. If it sizzles loudly, the oil is hot enough. The oil needs to be hot enough to "flash" fry the chicken and keep in the juice. Lukewarm oil means dry chicken.

9. Place the buttermilked and floured chicken in the oil. Cook 3 minutes on each side, then check for doneness by slicing one strip partway open. The chicken should be white all the way through. Unlike fish, which cooks all the way to the table, the chicken should be completely done when you take it from the pan.

10. Serve the chicken, french fries, and coleslaw all together.

11. When dinner is done, bring out the vanilla ice cream and chocolate sauce.

Bonus Points

Add sprinkles, walnuts, or cookies to the ice cream. If it really is the Fourth, little American flags on top would be jim-dandy.

Mom's Kitchen: Savory Meat Loaf

MEAT LOAF
CARROT AND RAISIN SALAD
BEER
CRISPY RICE SQUARES

When it comes to the Girl Next Door, Mom always knows best. That's why, when it came to this meal, we went to the source. Drew's mom came through with the meat loaf recipe that "Susan Druskin's mother always made" as well as her own patented Carrot and Raisin Salad. Getting recipes from Mom is a can't-miss proposition except for one thing. After cooking from the seat of her apron all these years, Mom finds it a little hard to actually tell us how much of each ingredient she uses. Her recipes are full of things like "Add a little sugar" and "Pour in the milk until it looks right." After a little coaxing, however, she actually brought out a dusty set of measuring cups and put some left-brained quantities to her right-brained cuisine. I think you will agree that the following is a meal fit for the Girl Next Door.

Thanks, Mom. And we promise to keep our elbows off the table.

To Buy

1 can beef consommé

1 pound ground beef

1 package bread crumbs

1 can condensed cream of mushroom soup

6 medium-size carrots

1 small box raisins

1 small jar mayonnaise (3 tablespoons)

1 bag miniature marshmallows (4 cups)

1 box crispy rice cereal (5 cups)

Staples

1 medium-size onion

1 egg

¼ teaspoon pepper

2 teaspoons sugar

1 tablespoon milk, plus two glasses to drink with dessert

4 tablespoons butter, plus 1 tablespoon to rub inside the dessert pan

From the Liquor Store

Well, Mom doesn't want you getting all lit up, but she says a beer would be OK.

Before she arrives:

6:30

1. Put the beers in the fridge.

2. You will need about an hour of cooking time for the meat loaf, so let's get that going first. Preheat the oven to 350 degrees.

3. Grate one medium-size onion into a large bowl and add 1 egg. Beat with a fork until it is all mixed together. Add half the consommé right out of the can. Add ¼ teaspoon pepper and stir. Add the ground beef and mix it up. Mom recommends just sticking your hands into it and "messing with it until it's all squishy."

4. Add bread crumbs a little at a time until the mixture is a consistency you can pat into a loaf. Put the loaf in a bread loaf pan. Pour half the can of condensed cream of mushroom soup over the top before baking. Don't add water to the soup—use it right out of the can.

5. Bake for an hour.

7:00

6. Grate the carrots coarsely. Mom says to tell you to use the bigger holes on your hand grater. Add ½ cup raisins.

7. In a cereal bowl, mix together 2 teaspoons sugar, 3 tablespoons mayonnaise, and 1 tablespoon milk. Add this mixture to the carrots and raisins and stir. Set the salad in the fridge to chill.

7:30

8. Melt 4 tablespoons butter in a medium saucepan over low heat. Add 4 cups of marshmallows and stir until melted. Cook for 3 minutes, stirring constantly. Remove from the stove and add 5 cups crispy rice cereal. Stir until coated. Use 1 tablespoon butter to

grease the inside of the 9x13-inch baking dish. Using a buttered spatula, press the mixture down into the pan and let it cool during dinner.

After she arrives:

8:00

9. Offer her a beer.

10. Serve the meat loaf with the carrot and raisin salad.

11. After dinner, cut the crispy rice mixture into 3-inch squares and serve with a glass of cold milk. Ah . . . home.

Bonus Points

Add a cup of chocolate chips to the crispy rice squares. Or add ¼ cup peanut butter while the marshmallows are melting.

Hometown Favorites: Pineapple Glazed Ham

PINEAPPLE GLAZED HAM
BAKED BEANS
DEVILED EGGS
LANCER ROSÉ
CHOCOLATE CHIP COOKIES

Pineapple glazed ham usually makes an appearance around our house at Thanksgiving, but when you're dating a Girl Next Door, you can give thanks every day. For one thing, you can give thanks that she's so easy to cook for. Let's face it, any meal that starts with "Buy a pre-cooked ham and a can of baked beans" isn't going to cause you serious stress. This meal needs to be started about an hour and a half before dinnertime, but heck, that'll give you time for a few hands of gin rummy before you sit down to a tasty meal any Girl Next Door will want to call home about.

To Buy

1 (2- to 3-pound) precooked ham

1 package chocolate chip cookie dough (from the refrigerator case)

1 package bacon (4 slices)

1 (12- to 16-ounce) can baked beans with pork

1 small bottle ketchup (¼ cup)

1 package brown sugar (½ cup plus ¼ cup)

1 small jar yellow mustard (1 tablespoon plus ¾ teaspoon)

1 (8-ounce) can pineapple slices

1 small jar mayonnaise (2 tablespoons)

1 container paprika

Staples

¾ cup chopped onion

6 eggs

¼ teaspoon salt

Pinch of pepper

Milk

From the Liquor Store

Lancer Rosé

Before she arrives:

6:30

1. Preheat the oven to 350 degrees.

2. Put the ham in a 9x13-inch baking dish and put it in the oven for an hour.

3. Follow the directions on the chocolate chip cookie dough and get the cookies on a baking sheet and in the oven. Keep an eye on the cookies and remove them from the oven when they are golden brown.

7:00

4. In a frying pan, cook 4 slices of bacon and ¾ cup chopped onion until the bacon is crisp. Drain the bacon on paper towels and chop it into small pieces. Drain the fat out of the frying pan (leaving the onion) and add the chopped bacon, the can of baked beans, ¼ cup ketchup, ½ cup brown sugar, and 1 tablespoon yellow mustard. Pour it into a 9-inch square glass baking dish.

7:15

5. When the ham has 10 minutes to go, put the beans in the oven with it. Then, in a small mixing bowl, combine half the juice from the can of pineapples with ¼ cup brown sugar. When the ham comes out, place as many pineapple slices as you can fit on top of it, then ladle on the juice-sugar mixture. Put it back in with the beans and bake another 30 minutes.

7:30

6. Meanwhile, put 6 eggs in a cold pan of water and bring it to a boil. Turn the heat down and let the eggs simmer for about 12 minutes. Put the pan in the sink and run cold water over the eggs. (That will help the shells release.) Peel the eggs and cut them in half, lengthwise. Hold each egg over a soup bowl and gently push on the outside to pop out the yolk. Set the egg whites aside. Mash the yolks with a fork and add 2 tablespoons mayonnaise, ¾ teaspoon yellow mustard, ¼ teaspoon salt, and a big pinch of pepper. Scoop a spoonful of the mixture back into each egg white. Sprinkle paprika on top for color and flavor.

7:45

7. Put the Lancer in the refrigerator to chill a little.

After she arrives:

8:00

8. By now, your ham and beans should be done and your kitchen should smell like a kitchen should when family comes to call. Offer her a glass of wine and carve the ham. Then spoon up the beans, add a couple of deviled eggs, and enjoy the good life.

9. Serve the chocolate chip cookies with, what else? Milk!

Bonus Points

We were serious about the card game. Make sure you have a deck in the house so you can play gin rummy or spades after dinner.

Lancer wines are a favorite of the Girl Next Door, partly because they are easy to like and inexpensive, and partly because they come in decorative clay bottles that, once emptied, can be used as decorative candleholders. After your successful date, save the bottle, put a candle in it for her next visit, and rock the Girl Next Door's world.

Sunday Dinner: Pot Roast

POT ROAST
GREEN SALAD
DINNER ROLLS
MERLOT
APPLE PIE

A pot roast is, in simple terms, a hunk of meat and a pile of vegetables, cooked for hours in the beef juices. In metaphoric, sense-memory terms, however, a pot roast is a warm family gathering, a laughing reunion with bustling matrons in the kitchen, bowling trophies on the hearth, babes in arms, and dogs underfoot. It is a statement of the America we used to be, before fast food, before e-mail, before CNN, before anybody realized that we couldn't possibly be happy until we bought a brand-new SUV. This recipe is a time machine, a Ghost of Sunday Past, a tender melt-in-your-mouth midwestern delicacy so down-home you may want to gather everybody in the parlor afterward for a piano recital.

The secret to making something tender is to cook it for a long time at a low temperature, and if that isn't good dating advice, we don't know what is. You will want to get this roast in the oven as early as you can, because it can take up to two hours to cook. As a matter of fact, it is almost impossible to overcook it. The longer you leave it in, the more tender it gets.

This is a good meal to make if you need some time to clean house. By 6:00, you've pretty much done all the cooking you need to do.

Lastly, this meal is one of the best leftovers in this book. Pot roast just keeps getting better the longer it sits (in the refrigerator, that is).

To Buy

1½ pound boneless chuck roast (try to get one that isn't thicker than an inch, so it will cook faster; thicker meat equals longer cooking time)

1 package dry onion soup mix

3 large carrots

3 red potatoes

Green leaf lettuce

1 large tomato

1 bottle salad dressing (buttermilk ranch or peppercorn ranch)

4 dinner rolls

1 apple pie (store-bought and prebaked)

Staples

1 teaspoon salt

½ teaspoon pepper

½ cup flour

1 tablespoon olive oil

1 large yellow onion

From the Liquor Store

Merlot

Before she arrives:

5:30

1. Preheat the oven to 350 degrees.

2. Mix 1 teaspoon salt and ½ teaspoon pepper into ½ cup flour in a wide, flat dish or dinner plate. Roll the roast in it to coat the meat. Put 1 tablespoon olive oil in the bottom of the oven-safe stockpot over low heat. Brown both sides of the roast. Take the roast out of the pan and set it on a plate.

3. In a small bowl, use the wire whisk to mix together 3 tablespoons of the flour mixture with 2 cups water. Stir until the lumps disappear, then dump it into the meat pan and stir it together with the meat drippings. Add enough water to make thin gravy, then stir in the onion soup mix and set the meat back down in the pan. The roast should be soaking in gravy, but not covered.

4. Cut up the carrots, potatoes, and onion into thumb-size chunks and dump them around and over the meat.

6:00

5. Stick it in the oven. Now you can clean the house.

After she arrives:

8:00

6. Offer her a glass of wine.

7. Rinse and tear up the lettuce, slice the tomato, and toss with the salad dressing. Start checking the meat at 1½ hours and keep sticking a fork in it every 15 to 30 minutes. When it is tender, wrap the dinner rolls in aluminum foil and stick them in the oven for 10 minutes to warm them.

8. Serve the salad.

9. When you're ready for the roast, take it out and arrange the meat on a plate, surrounded by vegetables. (Reduce the oven temperature to 300 degrees.) Bring the warmed rolls to the table. Serve it up and get ready to reminisce about your Iowa upbringing.

10. When you are halfway through dinner, excuse yourself for a moment and stick the pie in a 300-degree oven for 15 minutes. Serve warm with milk or coffee.

Bonus Points

If it isn't obvious, the bonus point here is to scoop some vanilla ice cream over the apple pie.

Hot Dish: Midwestern Tuna Casserole

TUNA CASSEROLE
COOKED CARROTS
AMBROSIA SALAD
MINNESOTA BEER

Ah, tuna casserole. This one is quick and easy, if you're pressed for time. Hey, maybe this is the right Girl Next Door meal if she really does live next door. Stick your head out the window and tell her you'll have the "hot dish" ready in half an hour. "Hot dish" is Minnesota slang for any one-dish casserole that you might bring to a potluck. While we're on the subject of Minnesota slang, we highly recommend the use of "You bet" in any conversation with a girl from the great Midwest. This useful bit of Minnesota slang has roughly the same all-purpose usefulness as "aloha" in Hawaii. For example:

"Hi there! You doin' alright?"
"You bet."

"See you later then."
"You bet!"

You might not think that Minnesota would be famous for beer, but you'd be wrong. Back in the nineteenth century, it actually attracted a string of upstart brewers from that other metropolis of suds—Milwaukee—who came to the Twin Cities of Minneapolis and St. Paul to try their fortunes. Using marketing slogans like "From the Land of Sky-Blue Waters," they brought out such classic Minnesota brands as Hamms and Joseph Schmidt, both now lamentably gone. If you can't get the quality Minnesota brands like Schell, Eureka, or Three Floyds where you are, go ahead and buy something from a local microbrewery, safe in the knowledge that you are supporting, if in spirit only, the grand tradition of Minnesota brewing.

To Buy

2 bananas
1 can mandarin oranges in syrup
1 bag shredded coconut (2 cups)

1 bag miniature marshmallows (2 cups)

8 ounces elbow macaroni noodles

1 (12-ounce) can of chunk tuna

1 block cheddar cheese (½ cup grated)

1 bag frozen peas (1 cup)

1 small tub grated Parmesan cheese (½ cup)

8 carrots

Staples

1 cup milk

4 tablespoons butter (plus some for greasing dish)

From the Liquor Store

Schell, Eureka, or Three Floyds beer or other local microbrew

Before she arrives:

7:00

1. Start with the ambrosia salad, which is dessert. Peel the bananas and chop them into bite-size pieces.

2. In a serving dish, make layers of the mandarin oranges, 2 cups coconut, 2 cups marshmallows, and the bananas. Drizzle a little of the syrup from the oranges over it all and refrigerate until you are ready—the colder the better.

7:15

3. Preheat the oven to 350 degrees.

4. In a medium saucepan, boil 6 cups water. Add the macaroni to the boiling water and follow cooking directions on package. Open and drain the tuna. Grate enough cheddar cheese to make ½ cup. Rinse the peas in lukewarm water. Once the macaroni is soft but not mushy, drain and rinse in cool water. Rinse the saucepan—you'll need it again in a minute.

5. In a medium mixing bowl, combine the macaroni, tuna, 1 cup milk, 2 tablespoons butter, ½ cup grated Parmesan cheese, ½ cup grated cheddar cheese, and peas.

6. Lightly butter a 9-inch-square baking dish. Pour mixture into the dish. Set aside.

7. Chop up the carrots into thumb-size pieces and set aside.

8. Bring 5 cups water to a boil in a medium saucepan. Cover it and turn off the burner.

After she arrives:

8:00

9. When she walks in the door, offer her a beer. Stick the casserole in the oven and bake for 15 minutes.

10. Bring the saucepan full of water back to a boil and add the carrots. Cook until soft, about 10 minutes.

11. Remove the carrots from the heat and rinse briefly with cold water to keep them from cooking further. Drain, then add 2 tablespoons butter and mix it around to cover the carrots.

12. Ladle out the tuna casserole and carrots onto plates and serve. When you are ready for the ambrosia, remove it from the fridge and serve.

Bonus Points

Add a bay leaf to the water when you cook the carrots, and/or sprinkle a little brown sugar over the carrots when you serve them. Put crushed saltine crackers on top of the casserole before you bake it.

The Party Girl

**I like to have a martini, two
at the very most—after three
I'm under the table; after
four, I'm under the host.**

—Dorothy Parker

Audrey Hepburn's character Holly Golightly in *Breakfast at Tiffany's* is the quintessential Party Girl. Truman Capote named her for a woman who creates a holiday of life, and who takes it lightly. That classic scene of her standing in front of Tiffany's eating her breakfast roll and sipping coffee after being out on the town all night, her fridge with nothing in it, those wild cocktail parties. All very Party Girl.

New York City is also very Party Girl. As are LA, Miami Beach, London, Amsterdam, and of course, Vegas, baby, Vegas. Party Girls hate rural areas, because their worst nightmare is to be somewhere where there's nothing going on. The Party Girl is an extrovert, and she's usually very popular. If you're the kind of guy who likes to spend his Saturday nights watching DVDs or playing Scrabble, the Party Girl may be a challenge. She likes to have F-U-N. If you want to keep up with this Girl, you will need to know how to make a killer margarita, how to cure a hangover, and how to find the energy not to pull a wet-blanket, negatron move like losing steam by the fifth club of the evening. (The answer to that last one is to have another vodka and Red Bull.)

You'll also need to learn some drinking games. Here are a couple of easy ones: "Hi, Bob," which is to be played while watching reruns of *The Bob Newhart Show* or his other show, *Newhart.* Whenever anyone walks in and says, "Hi, Bob," you drink. That's all there is to it. Another one is called "Roxanne," and basically you just listen to that song by the Police and whenever Sting goes, "Roxaaaaanne," you slam a shot. There are a zillion others on the Internet—just type in "drinking games" and find a good one.

She Might Be a Party Girl If:

1. **She drives:** a convertible or other sports car, or she rides on a "party bus" (you know, the ones that take you from bar to bar). Also: cabs and limousines.

2. **She can talk for more than ten minutes about:** the hottest bars, restaurants, and clubs—in short, "the scene."

3. **She begins her sentences with:** "Make it a double."

4. **She'd never, *ever*:** take up knitting.

5. **She owns any of the following:** cell phone, PDA or Filofax (to manage all her contacts), a sleeping mask and earplugs (since she often doesn't come home until the wee hours), travel-size toothbrushes and very dark sunglasses (for when she doesn't come home at all).

Where You'll Find Her

Out on the town. Salsa dancing. Being escorted past a velvet rope. In rock stars' hotel rooms. At book or CD release parties and movie premieres. This girl's a night owl, though, so don't expect to bump into her jogging in the park or having a picnic. She's not really into the whole daylight thing.

How to Spot Her

She's the one in sparkly, shiny fabrics and sequins. Or ripped-up T-shirts and Diesel jeans (she's often into labels). She may have her hair crimped and be wearing body glitter. A subset of the Party Girl is the Sorority Girl, for whom Greek is not a language but a lifestyle. The Sorority Girl often continues her Greek lifestyle beyond college, where Delta Tau becomes Merrill Lynch. The Sorority Girl is not the same as the Movie Premiere Girl with crimped hair and high heels—she's more the shot-slamming number in the little black dress who's dancing on the bar.

Famous Party Girls

Heiresses like the Hilton sisters and people from rock-star families, like Mick's ex, Bianca, and his daughter, Jade Jagger, as well as Courtney Love, Pamela Anderson, and Kelly Osbourne. Also Anna Nicole, Elizabeth Hurley, Carmen Electra, Jenna Bush, Madonna before motherhood, and Fergie before Weight Watchers. Samantha Jones on *Sex and the City* and Patsy and Edina on *Ab Fab*.

Your Place

This is the one case (and the only case) where the tower of beer bottles from your college dorm room may actually be appreciated. Okay, maybe not appreciated. Tolerated. Think festive: Christmas lights, palm trees, piñatas. And sexy: animal prints, fake fur rugs. The lounge or tiki looks from the '50s are also good. Or '60s mod: inflatable furniture, shagadelic shag carpeting, you know, the kind of thing you'd see in an Austin Powers movie. If you really want to fan this fox's flame, add a built-in bar, fully stocked with all sorts of liquor, as well as condiments: olives, pearl onions, maraschino cherries, tomolives. And of course, a water bed. Grr, baby, very grr.

The Conversation

Stay on fun topics. Don't get heavy with this Girl. Know any jokes? No? OK, here's one: A waiter asks a man, "May I take your order, sir?" The man says, "I'm just wondering, exactly how do you prepare your chickens?" And the waiter says, "Nothing special, sir. We just tell them straight out that they're going to die."

The Coffee Table

Interview, Paper, Time Out New York, Village Voice, or *LA Weekly* (or your equivalent local weekly paper).

The Music

Brazilian music, disco, rap, and hip-hop. Songs like Nelly's "Hot In Herre" or Pink's "Get the Party Started" are Party Girl classics. Go with anything sexy, fun, and danceable. Steer clear of jazz, classical, and folk. If she's the clubbing type, go with house music and techno. For some late-night couch tunes, try Barry White or Marvin Gaye.

The Drinks

Drinks are as important to the Party Girl as organic veggies are to the Granola Girl. Consider alcohol a staple. Focus on drinks that spell F-U-N. Anything tropical, anything with umbrellas, anything south of the border, and shots, shots, shots. Especially shots you can light on fire (such as the Flaming Dr Pepper—see the "Saucy and Sweet" pizza menu.) Think daiquiris, mai tais, and Jell-O shots. This is also your chance to serve drinks with a funny sexual innuendo, such as a Sex on the Beach, Buttery Nipple, or a Slow Screw Up Against the Wall. (Try these drinks with most other girls, and you'll get a cold reception.)

The Shoes

Flip-flops to make it look like you just got done surfing. Barefoot is also good—just make sure you wash your feet.

The Flowers

Go tropical. It will make her feel like she's on vacation. Get a bouquet of Hawaiian flowers including protea, anthurium, and bird-of-paradise. Even better, put a real lei around her neck when she walks in the door (no, we're not gonna make the joke about "getting lei'd"—oops, sorry, guess we just did).

Tex-Mex Fiesta: Fajitas and Spanish Fly Cocktails

FAJITAS ("FAH-HEE-TAS")
PICO DE GALLO ("PEEK-O DA GUY-O")
GUACAMOLE ("GWAWK-A-MOLE-AY")
SPANISH FLY COCKTAILS

Purists will tell you that fajitas are really not Mexican food, because they were first popularized in Houston, Texas. They will also tell you that "Tex-Mex" food is a culinary sham that ignores the inherent, flavorful qualities of true Mexican dishes, bastardizes them with American spices and low-fat ingredients, and does not allow the savory culture of Mexico to shine in all its hot-peppered, lard-laden glory.

Party Girls do not date purists.

Party Girls date guys who can make party food. Party Girls like things that sizzle and crackle when brought to the table. Party Girls like to assemble food and see how many different ways they can fill up a tortilla. Party Girls like food that reminds them of sand beaches, salsa music, and roses that are 50 cents to the dozen.

The original fajitas were skirt steak, but this recipe works for chicken as well, if your Party Girl prefers.

The famous aphrodisiac Spanish Fly is actually the pulverized bodies of blister beetles which, when ingested, do produce an arousal of sorts by irritating the urinary tract. When applied to the skin, they produce blisters 6 to 12 inches in diameter. Instead, we recommend the liquid version of the Spanish Fly made from tequila and amaretto.

To Buy

¾ pound boneless, skinless chicken breast or ¾ pound skirt steak

2 limes

1 small container Mexican seasoning (large pinch)

2 large tomatoes (about 1 pound)

1 bunch fresh cilantro leaves (2 tablespoons chopped)

3 fresh jalapeños

1 ripe avocado (buy Haas avocados—the ones with bumpy skin)

Cheddar cheese (2 cups grated)

1 package flour tortillas (4 needed)

1 bag tortilla chips

Staples

2 garlic cloves, chopped

2 tablespoons olive oil

Salt (to taste)

Pepper (to taste)

1 small white onion

From the Liquor Store

Tequila

Amaretto

Mexican beer (Corona or equivalent)

Before she arrives:

7:00

1. For the fajitas, combine uncooked chicken or steak with 1 chopped garlic clove, the juice of half a lime, a large pinch of Mexican seasoning, and 1 tablespoon olive oil in a medium-size mixing bowl. Sprinkle in some salt and pepper. Mix well. Marinate for at least 30 minutes at room temperature.

7:15

2. To make the pico de gallo, finely chop the tomatoes. Chop the onion in half, and finely chop one of the halves. Wash and chop the cilantro, enough for 2 tablespoons. Seed and finely chop 2 of the jalapeños. In a small serving bowl, mix the tomatoes, onion, cilantro, jalapeños, and 1 tablespoon lime juice. Sprinkle a little salt on top. Cover and refrigerate.

3. For the guacamole, peel and roughly mash the avocado in a serving bowl. Leave lumps. Mash 1 clove garlic. Chop the remaining jalapeño and add to the mashed avocado with the garlic. Mince the remaining onion, enough for 1 tablespoon. Stir in the minced onion and 1 tablespoon lime juice. Set aside.

4. Grate the cheddar cheese; place in a serving bowl and set aside.

After she arrives:

8:00

5. For the Spanish Fly, pour an ounce each of tequila and amaretto into a rocks glass filled with ice, stir, and serve. It's a good idea to have some beers on hand if she needs a chaser. Put a bowl of chips out for munching.

6. Cut the marinated chicken or steak into bite-size strips and fry in 1 tablespoon olive oil in large frying pan over high to medium-high heat. Cook until the meat is browned and cooked through.

7. Lay out a tortilla on each plate and place some cooked chicken or steak on it. Lay it out in a long row, so she can roll up the tortilla once she's got all her stuff in it.

8. Put the pico de gallo, guacamole, and cheese in bowls in the middle of the table. Serve the plates with the chicken- or steak-filled tortillas and let her assemble her meal.

Bonus Points

Cook the meat in a cast-iron skillet. Right before you serve it, sprinkle some lime juice over the meat to make it sizzle. Bring the skillet to the table and set it on a rack or a hot pad. Remember, sizzling is festive.

Saucy and Sweet: Pizza, Flaming Dr Peppers, and Banana Splits

PEPPERONI PIZZA
FLAMING DR PEPPERS
BANANA SPLITS

You can't do better than serving a pizza to a Party Girl. Unless you serve it with Flaming Dr Peppers and banana splits. The whole thing is so darn simple; you can do it while DJing the party and doing your Barry White imitation (only don't do the Barry White imitation, 'cause we've seen it and it could use some work).

The Boboli premade pizza crust is the greatest thing to happen to bachelors since the mirror ball. Plus the motor never burns out. You could mix the dough for the crust from scratch, but that's a pain, and we're pretty sure it isn't going to win points with the Party Girl. Of course, if you can't find the Boboli, you can always go for the premixed dough that looks like a stick of butter. Follow the directions for smooth pizza goodness.

The whipped cream is another area where you could go classier by buying fresh whipping cream and whipping it up with the mixer, but again, that's a lot of work for not a lot of notice. Not when it comes to the Party Girl. Better to spend your time putting together mixed CDs and shopping for tropical decorations.

To Buy

1 Boboli pizza crust *or* other premade pizza dough

1 (8-ounce) can pizza sauce

1 (12-ounce) bag grated mozzarella cheese

6 to 8 ounces pepperoni slices

2 bananas

1 jar fudge sauce, suitable for heating

1 jar caramel sauce, suitable for heating

1 pint Neapolitan ice cream

1 package chopped nuts or maraschino cherries

1 can whipped cream

From the Liquor Store

Amaretto

151 rum

Amber or dark beer

Special Equipment

Pizza pan

Before she arrives:

7:15

1. Preheat the oven to 350 degrees.

2. Open the Boboli crust and spread pizza sauce on it up to about ¾ inch from the edge. Cover the pizza with a layer of mozzarella, followed by a layer of pepperoni. Place it on a pizza pan (if you've bought one) or put a couple of sheets of aluminum foil on the rack in the oven. When you get ready to make the pizza, you can lay it on the foil. If you want the pizza crispier, you can put it directly on the rack and line the bottom of the oven with foil to catch the drips.

3. Set the prepared pizza aside.

After she arrives:

8:00

4. Pop the pizza into the oven for 8 to 10 minutes.

5. Fill a shot glass with amaretto, leaving ¼ inch at the top. Fill a beer mug ¾ of the way with beer.

6. Rest a spoon on top of the amaretto and gently pour a thin layer of 151 rum onto it. The spoon keeps the rum from flowing down into the amaretto.

7. Light the rum on fire and drop the whole shot into the beer mug. (It's easier to use a match than a lighter.)

8. Drink immediately.

9. Serve the pizza with plenty of napkins.

10. After the pizza, adjourn to the kitchen for the building of the banana split. Heat the fudge and the caramel for 30 seconds in the microwave.

11. Cut the bananas in half, lengthwise, and lay them in bowls. Fill the middle of the bowl with ice cream, then ladle on nuts, hot fudge, and caramel, and top with whipped cream.

Bonus Points

Add mushrooms, black olives, and other ingredients to the pizza. As our pizza chef friend points out, you can actually put any vegetable except a carrot on a pizza, so get creative. Keep in mind, however, that using garlic and onion may cause her to keep you at a distance later on in the evening.

Very Happy Hour: Bar Food and Screaming Orgasms

SHRIMP COCKTAIL
POTATO SKINS
BUFFALO CHICKEN WINGS
SCREAMING ORGASMS
LONG ISLAND ICED TEAS

Thank God It's Friday and thank God you don't have to go to the neighborhood meat market to enjoy Happy Hour. Lucky you, 'cause the Party Girl is dropping in for an early-evening munch before her weekend festivities begin. Who knows? Do this one up right and the festivities may happen closer to home. Then again, with the Party Girl, it's a good idea to know a local gin joint you can adjourn to if her toes start tapping.

By the way, don't be surprised if she arrives with a posse of lady friends on their way out on the town. Don't take it personally—the Party Girl often travels with a crowd, also known as her "entourage." Look at it as an opportunity. Double or triple this recipe and serve her whole group. Throw a shindig for her girlfriends and you've got the Party Girl in the palm of your hand.

To Buy

1 small bottle Tabasco sauce (2 tablespoons)

1 pound chicken wings or drumettes

4 large russet potatoes

1 box Shake 'n Bake, barbecue style

2 lemons

8 large precooked, peeled, and deveined shrimp

1 bottle cocktail sauce

8 ounces cheddar (or combined cheddar and jack) cheese

1 small tub sour cream

1 bottle blue cheese dressing

Staples

2 tablespoons olive oil

From the Liquor Store

Just about everything they have. You will need vodka, gin, run, tequila, triple sec, sour mix, cola, coffee liqueur, amaretto, Irish cream, milk, and soda water. Pick up some crushed ice, too, if your fridge freezer can't make it. You can opt to focus on one of the two party drinks or the other, but this is happy hour, so being able to make both elevates you to the exalted role of Bartender, so it might be worth the investment. Wouldn't hurt to have some beer and/or wine on hand, just in case she wants something less exotic as a second round.

Before she arrives:

7:00

1. Preheat the oven to 350 degrees.

2. Combine 2 tablespoons Tabasco sauce and 2 tablespoons water in a small mixing bowl. Add the chicken and turn several times to moisten. Let it sit for 30 minutes.

7:15

3. Wash and poke holes in the potatoes (to keep them from blowing up) and put them in the oven (directly on the oven rack) for an hour.

7:30

4. Put the chicken in a plastic bag and shake with the Shake 'n Bake as directed on the package. Pour 2 tablespoons olive oil into a 9x13-inch glass baking dish.

7:45

5. Place the chicken in the baking dish and put in the oven (with the potatoes) for 30 minutes.

After she arrives:

8:00

6. First of all, find out if she wants a Long Island Iced Tea or a Screaming Orgasm. Note that asking a girl you barely know if she wants a Screaming Orgasm is a good test of whether or not she is actually a Party Girl. If the response is frosty, you're (1) probably in the wrong part of this book and (2) going to be alone in a few minutes. If you survive the question, mix her a drink and proceed with the food.

Long Island Iced Tea

Fill a glass with ice. Add:

½ oz. vodka

½ oz. gin

½ oz. rum

½ oz. tequila

½ oz. triple sec

1 oz. sour mix

Top it off with cola and garnish with
    a lemon slice.

Screaming Orgasm

Fill a glass with ice. Add:

½ oz. vodka

½ oz. coffee liqueur

½ oz. amaretto

½ oz. Irish cream

Fill with equal parts milk and soda
    water.

7. Back to the food. Cut the lemon into wedges. Take out a couple of margarita glasses and fill them halfway with crushed ice. (If you don't have margarita glasses, you have no business dating a Party Girl.) Arrange the shrimp around the edge, with the front end in the ice and the tail hanging over the edge. Put the lemon wedges in the center and serve with a small dish of cocktail sauce.

8. Grate the 8 ounces of cheese.

9. The potatoes and wings should be done about the same time. Take them out and turn the oven to broil. Slice the potatoes open lengthwise and scoop out most of the innards. Cover the inside of the skins with cheese.

10. Put the cheese-covered potatoes under the broiler for 2 to 3 minutes. Bring the chicken to the table but keep a close eye on the skins—the cheese should melt and begin to bubble, but not burn.

11. When the potatoes come out, serve them immediately with sour cream.

The best effect will come from bringing out each item one at a time: first the shrimp, then the wings, then the skins. Then the dartboard, the pool table, and, at the opportune moment, the hot tub! See? This party goes to eleven.

Bonus Points

Stock up on fixings for those potato skins! Chives are first on the list, followed by bacon, mushrooms, and salsa.

Spring Break South of the Border: Ultimate Nachos and Body Shots

BODY SHOTS
ULTIMATE NACHOS
MARGARITAS

No doubt about it—Party Girls like finger food. Finger food is the kind of food you can eat without silverware, but more important, it is food that doesn't get in the way of the real business at hand: drinking. We've taken the party south of the border with the ultimate ten-ingredient nachos and margies on the rocks.

Body Shots is a drinking game that is a variation on Spin the Bottle, but with tequila. In other words, it's an excuse for simultaneous bodily contact while chugging down large quantities of highly powerful alcohol. Is the Party Girl fun or what?

Here are the basic Body Shots instructions: Sit in a circle with four or more people, a bottle of tequila, a bowl of lime wedges, and salt. When it's your turn, choose someone you want to do a "body shot" off of. Just in case you grew up in a monastery, a proper tequila shot starts with a lick of salt, then the alcohol, then a bite of lime. In this case, the lime wedge goes between her teeth, the salt goes somewhere on her body (the fun part comes when you choose which part), and the glass goes in your hand. Lick the salt off her body, toss the drink, then grab the slice of lime from her mouth with your teeth. If there is a purpose to this other than drunkenness and sexual titillation, we can't think of one. Which is fine.

So, you're asking, can we still play if there are only two of us, just me and my date? Dude.

Warning: Do not try playing this game with any other type of Girl. If she's not a Party Girl and you push this as an activity, she will nuke you back into the Stone Age. Here's what you can do to prevent annihilation: After the second margarita, jokingly suggest a little game of Body Shots. If she enthusiastically agrees, she's a true Party Girl. If she makes a face, drop the matter entirely and just focus on the margaritas. You have obviously made a tactical error in figuring out what type of Girl she is. Get through the date as best you can, and then start over on page 1 of this book.

One last note: If you are planning to serve chicken nachos, try to put the chicken in the barbeque sauce first thing in the morning so it has plenty of time to soak up the flavor.

To Buy

2 ripe (tender to the touch) avocados
A whole lot of limes—1 for the nachos, the rest for Body Shots

½ pound ground beef or boneless, skinless chicken breasts

1 container ground ginger, for beef (2 teaspoons) *or* 1 bottle mesquite barbeque sauce, for chicken (1 cup)

1 can refried beans (16 ounces)

16 ounces cheddar cheese

1 big bag tortilla chips, preferably the "restaurant-style" ones; not Doritos

1 small container sour cream

1 container fresh, refrigerated salsa

1 small can jalapeño peppers

Staples

2 tablespoons olive oil

1 white onion

1 clove garlic

Salt (to taste)

Pepper (to taste)

From the Liquor Store

Margarita salt

Margarita mix

Tequila

Ice (cubed)

Mexican beer

Before she arrives:

7:00

1. To make the guacamole, cut an onion into quarters and mince one of the quarters. Slice the avocados in half and remove the pit. Rather than digging out the pit with a spoon, just bury the knife into the pit with a firm chop. Then twist the knife, and *voilà!* The pit will slip loose like buttah. Scoop out the avocado into a medium mixing bowl or food processor. Process or mash with a fork until smooth (unless you like it chunky). Add the juice of half a lime (or a whole one, depending on how you like it) and the minced quarter onion. Smash or press a clove of garlic and mix it all together. Salt and pepper to taste.

7:30

2. If you are making beef nachos, sprinkle the ginger over the meat and brown it in 2 tablespoons olive oil in a frying pan. If you are making chicken, drench the birds in the mesquite sauce before cooking (put them in a small mixing bowl in the morning and let them soak all day in the refrigerator, if you can). Slice the chicken into strips and cook in a frying pan over low heat, turning occasionally, until cooked through.

7:45

3. Heat the beans in a small saucepan over low heat. Cover and keep warm. Grate the cheese.

After she arrives:

8:00

4. Get her started with a margarita. You can play Body Shots before, after, or instead of dinner; your call. For the margaritas, don't be afraid to buy premixed. Cuervo now sells margarita mix in a bottle with the tequila already added. Remember, the Party Girl is all about fun, not fuss. Try this trick with a Gourmet Girl and it will be your last date, but the Party Girl would rather have the second round of drinks be quick, not homemade. Of course, if you invested in bartending school and you've got the blender to prove it, knock yourself out.

8:15

5. Get the biggest glass baking dish you can find that will still fit in your microwave. Cover the bottom with a thick layer of tortilla chips. Cover with the meat, then the beans, then a thick layer of cheese. Slide it into the microwave for 1 to 2 minutes. If you prefer, you can also use the regular oven—it'll take about 10 to 15 minutes in there (and will brown a little on top).

6. Put the guacamole, sour cream, salsa, and jalapeño peppers in small serving dishes and bring them to the table. Put a spoon in each dish. Serve the nachos when the cheese is melted and let her ladle on her own toppings.

Bonus Points

If you really want to get that spring break feeling, a little Jacuzzi action is in order. Yes, that's right, gettin' hot in the hot tub. You don't have one? Is there a nearby hotel or apartment complex that has one you could "borrow"? Think, man! (Note: *Cooking to Hook Up* does not condone sneaking into private hot tubs.)

[easy]
Fun-due: Cheese Fondue and Wine Coolers

CHEESE FONDUE
GREEN APPLES
FRENCH BREAD
CHERRY TOMATOES
CHICKEN SAUSAGES
CHOCOLATE FONDUE
WINE COOLERS

We've said it once, we'll say it again—the Party Girl is all about fun, or in this case, Fun-due. You can improvise a fondue set with a camping stove, a hot plate, or tea light candles, but considering the bonus points you will get, we highly recommend dropping the $25 to $30 for a basic fondue set.

There is a French tradition that says that anyone who loses the contents of their fondue fork into the fondue must kiss the host. Now that you know this, we fully expect you to develop a severe case of butterfingers. Be aware that she will probably catch on after the fourth or fifth time, but who knows, by then she may be swept up in the je ne sais quoi of the whole thing. The literal meaning of *fondue* is "melted," and, if you can kiss worth a damn, the cheese may not be the only thing melting at your place.

To Buy

2 precooked chicken sausages

2 green apples

1 loaf French bread

1 pound (16 ounces) Gruyère cheese

1 small box cornstarch (4 tablespoons)

2 oranges

1 lemon

12 ounces Swiss chocolate

1 cup (8 fluid ounces) heavy cream

Staples

1 tablespoon olive oil

1 clove garlic

¼ teaspoon pepper

From the Liquor Store

Brandy or rum (2 tablespoons)

Dry white wine (1½ cups for the recipe as well as some to drink)

Ginger ale

Before she arrives:

7:15

1. Heat 1 tablespoon olive oil in a pan and cook the sausages until they are cooked through.

2. Cut up the sausages, apples, and bread into bite-size cubes. Set up the fondue burner on the table and array the sausages, apples, and bread around it. Some fondue sets have room around the burner for this. If yours doesn't, put the sausages, etc. in separate serving or soup bowls.

7:30

3. Grate the entire pound of Gruyère cheese into a large mixing bowl. Add 4 teaspoons cornstarch and mix together. Set aside.

4. Rub a halved clove of garlic around the inside of a medium-size saucepan and then discard the garlic.

7:45

5. Peel and chop up the oranges. Put them on a plate, cover with plastic wrap, and leave them in the refrigerator until it is time for dessert.

After she arrives:

8:00

6. Hey, this is the Party Girl! Start by mixing her a drink. Put ice into a tall glass and fill it ¾ of the way up with white wine, then stir in ginger ale to make a wine cooler.

8:15

7. Cut the lemon in half widthwise and squeeze the juice into a small glass. Put 1½ cups wine and 2 teaspoons lemon juice in the saucepan and bring the mixture to a light boil over medium heat. Gradually stir in the grated cheese. Add ¼ teaspoon pepper. Cook the mixture for 2 to 3 minutes before pouring it into the fondue pan. Carry the pan to the table, light the flame underneath it, and voilà!

8. When the cheese fondue is exhausted, carry the pan to the kitchen and wash it out. Then, put the fondue pot on the stove at low heat. Break up the chocolate bars into the pot. Add 1 cup of cream and stir gently until the chocolate melts. Stir in 2 tablespoons brandy or rum and move the pot back to the fondue stand on the table.

9. Bring out the platter of chopped oranges and repeat the whole dunking thing, this time dunking the oranges into the chocolate. Then repeat the whole "Gee, I seem to have lost my orange in the chocolate" thing. If you didn't overdo it with the cheese, it might be funny one more time.

Bonus Points

Jell-O shots are just outrageous enough to serve along with this meal. Substitute vodka for about a quarter of the water in a standard Jell-O recipe to create this frat-house standard. Pour the Jell-O mixture into small paper cups and put in the refrigerator to set at least an hour before she arrives.

You may want to shift drinks when the dessert comes out. Try coffee spiked with amaretto or Bailey's Irish Cream.

The Athletic Girl

No diet will remove all the fat from your body because the brain is entirely fat. Without a brain you might look good, but all you could do is run for public office.

—Covert Bailey, fitness expert

The Athletic Girl is tuned into her body, and probably has the Mighty Abs of Death to show for it. She is energetic and has little time for those who are not. Even outside of the workout room, you will find her energy level surprising, even exhausting, especially if you are the resident Rip Van Winkle at your gym—only showing up once every twenty years to steal another towel. An afternoon hike in the woods might turn into a ten-hour, 7-mile orienteering expedition any army ranger would be proud of.

The hallmark of the Athletic Girl is a lifelong competition to be her ultimate best. Don't go looking for the other contestants in her race, however; the Athletic Girl is only competing against herself, and she certainly isn't competing against you. Bragging about your 10K personal best is a quick trip to boyfriend prison. Leave that conversation for the guys in the locker room. When it comes to winning, this time it's personal. She loves a *challenge*.

The Athletic Girl rewards action more than words. No matter what you *say*, her eye is trained on what you *do*. Research data is hard to come by, but we suspect that all Athletic Girls are descendants of the Oklahoma "Show Me" tribe. She is most attracted to men who have that deep look of determination that comes from an ain't-no-mountain-high-enough attitude. Ever watch Lance Armstrong attack a Category 1 hill climb when the Tour de France is on the line? That look. Take note, however. While she may appreciate a workout partner, you don't have to be a gym rat to impress her. You can be typing up the Great American Novel or starting a llama-trekking business for all she cares. This woman just wants you to be striving toward *something.* Slackers will get a smile and a wave as she sweetly pedals on.

The Athletic Girl's regular workout boosts the levels of endorphins in her blood, making her optimistic, cheerful, and sanguine. Her 6:00 A.M. body-sculpting class is part of her strategy for staying on the sunny side of life. Make her miss her workout and you are courting disaster. Some Athletic Girls are so committed to their workout that they seem a bit obsessive, even addicted. Needless to say, there are worse things than being hooked on leaping out of bed at 5:30 to do crunches with a disturbingly perky kickboxing instructor. We can't think of any at this particular moment, but that's just because we're just too Indie-Progressive to even ponder this sort of thing.

Cooking healthy will certainly benefit you, but the confusion comes when you try to figure out which healthy camp your Athletic Girl belongs to. Exercise and diet plans come and go at various speeds, depending on which Hollywood stars embrace or reject them. We've given you a wide list of plans to choose from here, depending on which flavor of diet she follows, so do a little research ahead of time to find out which one she is on. Here's the rundown:

The Zone, or 40-30-30: Based on the idea that you should have 40 percent carbohydrates, 30 percent protein, and 30 percent fat. These women actually read those nutritional charts on the sides of the cartons.

The Atkins Diet: This is the low-carb, high-protein, and who-cares-about-the-fat diet. Steak and eggs are common, along with cheese, eggs, chicken, and fish. If it grazed, flew, swam, or was extracted from something that did, it's probably on the Atkins Girl plate.

Body for Life: Similar to the Zone but nowhere near as complicated; it also includes a lot of weight training, as well as muscle-building nutritional supplements, like creatine.

Carb Loading: The opposite of the Atkins, this is the high-carb meal that endurance athletes eat right before a major competition. Think pasta, bread, vegetables, and, sakes alive, *pizza.* Only for the night-before-the-race meal.

Low Fat: If your Girl is a member of Weight Watchers and is always counting calories or points, go with the low-fat meal. You'll know you've picked the right one when she whips out her point calculator before dinner. (Women who use the Jenny Craig system can only eat the food sold by that organization, so, unless you can convince your JC Girl to cheat, her dinner tonight is BYO.)

She Might Be an Athletic Girl If:

1. **She drives:** Rollerblades, a Trek mountain bike, or a Jeep Wrangler.

2. **She can talk for more than ten minutes about:** resistance training.

3. **She begins her sentences with:** "My Pilates teacher says . . ."

4. **She'd never, *ever:*** watch an all-day TV marathon.

5. **She owns any of the following:** a treadmill, jogging hand weights, high-protein shakes or vitamin supplements like creatine, a "Frequent Lifter" card at her gym, a water bottle signed by Mia Hamm.

Where You'll Find Her

She is easy to find, if you hang out at gyms, jogging paths, and the "Health and Diet" section of the bookstore. You can also find her hiking mountain trails, running a marathon, or playing soccer. Wherever she is, she won't be there long, so make your move before she starts her next set of wind sprints.

How to Spot Her

Look for Lycra, spandex, and other microfiber high-tech fabrics sold at places like REI and Foot Locker. Accessories include headbands, ponytail scrunchies, and cardio straps (the ones that tell you your heart rate). She will *always* have a bottle of water within easy reach, even in the car.

There are three common subsets of the Athletic Girl: Yoga, Outward Bound, and Actress. The Yoga Girl is so grounded, she's almost a hillside. She is usually in a leotard, carries her mat everywhere, and prefers to be barefoot whenever possible. Her energy is tempered by a relaxed serenity, but she can bend into shapes that would put you in traction.

Although not all Outward Bound Girls actually worked for that organization, they have all thought about it. Those who passed on the wilderness jobs still run "ropes" courses for high-school kids or corporate executives. The Outward Bound Girl lives in ankle-high hiking boots and usually has a bandanna tied on some part of her body. If it isn't on her, it's probably on her dog. Don't try to coop her up inside for more than a few hours. She needs the sun on her face and a mountain view.

The Actress is body-conscious for an entirely different reason: The camera doesn't lie. She may seem obsessed with keeping her figure, but it is a sad reality that her career may depend on it. TV people are fond of saying the camera adds ten pounds, but whether you believe that or not, there's no way to hide anything when your body is projected 30 feet tall.

Famous Athletic Girls

Naturally, all well-known athletes fit this category, as do all well-known Hollywood actresses, but especially the likes of Demi Moore, Linda Hamilton, Angelina Jolie, and Madonna (both Angelina and Madonna are hybrids). Jennifer Aniston, Renee Zellweger, and Cindy Crawford are all 40-30-30 proponents, while Catherine Zeta-Jones follows the Atkins Diet. Fran Drescher goes low-fat, while Sarah Ferguson does ads for (and presumably uses) Weight Watchers. At least this is what we read in *Us* magazine.

Your Place

The Athletic Girl's diet is strictly controlled, so ditch anything that might tempt her or lead her to believe that you actually eat that stuff. No candy bars, chips, or sugared sodas. Having a water cooler and home delivery of bottles is a good choice. Show some signs that you are active, healthy, and energetic (at least once a month). Having a set of free weights in the bedroom is good, if a bit cliché. Having other kinds of athletic equipment, like tennis rackets, hiking shoes, cross trainers, or a mountain bike (preferably things you actually use) lying around is good, but remember, the Athletic Girl can smell a talker who isn't a walker. Athletic Girls like fresh air, so unless you live next to a Dumpster, open the windows and let the outside in.

The Conversation

Remember, the endorphins are pumping through her body from her last workout, so go along with her bright, optimistic attitude. Might even do you good. Talking about training can be useful, as long as you don't sound like you are competing with her. If you are going to discuss workout regimens and diets, try asking her opinion instead of just offering up yours. Talking about pro sports is good, although be aware that just because she works out doesn't mean she is a fan of male team sports. Dropping comments about a few professional female athletes, however, like Jackie Joyner-Kersee or the Williams sisters, is probably a safe bet. Yoga women might like to discuss the various styles of yoga, like Ashtanga, integral, or kundalini. If you are hosting the Outward Bound subset, talk about the mountains or preserving the coastline. If you are dating an Actress, it could go a lot of ways, but remember, anything you say can and will be used in her scene study class.

The Coffee Table

Sports Illustrated, Men's Health, Health or any magazine devoted to a particular sport like *Cycling, Runner's World,* or *Triathlon* magazine. *Golf* doesn't count, no matter how good of a workout you think it is.

The Music

Stay upbeat, but remember, she just got done aerobicizing to Britney Spears, so she's probably ready to wind down. The Athletic Girl is pretty easy to please around her music, though. Keep it mainstream and pop-y. Like the Girl Next Door (and unlike the Indie), the Athletic Girl isn't going to lay judgments on your tunes.

The Drinks

If she's in training, she will most likely not be drinking alcohol. Whether she drinks or not, she will most definitely prefer low-calorie, fat-free libations such as mineral water, diet soft drinks, or unsweetened iced tea (provide packets of Equal or Sweet & Low just in case she uses those sweeteners). If she does drink, she might like a light beer. Wine is loaded with sugar, which equals calories, so proceed with caution.

The Shoes

Cross trainers, day-hiking boots, or clean sneakers. Fila sandals are good, if you just finished your own workout.

The Flowers

A spring bouquet would work great. Something that says bright, cheerful, and energetic. Like music, this is an area where the Athletic Girl is easy to please.

In The Zone: Chicken in Orange Sauce

CHICKEN IN ORANGE SAUCE
FRUIT SLICES
ALMONDS

The Zone diet, made popular by Dr. Barry Sears but taken up by others, teaches the gospel of 40-30-30. When you've got 40 percent carbohydrates, 30 percent protein, and 30 percent fat in your diet, you are "in the Zone." Generally, you can put together a Zone-friendly meal using a sophisticated measuring instrument—your hand. You need a portion of protein (meat, fish, soy, etc.) that's about the size and thickness of your palm and a portion of carbohydrates (vegetables, pasta, etc.) about the size of your fist. The fats tend to take care of themselves with a few nuts or some olive oil. While this method isn't precise, it does give you an opportunity to hold her hand early in the date. "I'm just measuring for the protein . . ." You dog.

To Buy

8 to 10 ounces boneless, skinless chicken, cut up

1 container frozen orange juice concentrate (3 tablespoons)

1 container whole cloves (2 cloves)

1 cinnamon stick

Pinch of cayenne pepper

1 box cornstarch (½ teaspoon)

2 peaches

1 nectarine

1¼ cup slivered almonds

Staples

Pinch of black pepper

Before she arrives:

1. Combine 3 tablespoons orange juice concentrate and ⅓ cup water in a nonstick frying pan over medium-high heat. Add chicken breast and brown both sides for about 8 to 10 minutes each side. Add the cloves, cinnamon stick, cayenne pepper and black pepper. Bring to a boil, then reduce the heat to medium-low and simmer for 7 to 10 minutes or until the chicken is just barely white all the way through.

2. In a small bowl, mix ½ teaspoon cornstarch together with another ¼ cup water. Add this mixture to the skillet and stir until the sauce thickens and begins to bubble.

7:45

3. Pit and cut up the peaches and nectarine.

After she arrives:

8:15

4. Arrange the chicken on two plates and surround it with the fruit pieces. Sprinkle the almonds over the top. Pour the rest of the sauce into a small bowl and serve it alongside so she can ladle it on herself. That's 40 percent fruits, 30 percent chicken, and 30 percent fat from the almonds and the chicken fat. Congratulations, you're in the Zone!

Bonus Points

Get a couple of ZonePerfect bars or other 40-30-30 nutritional bar. Zone Girls aren't supposed to let more than five hours go by between meals, so if things go well, you might need a midnight snack.

The Atkins Diet: Low-Carb Crab Cakes

LOW-CARB CRAB CAKES
ROASTED ASPARAGUS
LOW-CARB CHOCOLATE-COVERED STRAWBERRIES

When the Atkins diet started to really catch on a few years back, *Time* magazine put a photo on the front cover showing a hamburger the size of a dinner plate sitting on a bun the size of a silver dollar. While they were playfully exaggerating, most people are in for a surprise when they start eating on the Atkins diet. The emphasis on protein is based on the body's tendency to call out the insulin reserves when a large amount of carbohydrates appears. Insulin converts the carbs to fat cells and stores them away without burning them up. The Atkins theory says that focusing on protein and avoiding carbohydrates causes your body to use up those fat cells rather than storing away new ones. In any case, your goal isn't to provide a physiology lecture, your job is to keep her on her program, and maybe keep her around after midnight, so forget the details and dive into the meal.

The one shopping challenge here might be low-carb bread. Look for it in better grocery stores or visit the Atkins Web site at www.atkins.com for a store locator.

To Buy

1 loaf low-carb bread (4 grams carb per slice or less) (3 slices)

3 Atkins "Indulge" chocolate candy bars

6 large, long-stemmed strawberries

1 bunch celery (1 stalk)

1 bunch green onions (2 onions)

2 (6-ounce) cans crabmeat

1 small jar mayonnaise (½ cup)

1 container Old Bay seasoning (1 teaspoon)

¾ pound asparagus

Staples

2 tablespoons olive oil, plus some for sprinkling

Salt

Black pepper

Before she arrives:

5:15

1. Put 3 slices of bread in the freezer.

5:30

2. Preheat the oven to 350 degrees.

3. Line a large plate with aluminum foil or waxed paper. Unwrap the candy bars, place them in a bowl, and microwave on high until completely melted, 40 to 60 seconds. You may have to stir once or twice. Rinse and pat dry the strawberries. Holding each strawberry by its stem, dip it in the chocolate, leaving a bit of uncovered strawberry around the stem. Gently shake off excess chocolate and place the strawberry on its side on the foil. Repeat with the rest of the berries and stick the plate in the refrigerator.

6:00

4. Cut the frozen bread into cubes. Spread in a single layer on a baking sheet and bake 15 minutes until completely dry but not brown. Let cool. If you have a food processor, chop the bread until most of it is in fine crumbs. If you don't have the technology, put the bread in a Ziplock bag and mash with a coffee cup until the crumbs are as fine as possible.

6:15

5. Heat 1 tablespoon olive oil in a large frying pan over medium heat. Chop 1 stalk celery and 2 green onions and cook them until softened, about 3 minutes. Transfer to a large bowl. To the bowl add the 2 cans of crabmeat, 1 tablespoon of bread crumbs, ½ cup mayonnaise, and 1 teaspoon Old Bay seasoning. Save one of the crabmeat cans and rinse it out. You will need it in a minute.

6. Mix up the crab concoction with a fork until combined. Cover and refrigerate 20 minutes.

7:00

7. Time to get artsy. Sprinkle a thin layer of bread crumbs in the bottom of the crabmeat can. Fill the can with a 1-inch layer of the crab mixture, tamping it down with the bottom of a measuring cup. Once it is packed in, add another layer of bread crumbs on top. Gently shake the crab cake (for that is what it is) onto a plastic wrap–covered

baking sheet. If you are using the same sheet as you used for the bread, make sure it is cool, or you will have melting plastic wrap. Repeat this process for the rest of the crab cakes—you should get three or four from this mixture. Cover the crab cakes and refrigerate. Leave them in for an hour, if you can. If you are short on time, stick them in the freezer for 15 minutes.

7:30

8. Preheat the oven to 400 degrees.

9. Cut off the hard ends of the asparagus. Rinse and lightly pat dry. Line a 9x13-inch baking dish with aluminum foil. Spread the asparagus in the dish and sprinkle with a little olive oil, salt, and pepper. Mix with your hands to distribute the seasoning and spread the veggies out in a single layer. Set aside until she crosses the threshold.

After she arrives:

8:00

10. Put the asparagus in the oven and bake until tender and a little crisp, about 15 minutes. Shake the pan once or twice while cooking.

11. Once you have the asparagus going in the oven, heat 1 tablespoon olive oil in the frying pan over medium heat. Gently transfer the crab cakes to the frying pan with a wide, metal spatula. Cook 5 minutes, flip, and cook 5 minutes more.

12. If you are on schedule, the crab cakes and asparagus should reach doneness at about the same time. Transfer them both to plates and serve.

13. Once you have enjoyed your successful meal, bring out the chocolate-dipped strawberries as a finale. She might freak out when she sees the chocolate. Make sure you tell her that it's Atkins-approved or you may have to chase her as she flees the scene.

Bonus Points

The Atkins plan highly recommends a program of light exercise with the diet, so now's your chance for a romantic postdinner walk. Sharing a midnight smooch under the moonlight is a real calorie-burner, too, so tell her you'd like to help her program in any way you can. You're a giver, aren't you?

[easy]

Body-for-Life: Chicken Parmesan

BAKED CHICKEN PARMESAN
STEAMED SUMMER SQUASH
SIDE OF CREATINE

Bodybuilder Bill Phillips started an empire when he wrote *Body for Life,* a twelve-week guide to remaking your body and your mind through diet, exercise, and nutritional supplements. He then started giving away a million dollars a year to the winners of his muscle-building challenges. Whether your Athletic Girl is motivated by muscle or money, it's a sure bet you can impress her by helping her get through these three months. Avoid the butter and the egg yolks, balance the carbs and the proteins, and finish it off with Phillips's favorite supplement: creatine. You may have to go to a health food store to find that last one, but trust us, you'll get your Girl's attention by paying attention to her program.

To Buy

1 small container bread crumbs

1 container Italian seasoning (1 teaspoon)

2 skinless, boneless chicken breasts

1 package grated mozzarella cheese (½ cup)

1 jar tomato pasta sauce (2 cups)

2 summer squash

1 container bay leaves (3 leaves)

1 (8-ounce) box spinach or whole-wheat linguine

2 tablespoons creatine

Staples

1 teaspoon salt

½ teaspoon pepper

2 eggs

1 tablespoon olive oil

Before she arrives:

7:15

1. Preheat the oven to 400 degrees.

2. Start by separating 2 eggs. The best way to separate eggs is by gently cracking open the shell, keeping the yolk in one half. Pass the yolk back and forth between the two halves, letting the white drip into a bowl. Once all the white is out, throw away the shells and the yolks. Set the egg whites aside.

3. Mix together the bread crumbs, 1 teaspoon salt, ½ teaspoon pepper, and 1 teaspoon Italian seasoning. Cover the bottom of a dinner plate with the mixture.

4. Dip each piece of chicken into the egg whites, covering it with a good coating of egg. Roll the chicken in the bread crumb mixture until you have a good layer of breading.

5. Put 1 tablespoon olive oil into a frying pan and warm it up. Place the chicken in the pan and cook it, keeping the heat high enough to sizzle but not high enough to burn. Two minutes on each side should do it. It should not be completely cooked, just browned.

7:45

6. Into a 9x13-inch baking dish, pour 1 cup tomato sauce. Place the chicken in the sauce, then pour another 1 cup sauce on top. Sprinkle ½ cup mozzarella cheese on top of the chicken. Bake until the cheese is melted and the sauce is hot, about 10 to 15 minutes.

7. Once you have put the chicken in the oven, put some water (about two horizontal fingers high) into a basket steamer, along with the 3 bay leaves, and bring to a boil. Chop the summer squash into ¼-inch-thick rounds and put them in the steamer. The squash should be cooked through but still firm when done.

After she arrives:

8:00

8. Prepare the pasta according to the directions on the package. Ideally pasta should be *al dente,* which is Italian for "to the tooth." The noodles should be flexible but with a little resistance in the center.

8:15

9. When the pasta is done, drain it in a colander and make a pile on each plate. Put the chicken on top of the pasta bed. Add the veggies on the side and you are ready to go. Serve the meal with two glasses of water—one plain and one containing a heaping teaspoon of creatine. Enjoy your meal while talking about your favorite ab crunchers.

Bonus Points

Phillips markets his own line of nutritional supplements called Myoplex. You can make points with the Body-for-Life Girl by mixing a serving of chocolate Myoplex with one serving of fat-free, sugar-free hot cocoa mix and three ice cubes in a blender. Mix for 45 seconds and serve the chocolaty goodness for dessert.

Carb Loading: Sun-dried and Roasted Tomato Fettuccine

SUN-DRIED AND ROASTED TOMATO FETTUCCINE
ROASTED GARLIC
ITALIAN COUNTRY BREAD

Generally, athletes balance their proteins and carbs pretty carefully, but on the eve of a big event, they sometimes want to stock up their system with pasta, potatoes, bread, and rice. These complex carbohydrates provide bodily fuel for endurance-oriented sporting events like running, biking, and soccer. For example, Lance Armstrong's team of elite bike riders live on almost nothing but pasta for the two weeks of the Tour de France. Then again, they burn 9,000 to 10,000 calories a day sprinting through the countryside of France, while the more human of us burn 2,000 to 2,500 sprinting through the aisleways of Cubelandia. Under most circumstances, an Athletic Girl would shy away from this high-carb, low-protein meal, but if she's got a marathon in the morning, inviting her over tonight for a little "carb loading" might be downright romantic.

Because you need to buy a lot of it, the garlic is listed under "To Buy" this time around. Make sure you have some in the "staples" list as well, because you will need a small amount of minced garlic in addition to the 6 whole heads.

To Buy

6 whole heads of garlic

1 pound plum tomatoes

1 bunch fresh basil leaves

1 small jar oil-packed, sun-dried tomatoes (¼ cup)

1 small bottle white wine (¼ cup)

8 ounces fettuccine

Italian bread, preferably "rustico" or "country" style

Parmesan cheese (½ cup freshly grated)

Staples

3 tablespoons olive oil, divided

Pinch of salt

Pinch of pepper

2 tablespoons minced garlic

¼ cup chicken broth

Before she arrives:

6:15

1. Preheat oven to 350 degrees.

2. Wrap each head of garlic separately in aluminum foil and place them in the center of the oven. Bake for 45 minutes. When done, set them aside to cool, but leave them in the foil.

7:15

3. Boost the oven temperature to 400 degrees. Cut the plum tomatoes into wedges and toss them in a bowl with 1 tablespoon olive oil and a little salt and pepper until everything is coated. Roast them in a 9-inch square glass baking dish in the oven until the skins are slightly browned, about 10 to 15 minutes.

7:30

4. While the plum tomatoes are cooking, coarsely chop the basil until you've got ½ cup. To make the sauce, in a frying pan combine 2 tablespoons minced fresh garlic with 2 tablespoons olive oil, the roasted tomatoes (once they are out of the oven), ¼ cup sun-dried tomatoes, and ½ cup chopped basil leaves. Add ¼ cup white wine and ¼ cup chicken broth and simmer for 5 to 10 minutes. Turn the heat off under the sauce, cover, and let sit until dinnertime.

7:45

5. Bring at least 8 cups water to a boil in a large saucepan, then turn off the heat, cover, and let it sit. That way, it will be ready to go for the pasta when she arrives.

After she arrives:

8:00

6. Turn the heat back on under the water and bring it back to a boil. Add the fettuccine and cook until it is al dente, flexible but still firm in the middle, about 3 to 5 minutes.

7. Slice the bread while the pasta is cooking. Lay a clean kitchen towel over a small bowl, put the bread in the bowl, then close up the towel over the top.

8. Warm up the sauce if it has gotten cool.

9. Unwrap the garlic heads, cut off the top ¾ inch so those little cloves are peeking out, and arrange them on a small plate.

10. Place the pasta in a serving bowl, pour the sauce over the top, then sprinkle ½ cup Parmesan cheese over all of it. Bring it all to the table. Show her how to stick a fork into a clove of garlic, pop it out of the head, then spread it on the bread.

11. Ladle out the pasta and ask her about her personal best in the marathon. Remember, just because her last one was better than yours is no reason to get all huffy. You can lose the race and still win the Girl.

Bonus Points

She should go to bed limber before the race, so take a long, slow walk after dinner, then do some slow stretching on the living room floor. If you really want to be Mr. Perfect, massage her calves. Don't get frisky without permission, though. She may need that energy tomorrow.

Weight Watchers: Lemon-Pepper Halibut

LEMON-PEPPER HALIBUT
BASIL ZUCCHINI
APPLE CRISP

Most women are watching their weight one way or another; the Weight Watcher woman is just being more systematic about it. The Weight Watcher system assigns a certain number of "points" to each food item, depending on its nutritional or sin value. Each woman is given a certain number of points per day, depending on her weight, body type, and weight-loss goals. Weight Watcher women often carry point calculators that look like those slide rules the NASA guys used to carry around, but we recommend avoiding the "pocket protector" jokes.

The meal we have outlined here is only 8 points on the Weight Watcher scale, thus keeping her on track and making you the popular one.

Weight Watchers isn't the only weight-loss system out there, but, if your Girl is trying to slim down, it's a safe way to go. If she's doing Jenny Craig, she has to buy all her food from them, so she either has to cheat at your place or go potluck. We're betting she'll cheat, especially since you have gone to such lengths to give her a low-fat dinner.

To Buy

1 small box raisins (1 point per serving)

4 apples (McIntosh are best, 1 point per serving)

1 small container ground cinnamon (½ teaspoon)

1 (16-ounce) package long-grain white or basmati rice

2 (6-ounce) halibut fillets (5 points each)

1 lemon

1 small container lemon pepper seasoning (1 tablespoon)

1 large or 2 small zucchini (0 points)

1 small container dried basil (1 tablespoon)

1 small box fat-free granola (about 2 cups; 1 point per serving)

Before she arrives:

7:15

1. Preheat the oven to 350 degrees.

2. Put about two cups water in a small saucepan and bring to a boil over high heat. Pour the boiling water over ¼ cup raisins and let them sit for 5 minutes. Core and cut the four apples into thick slices and place in a 9x13-inch glass baking dish. Drain the raisins into a colander and mix in with the apples. Sprinkle on cinnamon (about ½ teaspoon). Cover with foil.

3. Bake covered for 30 to 40 minutes. At this point the apples should be tender but not mushy.

7:30

4. Rinse the small saucepan. Combine water and rice in the saucepan according to package directions and get it cooking.

7:45

5. Get out the 9-inch square glass baking dish and lay the halibut in it. Cut the lemon in half and squeeze both halves over the fish. Make sure you remove any seeds. Sprinkle 1 tablespoon lemon pepper seasoning over it. Set it aside until she arrives.

After she arrives:

8:00

6. Take the apple crisp out of the oven and set aside. Leave the foil on.

8:15

7. Put the fish in the 350-degree oven and check it after 8 minutes. The trick with fish is always to avoid overcooking, so keep a close eye on it and remove it from the oven when it is flaky and almost cooked through. Remember, it will cook a little on the way to the table, too.

8. While the fish is baking, put about an inch of water in the medium saucepan and bring it to a boil. Cut the ends off the zucchini, slice it into ⅛-inch-thick rounds, and put them in the basket steamer. Pour 1 tablespoon basil into your palm and crush it with your

thumb until it is very fine. Sprinkle it over the zucchini and drop the steamer into the saucepan. Check it every couple of minutes. You want the zukes to be tender but not mushy. They won't take more than 5 minutes.

9. Once the fish comes out of the oven, go back to the apple crisp. Remove the foil and add enough granola (about 2 cups) to cover the apples, then put it back in the oven without the foil for about 15 minutes or until the granola is browned.

8:30

10. At this point, the fish, the zucchini, and the rice should all be ready. Pile them onto plates and serve.

11. When the apple crisp is ready, remove it from the oven and set it out on the counter. When dinner is done, serve the still-warm crisp.

Bonus Points

Sprinkle a pinch of ground cloves on the apples along with the cinnamon to add more spice to your evening. Also serve a small cup of nonfat warm milk on the side with the apple crisp. She can pour a little over the crisp and it will cost only a point or two.

The Academic Girl

La-la-la I'm in love with a four-eyed girl.
—Rhett Miller song, "Four-Eyed Girl"

I f you want to date the Academic Girl, it's time to hit the books, or at least hit the bookstore. This is the Girl you never met in college because you never spent an evening in the Rare Books Room. Or, if you did, you were too busy reading rare books.

Actually, the Academic Girl has never really left the university, not because she's still chugging margaritas (see the Party Girl chapter) or wearing her college colors (see the Girl Next Door chapter), but because the Academic Girl is a lifelong learner, eternally seeking knowledge and culture and the answers to the Big Questions. This is the Girl whose favorite date is a lecture, whose cat is named Plato, and whose favorite love note is a footnote.

Stock up on a few choice quotations, preferably obscure, like:

> *There be none of Beauty's daughters, with a Magic like thee;*
> *and like music on the waters is thy sweet voice to me.*[1]

Yeah, that'll get her.

Or, if you are looking to get a bit bawdy, try dipping into Shakespeare, an ever flowing fountain of sexual references:

---

1. Lord Byron, the author of this poem, was (along with Percy Bysshe Shelley and John Keats), part of the early nineteenth-century British Romantic movement. Besides his extensive writings, he is also known as the man who challenged Mary Shelley to write a ghost story. She responded with a little thing she called *Frankenstein*.

Madam, before you teach the instrument,
To learn the order of my fingering,
I must begin with the rudiments of art.[2]

Isn't this great? You can actually look a woman you barely know in the eye, tell her that you are about to give her a lesson in pleasing you sexually, and live to tell your friends about it. Of course, if she is a Shakespearean scholar, she will know exactly what you mean (and understand the sexist attitude this remark portrays), but she will probably give you points for being well read and refrain from slapping you. Too hard.

Academic Girls like to delve, discover, and elaborate. They love it when you can dig into something arcane and discover a new piece of the liberal arts universe. This isn't only true in books. They appreciate the discovery of a good cafe or a remote medieval village in the Czech Republic. They are also argumentative. Let's not forget that PhD candidates do not turn in their theses, they "defend" them. The Academic Girl does not appreciate a casual opinion without some research behind it, so if you are going to go shoot off your mouth, you better have the reference chops to back it up.

One final note: Foreign languages are sexy to just about every kind of Girl, but they hold special significance for the Academic Girl, especially if you are American born. Sure, Europeans all speak six languages, but a homegrown boy who can quote Pablo Neruda in Spanish? Dude, you are *in*.

She Might Be an Academic Girl If:

1. **She drives:** a Volvo, a Saab, or a Toyota.

2. **She can talk for more than ten minutes about:** her thesis.

3. **She begins her sentences with:** "Noam Chomsky[3] says . . ."

4. **She'd never:** read *Cosmo*.

5. **She owns any of the following:** an *Oxford English Dictionary (OED)*, any book written in a "dead" language (Greek, Latin, Aramaic, etc.), a lifetime membership to Mensa.

---

2. William Shakespeare, *The Taming of the Shrew,* act 3, scene 1.

3. Noam Chomsky, professor of Linguistics at MIT, has written extensively on linguistics, philosophy, intellectual history, contemporary issues, international affairs, and U.S. foreign policy. He is known for being an educated conscience on foreign policy issues with such books as *Middle East Illusions* (Lanham, Md.: Rowman and Littlefield, 2003). The *New York Times Book Review* has described him as "arguably the most important intellectual alive."

Where You'll Find Her

Lectures, bookstores, libraries, cafes, anywhere people are talking about the Big Ideas.

How to Spot Her

She's the one reading the book and taking notes on a legal pad. Look for simple cardigans, comfortable shoes, and no-nonsense hair. Yes, think *librarian.* Academic Girls are not known for putting a whole lot of time and effort into their looks. You won't see them getting Botox injections or lining up at the Mac lipstick counter to check out the newest arrivals. We know one Academic Girl who, when she was in the throes of writing her dissertation on medieval literature, couldn't be bothered to break away for a haircut. When her bangs got long enough to obscure her vision, she just grabbed a pair of scissors from her desk and hacked them off.

Famous Academic Girls

Diane Chambers on *Cheers,* Hermione in *Harry Potter* (once she's old enough), Ione Skye in the movie *Say Anything,* Belle in Disney's *Beauty and the Beast,* Marian the Librarian in *The Music Man.*

Your Place

If you don't have a bookshelf full of books, you are probably after the wrong girl, but in a pinch, check out every weighty tome you can carry from the library. Reference books are key, like *The Oxford Companion to the English Language* and *The New York Public Library Desk Reference.* The complete works of Shakespeare is de rigueur, as is a large, unabridged dictionary.

The Conversation

For starters, ask her about her master's thesis. Then use lots of words that end in "ism." The Academic Girl is both romantic and Romantic, so thrill her by knowing the difference.[4] If you are feeling lucky, try faking your way through the classic books you read

---

4. Spelled with a lower case "r," *romantic* means having a preoccupation with love and with idealizing one's beloved. Spelled with a capital, *Romantic* refers to an eighteenth-century social, artistic, musical, and philosophical movement characterized by strongly personal, subjective, and organic thought. In it the individual is superior and feeling is superior to reason.

when you were much too young to understand them, like *David Copperfield* and *Moby Dick*. If you've seen the movie version, you can probably get away with it, unless you talk about the "Demi Moore" character in *The Scarlet Letter*. If you blow that one, we can't help you. One other tip: If she is at all theatrical, never quote *Macbeth*. It is surrounded by myth and superstition, and bad things happen to those who quote it. Don't even say the name. Refer to it only as "the Scottish play."

The Coffee Table

Magazines like *Smithsonian, Scientific American,* the *New York Times Book Review* or the *New Yorker*. For bonus points, finish the crossword in the *New York Times*. For *huge* bonus points, finish the Sunday one. In pen.

The Music

The genus *Femmus academicus* has several subspecies, including Musician. Far from the black-lipsticked, Stratocaster-strumming Indie Girl rocker, however, the musical AG plays Bach, Britten, and Gluck. They do both have a fondness for early Coltrane, though, so you're safe there. Whatever breed of academician she is, stay classical or classic jazz until told otherwise. We are told that some AGs have a hidden fancy for early Motown, but this trait has rarely been observed in the wild.

The Drinks

Scotch whisky (single malt, never blended) is the official drink of the Academic Girl, but if she's not into the hard stuff, Guinness is always good. If you would find it in an old Oxford pub, you are probably safe. Sherries and cognacs are also good. Unless the recipe tells you otherwise, stick with wines like Cabernet or Bordeaux.

The Shoes

Stay simple and comfortable. Pick shoes you can sit at your desk and think in. Stay away from expensive dress shoes or heavy boots. Remember those shoes your English teacher always wore? Those.

The Flowers

Pick your Shakespearean reference!

"A rose by any other name would smell as sweet." (*Romeo and Juliet,* act 2, scene 2)

" . . . prouder than Blue Iris." (*Troilus and Cressida,* act 1, scene 3)

"There's rosemary for remembrance." (*Hamlet,* act 4, scene 5)

" . . . honeysuckles ripen'd by the sun forbid the sun to enter." (*Much Ado about Nothing,* act 3, scene 1)

And what would a chapter about Academic Girls be without a . . .

Bibliography

Achbar, Mark, ed. *Manufacturing Consent: Noam Chomsky and the Media.* Montreal: Institute of Policy Alternatives, Black Rose Books, 1996.

Berington, David M., ed. *The Complete Works of Shakespeare.* 4th ed. New York: Harper Collins, 1996.

Brown, David Blayney. *Romanticism (Art and Ideas).* New York: Phaidon Press, 2001.

Byron, George Noel Gordon, Lord, and Jerome J. McGann, ed. *Lord Byron: The Complete Poetical Works.* Oxford: Oxford University Press, 1986.

Fargis, Paul, and Sheree Bykofsky, editorial directors. *The New York Public Library Desk Reference.* 2d ed. New York: Stonesong Press, 1993.

Gove, Philip Babcock, ed. *Webster's Third New International Dictionary of the English Language, Unabridged.* 3d ed. New York: Merriam-Webster, Inc., January 2002.

Jackson, Michael. *Michael Jackson's Complete Guide to Single Malt Scotch: The Connoisseur's Guide to the Single Malt Whiskies of Scotland.* 4th ed. London: Running Press, 1999.

John, Justin, and Kaplan Bartlett, eds. *Bartlett's Familiar Quotations: A Collection of Passages, Phrases, and Proverbs Traced to Their Sources in Ancient and Modern Literature.* 17th ed. New York: Little Brown & Company, 2002.

McArthur, Tom, ed. *The Oxford Companion to the English Language.* Oxford: Oxford University Press, 1992.

Randel, Don Michael, ed. *The New Harvard Dictionary of Music.* Cambridge: Belknap Press, 1986.

A Chaucerian Feast: Chiknes with the Marybones

CHICKEN WITH MARROW-BONES
BRAISED SPINACH
STILTON CHEESE
FLAVORED ALES OR WINE
STRAWBERRIES WITH WHITE CUSTARD SAUCE

And with his wyf he maketh feeste and cheere

—The Shipman's Tale, Canterbury Tales

Be ye redy forr a peelgrimege to Canterrberry? OK, reading Chaucer's poetic trave-logue, *The Canterbury Tales,* may get a little tough on the eyes, but lo, there are treasures to be found within, if ye go seeking recipes. How about "Take halfe a dosyn Chykonys, & putte hem in-to a potte; then putte ther-to a gode gobet of freysshe Beef"[5] for starters? Medieval feasting was a glorious sport, full of rowdy music, energetic dancing, and bawdy jests. You don't have to be a knight-errant to sweep your courtly maiden off her feete. Follow the tips we offer to make a Chaucerian banquet out of express-lane fare.

The table setting should have no silverware. Spoons were used for soups, but the fork is actually an Italian invention that didn't find its way to England until the late Renais-sance. Instead, the English employed an involved set of rituals to eat with their fingers. Certain fingers were used with certain foods, so as to ensure a supply of grease-free dig-its for future courses. Modern culinary inventors have seen fit to introduce the napkin, but we still suggest dispensing with the forks, both as a conversation piece and because eat-ing with your fingers is just too darn romantic. Listen to this little Chaucerian love note:

> *Wel koude she caire a morsel and wel kepe*
> *That no drope ne fille upon here brest.*[6]

Plates were also a rarity. Servers would place a round piece of bread, a *trencher,* before you and plop the food upon it. When you were done, the gravy-soaked bread would be fed to the dog at your feet or, at fancier castles, carried down to the gate and

---

5. Thomas Austin, *Two Fifteenth-Century Cookery-Books* (London: N. Trübner & Co., 1888).
6. Chaucer, "General Prologue," *Canterbury Tales,* line 130.

given to the peasants as alms.[7] We recommend using plates, although we still serve the meat on top of bread. It's still not a bad idea to have a dog around, to provide atmosphere and handle spills.

Each course began with a trumpet fanfare, rolling of drums or a pipe tune. In fact, music was important throughout the meal. Minstrels would sing, accompanied by a lute or harp; instrumentalists would accompany troupes of dancing guests or hired performers.[8] Crank up that early music collection for a real mood setter.

When you visit the grocery store, you will need to talk to the butcher to get a cracked beef shank. Cracking it just means cutting it open, so the flavor of the marrow will seep into the chicken. Cheese was typically served after a meat course, a practice recommended by physicians to aid with digestion.

To Buy

1 container honey (2 tablespoons)

1 whole chicken, in pieces

1 beef shank bone, split open

Fresh parsley (1 tablespoon chopped)

Fresh sage (2 teaspoons chopped)

1 bag baby spinach

1 loaf bread, preferably country-style multigrain or black bread, sliced

½ pound Stilton cheese

1 quart strawberries

Staples

2 eggs

1 cup and 2 teaspoons milk

1 teaspoon and some pinches of salt

2 teaspoons sugar

1½ tablespoons butter

3 tablespoons finely chopped onions

Pinch of pepper

1 clove garlic

1½ tablespoons flour

2 cups vegetable broth, divided

---

7. Madeline Pelner Cosman, *Fabulous Feasts* (New York: George Braziller, 1976), 180.

8. Ibid, 94.

From the Liquor Store

Flavored ales are very much in the period style, as are both red and white wine. You could go with a German Reisling, a sweet white wine, which would be very similar to Vernage, which was popular in Chaucer's day.

Before she arrives:

6:45

1. If you have chosen white wine or ale, put it in the refrigerator to chill. Rinse the strawberries and remove the stems. Leave them in the refrigerator.

2. Start with dessert. Separate two egg whites and put them in a small saucepan with 1 cup milk. To separate eggs, crack the egg in two over the mixing bowl. Pass the yolk back and forth between the two eggshell halves, allowing the egg white to fall into the bowl. When all the egg whites are in the bowl, throw the eggshells and the yolk away.

3. Cook the milk and egg mixture over medium heat, stirring often, until boiling gently. Lower heat and simmer for 5 minutes while stirring continuously, then add 2 tablespoons honey and a pinch of salt. Simmer another minute, then blend in a blender. Add 2 more teaspoons of milk and 2 teaspoons of sugar. Stick the blender pitcher in the refrigerator to chill.

7:15

4. Place the chicken and beef bones in a large stockpot and cover with water. Bring to a boil. Reduce the heat to a simmer; stir in the parsley, sage, and 1 teaspoon salt; and cook slowly until the chicken is tender, about an hour.

After she arrives:

8:00

5. Offer her a drink. On to the spinach. Melt 1½ tablespoons of butter in a frying pan over medium heat, add 3 tablespoons finely chopped onion and a pinch of salt and pepper, and sauté until light golden colored. Mince 1 clove garlic (or, if you have one, use a garlic press), add it to the pan and let it cook for a minute. Toss in the spinach and mix it in well with the sauce. Turn the heat up to medium-high and continue cooking until the spinach has shrunk and most of the liquid is gone. Sprinkle with 1½ tablespoons flour and cook for 2 more minutes. Reduce the heat to low and slowly stir in 1 cup broth. Bring to a simmer and cook, stirring occasionally, for 10 to 15 minutes. Toast four slices of bread.

6. Heat a cup of broth on the stove or in the microwave. Divide toasted bread onto two dinner plates. Pour the warm broth over the bread and arrange the chicken on top. Use a slotted spoon to serve the spinach beside the bread.

7. When the course is finished, bring out a plate of Stilton cheese to settle your stomachs. Put a small knife on the cheese plate so she can cut her own slices. After the cheese, spoon out the strawberries on two small plates and pour the cream mixture over the top. Don't even *think* of using forks to eat them. These are the ultimate finger foods.

Bonus Points

A contemporary of Chaucer, Francesco Petrarca (Petrarch), was considered the first modern poet. His collection of poems, entitled the *Canzoniere,* was inspired by a woman named Laura (probably Laura de Noves), a young woman he saw for the first time in church on Good Friday when he was twenty-three and she was nineteen. He felt so much love for her that over the next twenty years, he wrote 366 sonnets for her. A sonnet is a lyric poem of fourteen lines with a formal rhyming scheme. Although Petrarca did not invent the sonnet (Dante did), he is said to have been the one to perfect it.

One common tradition in a medieval feast was to serve small, flat platters, called *roundels*, made of porcelain or stiff paper, with the final course. When the dish had been eaten, guests turned the roundel over to find a poem or text pasted to the bottom. The music would strike up and each guest would sing the text to an improvised melody.

While neither one of you may be brave (or drunk) enough to improv medieval karaoke, you could pick up a copy of Petrarca's *Canzoniere*, make a photocopy of one of the sonnets, and paste it to the bottom of her dessert plate.

Bibliography

Austin, Thomas. *Two Fifteenth-Century Cookery-Books. Harleian MS. 279 & Harl. MS. 4016, with extracts from Ashmole MS. 1429, Laud MS. 553, & Douce MS 55.* London: For the Early English Text Society by N. Trübner & Co., 1888.

Black, Maggie. *The Medieval Cookbook.* New York: Thames and Hudson, 1992.

Chaucer, Geoffrey. *The Canterbury Tales.* Edited by V. A. Kolve and Glending Olson. New York: W. W. Norton, 1989.

Cosman, Madeleine Pelner. *Fabulous Feasts.* New York: George Braziller, 1976.

Hammond, P. W. *Food & Feast in Medieval England.* Dover: Alan Sutton Publishing, 1993.

Hieatt, Constance B., Brenda Hosington, and Sharon Butler. *Pleyn Delit: Medieval Cookery for Modern Cooks.* 2d ed. Toronto: University of Toronto Press, 1996.

Petrarca, Francesco (Petrarch). *Petrarch: The Canzoniere, or Rerum vulgarium fragmenta.* Translated by Mark Musa. Bloomington, Ind.: Indiana University Press, 1999.

Renfrow, Cindy. *Take a Thousand Eggs or More: A Translation of Medieval Recipes from Harleian Ms. 279, Harleian Ms. 4016, and Extracts of Ashmole Ms. 1439, Laud Ms.* Unionville, N.Y.: Royal Fireworks Press, 2003.

[easy]

Papa's Tapas, or A Moveable Feast: Hemingway's Picnic of Spanish Tapas

SPANISH OLIVES
MANCHEGO CHEESE
SERRANO JAMON (HAM)
POTATAS BRAVAS (POTATOES WITH PAPRIKA SAUCE)
PAN CON TOMATE Y AJO (BREAD WITH TOMATO AND GARLIC)
SPANISH RIOJA

These are tapas that may very well have been eaten in *The Sun Also Rises,* Hemingway's classic novel about Spain. We've made them picnic-friendly, *A Moveable Feast,* if you will. Academic Girls don't tend to get much sunshine—so tempt her away from her dissertation by surprising her with a picnic basket full of sexy finger foods and a good bottle of Rioja. You don't have to travel to *The Green Hills of Africa* or *The Snows of Kilimanjaro,* just find a nice grassy spot where you can spread a blanket.

The word *tapa* is Spanish for "top," or "lid." No one knows for sure where the name originated, but most think that it came from the eighteenth century when bartenders would cover a glass of wine or sherry with a lid—a slice of bread or ham—to keep the flies away. It was also a way to make customers thirsty (and thus, get them to order more drinks), since the tapas were often salty.

While your Academic Girl will be impressed by facts such as these, the meal itself is a lot easier than your chemistry midterm. Make this recipe and we promise, it'll do all the work for you. Ask not for whom the meal toils—it toils for thee.

Note: The schedule will have you ready to go by noon.

To Buy

5 medium-size tomatoes

2 large Russet potatoes

1 container paprika ($\frac{1}{2}$ teaspoon)

1 French baguette

8 ounces Manchego cheese

8 ounces sliced Serrano ham (available at gourmet food stores)

1 small jar Spanish olives

Paper plates

Plastic cups

Plastic silverware

Staples

2 tablespoons olive oil, plus some for drizzling

5 cloves garlic

1 dash balsamic vinegar

1 teaspoon flour

Salt (to taste)

Pepper (to taste)

From the Liquor Store

A good bottle of Spanish Rioja

Special Equipment

1 plastic (1-quart) container with lid

The Day Before (Or The Same Day If You Work Fast):

1. Map out a place to have a picnic. It could be your backyard or in a local park, or by the lake—anywhere scenic and comfortable with grass, trees, water. Find a large basket or bag to hold all the goodies and a blanket to sit on.

The Day of the Date:

10:00

2. Preheat the oven to 350 degrees. Rinse 2 of the tomatoes and quarter them. Rinse the potatoes and cut them into bite-size cubes. In a medium saucepan over medium heat, add 1 tablespoon olive oil, 2 cloves smashed garlic, and 2 chopped potatoes. Cook on medium heat, stirring often, until potatoes are brown and cooked all the way through, about 15 minutes. Then remove from heat and drain potatoes on paper towels. When completely drained, transfer to a medium bowl.

3. Add another tablespoon olive oil to the saucepan; add 2 cloves smashed garlic, followed by the quartered tomatoes and ½ teaspoon of paprika. Cook for about 5 minutes; add a dash of balsamic vinegar, a teaspoon of flour, and some salt and pepper (to taste); and mix well. Pour the tomato mixture over the potatoes and stir. Transfer to a plastic container with a lid. This is the Potatas Bravas.

11:00

4. Slice the baguette into 1-inch-thick slices. Smash 1 garlic clove and set aside. Drizzle a little bit of olive oil on each of the slices of bread. Put in the oven for 10 to 15 minutes. Roughly chop the remaining 3 tomatoes and stir in the crushed garlic. Remove the bread slices from the oven, spread on the chopped tomatoes and garlic, and wrap in foil to keep warm.

11:30

5. Time to pack. Unwrap the Manchego cheese and cut into half-inch slices. Put into a Ziplock or other resealable plastic bag. Open the package of ham and put it into a Ziplock bag (so you won't struggle trying to open the package later). Pack your bag with the container of Potatas Bravas, the foil-wrapped bread, the plastic bag of Manchego cheese, the plastic bag of ham, the jar of olives, and the paper plates and plastic cups and silverware. Don't forget the wine and a corkscrew. You're good to go!

Bonus Points

Throw in some fresh fruit for dessert. Spain is famous for its oranges, but you could also bring pears, apples, or figs. Manchego cheese is traditionally served with Membrillo Quince Paste, so pick up a few ounces at a better quality deli or gourmet shop.

Bibliography

Hemingway, Ernest. *For Whom the Bell Tolls.* New York: Scribner; reprint edition, 1995.

———. *The Green Hills of Africa.* New York: Scribner, reprint edition, 1996.

———. *A Moveable Feast.* New York: Scribner, 1996.

———. *The Snows of Kilimanjaro.* New York: Scribner, 1995.

———. *The Sun Also Rises.* New York: Scribner, reprint edition, 1995.

Pub Grub I: Pygmalion Bangers & Mash

BANGERS & MASH
HARD CIDER
TRIFLE PUDDING
HOT BUTTERED RUM

Here's a little meal inspired by George Bernard Shaw's classic play, *Pygmalion* (later made into the musical *My Fair Lady*), in which phonetics professor Henry Higgins teaches Eliza Doolittle, a Cockney girl, to speak proper English. Cockneys are especially interesting to linguists, because they invented their own dialect called Cockney rhyming slang. It originated in the mid-nineteenth century as a way for illegal street traders to talk in code.

The way it works is that they replace a word with a rhyming phrase. So instead of using the word *eyes,* they'll say "mince pies." The expression "Let's get down to brass tacks" comes from Cockney rhyming slang: "Brass tacks" rhymes with *facts.* It can get a little confusing when the rhyme becomes truncated. For example, "loaf of bread" is Cockney rhyming slang for *head.* Instead of "Use your head," they'll say, "Use your loaf." New rhyming slang is being invented all the time, such as "Mork and Mindy" for *windy* and "Judi" for *wrench* (*wrench* rhymes with "Judi Dench").

This is the kind of language you will hear at an East End pub, and most Academic Girls would be utterly fascinated by it, just as old Higgins was. We've included a glossary at the end of the recipe to help you with the lingo.

Right, so you're *down the nuclear* over by the *uni, on the pull,* you know, *checking out the talent,* when you see a *tidy* Academic *Bird* you *fancy.* You're *keen as mustard* to *chat her up,* but you never even passed your *bloody A-level. Bollocks!* What's a *bloke* to do?

No probs, old *china,* we've got it *sorted.* We'll *gen you up* with just the thing to get her mind off her *marks.* Just *ring* her up and ask her over your *flat* for a good *nosh up. Babble* this *lilly and skinner,* a *cracking* dish when it's *parky* outside. She's probably *right knackered* from *swotting,* and *Hank Marvin* since she only eats over at the *buttery.* And everyone knows that food is *total pants.*

Some *luvvly-jubbly* comfort food is what this *hen* needs. Bangers & Mash is *brill* comfort food—*dead scrummy* and *cheap as chips.* It's just sausage and *taters,* covered in *army.* After a few pints of *Winona,* she'll be *bloody elephant's.* Give 'er a bit of this *moreish* pudding, and *Bob's your uncle, mate. Easy peasy lemon squeezy.* After a *nosh* like that, you'll soon be *getting her kit off*. Since she's bound to be *gagging for it,* you're sure to get in a bit of *snogging.* If you're really *jammy,* you could end up *on the job,* a bit of the old *How's Your Father,* you know, the old *rumpy pumpy.* Trust us, *mate,* with this grub, you'll be *sound as a pound.*

Right, enough of this *fannying around*—let's *get cracking!*

To Buy

1 (3-ounce) box vanilla pudding (not instant pudding)

6 large baking potatoes

1 pound pork or beef sausages

1 package brown gravy mix

1 (16-ounce) carton heavy cream

1 store-bought angel food cake

Raspberry preserves (4 tablespoons)

1 package fresh raspberries or strawberries

2 cinnamon sticks

Staples

2 cups plus ½ cup milk

½ onion

3 tablespoons butter, divided

Salt (to taste)

Pepper (to taste)

1 tablespoon olive oil

3 tablespoons plus 2 teaspoons sugar

From the Liquor Store

A few bottles of British cider ale

1 bottle rum (11 tablespoons)

1 small bottle brandy (6 tablespoons, you can get the cheap stuff)

Before she arrives:

4:45

1. Set the cider on the counter, not in the fridge. (You'll want to serve it just below room temperature, so we'll have you put it in the fridge at the last minute.)

2. Put a medium saucepan on the stove on low heat. Empty the box of pudding mix into the pot and add 2 cups milk. Cook for 10 to 15 minutes, stirring occasionally, until it becomes thick and, well, puddinglike. Remove from heat, transfer to a medium mixing bowl, mix in 3 tablespoons rum, and stick in the fridge to cool while you make the Bangers & Mash.

5:15

3. Peel the potatoes, put them on a plate, and stick them in the microwave for 15 to 20 minutes on high, or until they are soft.

4. While the potatoes are cooking, chop up ½ an onion.

5. When the potatoes are done, put in a food processor and add ½ cup milk and 1 tablespoon butter and mix until smooth. Add a bit of salt and pepper to taste.

6:00

6. Heat 1 tablespoon olive oil in a frying pan on medium heat. Cook the sausages until heated all the way through, about 10 to 15 minutes. Set the sausages aside.

7. Add 1 tablespoon butter to the pan, and cook the chopped onion over medium heat until soft. To the pan add the gravy mix and water as directed on the package. Stir constantly and cook until you get a thick gravy.

8. Pour half the gravy into a 9x13-inch glass baking dish. Slice the sausages in half (butterfly) and add them to the dish of gravy. Pour the rest of the gravy over the top, then top with your mashed potatoes. Cover with foil and set aside. Preheat oven to 350 degrees.

6:45

9. Let's get back to the pudding, shall we? Take the chilled pudding out of the fridge and set it on the counter. In a large mixing bowl, whip 1 cup of the heavy cream and 1 tablespoon sugar with an electric hand mixer until stiff. Add to the pudding and stir just enough to incorporate. Do not overmix.

10. Slice the angel food cake horizontally in half. Take the top piece and, on the crust side, coat it with 2 tablespoons raspberry preserves. Now put it crust-side down (yes, your preserves are going smack against the plate) on a large serving dish. Pour 2 tablespoons brandy on the layer of cake and then spoon on half the pudding mixture.

11. Take the other cake slice, coat the crust side with 2 tablespoons raspberry pre-serves, and lay it crust-side down on top of the first layer. Add 2 more tablespoons brandy and the other half of the pudding mixture. Cover with most of the berries (set aside a handful—you'll need them later) and add yet 2 more tablespoons of brandy (hmm . . . now we know why those Brits are always so darn cheerful).

7:30

12. Pour the other cup of heavy cream into a mixing bowl, add 2 tablespoons sugar, and whip with an electric hand mixer until stiff. Decorate the top of the pudding with the whipped cream and top with the berries you set aside. Stick in the refrigerator until you are ready to serve.

7:45

13. Set the timer and bake the Bangers & Mash at 350 degrees for 20 minutes. Stick the cider in the fridge for 15 minutes to cool it slightly.

After she arrives:

8:00

14. Serve the Bangers & Mash with a glass of cider.

15. After you're finished with the first course, prepare the hot buttered rum: Get out 2 mugs and fill about ¾ full with water. Stick in the microwave on high for 1 to 2 minutes, until piping hot. To each mug of hot water, add 4 tablespoons rum, 1 teaspoon sugar, and 1 cinnamon stick. Float a small pat (½ tablespoon) of butter on top.

16. Serve the trifle pudding with the mugs of hot buttered rum.

Bonus Points

Rent *My Fair Lady.* Or, here's an even smarter pick: *Educating Rita*, a brilliant 1980s sleeper. The story of a working-class hairdresser who goes back to college, it won the British Academy Award for Best Picture, Best Actor (Michael Caine), and Best Actress (Julie Walters).

Glossary

A-level. (noun) exam given at the end of high school.

army. (noun, Cockney rhyming slang, from "army and navy") gravy.

babble. (verb, Cockney rhyming slang, from "babbling brook") cook.

bird. (noun) female.

bloke. (noun) guy.

bloody. (1) (adjective) stupid, (2) (adverb) very.

Bob's your uncle. (phrase) British slang for "you've got it made" or "you're all set."

bollocks. (exclamation) literally means "testicles."

brill. (adjective) excellent, abbreviation of *brilliant*.

buttery. (noun) cafeteria.

chat (someone) up. (verb) to hit on someone of the opposite sex.

cheap as chips. (phrase) inexpensive.

checking out the talent. (phrase) looking at women.

china. (noun, Cockney rhyming slang, from "china plate") mate, or friend.

cracking. (adjective) great, excellent.

dead. (adverb) extremely.

down the nuclear. (phrase, Cockney rhyming slang, from "nuclear sub") at the pub, or at a bar.

easy peasy lemon squeezy. (adjective, Cockney rhyming slang) easy, simple.

elephant's. (noun, Cockney rhyming slang, from "elephant's trunk") drunk.

fancy. (verb) like, desire.

fannying around. (phrase) screwing around, wasting time.

flat. (noun) apartment.

gagging for it. (phrase) eager to have sex.

gen (someone) up. (verb) give (someone) information.

get cracking. (phrase) get going, get started.

get (someone's) kit off. (phrase) taking (someone's) clothes off.

Hank Marvin. (adjective, Cockney rhyming slang) starving.

hen. (noun) woman.

How's Your Father. (phrase) have sex.

jammy. (adjective) lucky.

keen as mustard. (phrase) eager.

knackered. (adjective) exhausted.

lilly and skinner. (noun, Cockney rhyming slang) dinner.

luvvly-jubbly. (adjective) lovely.

marks. (noun) grades (in school).

mate. (noun) friend.

moreish. (adjective) tasty, delicious (meaning so good you want more).

no probs. (phrase) no problem.

nosh or nosh up. (noun) meal.

on the job. (phrase) have sex.

on the pull. (phrase) looking for a date, trying to pick up women.

parky. (adjective) cold weather.

right. (1) (figure of speech) OK, (2) (adjective) very.

ring (someone) up. (phrase) call (someone) on the phone.

rumpy-pumpy. (noun) sex.

scrummy. (adjective) delicious; abbreviation of *scrumptious.*

smashing. (adjective) excellent.

snogging. (verb) kissing, making out.

sorted. (adjective) worked out, figured out.

sound as a pound. (phrase) British version of American slang "good as gold" or "golden."

swotting. (verb) studying.

taters. (noun) potatoes.

tidy. (adjective) attractive, sexy.

total pants. (phrase) total crap.

uni. (noun, abbr.) university.

Winona. (noun, Cockney rhyming slang, from "Winona Ryder") cider.

Pub Grub II: Welsh Rabbit vs. Rarebit

WELSH RABBIT/RAREBIT (MELTED CHEESE ON TOAST)
WALNUTS AND SLICED PEARS
BLACK & TANS
STICKY TOFFEE PUDDING (DATE CAKE WITH HOT TOFFEE SAUCE)
SINGLE MALT SCOTCH WHISKY

Here's your chance to render your Academic Girl speechless with a little etymology (that's the study of word origins). The issue: Is it Welsh *rabbit* or *rarebit?* Most people think *rarebit* is correct, but those folks are wrong. The *OED (Oxford English Dictionary)* cites the origin of the term *Welsh rabbit* as 1725, whereas *Welsh rarebit* was not used until 1785.

The term *Welsh rabbit* was actually an ethnic slur, the joke being that the Welsh were so poor, they couldn't afford meat, so cheese on toast was their version of ''rabbit.'' The Welsh were so scapegoated, in fact, that the verb *welch* came about in 1857, slang in the sport of racing for refusing to pay money put down on a bet. But back to the rarebit. The switchover was either a miscommunication or someone's attempt to make it politically correct. Either way, *rabbit* is the correct term. However, if you go to Wales, you won't see it on a menu—they call it *rarebit.* I guess they're still a little sensitive about the whole thing.

Here is a very old version of the recipe for Welsh Rabbit, from a cookbook written in 1669:

Savoury Tosted or Melted Cheese

(From Sir Kenelme Digbie's *The Closet Opened*)
Cut pieces of quick, fat, rich, well tasted cheese, (as the best of Brye, Cheshire, &c. or sharp thick Cream-Cheese) into a dish of thick beaten melted Butter, that hath served for Sparages or the like, or pease, or other boiled Sallet, or ragout of meat, or gravy of Mutton : and , if you will, Chop some of the Asparages among it, or slices of Gambon of Bacon, or fresh-collops, or Onions, or Sibboulets, or Anchovis, and set all this to melt upon a Chafing-dish of coals, and stir all well together, to Incorporate them ; and when all is of an equal consistence, strew some gross White-pepper on it, and eat it with tosts or crusts of White-breat. You may scorch it at the top with a hot Fire-Shovel.

Don't worry, we won't make you go buy a "Chafing-dish of coals" or a "hot Fire-Shovel." We've simplified the entire process, and we've even rewritten the menu so you'll be able to make some sense of it.

But before we get into the food, just a little more etymology. The Black & Tan, also called a Half & Half, is a favorite in pubs. It's basically a pint glass with half Guinness or other stout beer and half Bass or other ale. The Black & Tan is named after a breed of beagles used as hunting dogs in Ireland. It was also used to refer to a regiment of British soldiers sent to Ireland in 1921 (their uniforms were black and tan). Meanwhile, *whisky* (yes, the *e* was left out on purpose—this is how it is spelled in Scotland) in Gaelic means "water of life." The Scots are so proud of their whisky, in fact, that in Scotland they don't call it Scotch. They call it whisky. Whisky that comes from Ireland is called "Irish whisky," whisky from the United States, "American whisky." But Scotch whisky is just "whisky."

To Buy

8 ounces pitted, dried dates

1 box baking soda (1 teaspoon)

1 small bottle vanilla (1 teaspoon)

8 ounces sharp cheddar cheese

1 small container dry mustard (½ teaspoon)

1 small bottle Worcestershire sauce (2 tablespoons)

4 slices bread, preferably whole-grain or brown

2 pears

½ pound walnuts

Staples:

10 tablespoons (1¼ sticks) butter, plus a little extra to butter a pan

¾ cup sugar plus 6 tablespoons

1 egg

2 cups plus 2 tablespoons flour

Pepper (to taste)

3 tablespoons milk

From the Liquor Store

Guinness Stout (at least 1 pint plus 1 cup)

Bass Pale Ale (at least 1 pint)

Single malt Scotch whisky

Before she arrives:

7:00

1. Preheat oven to 350 degrees.

2. Let 4 tablespoons (half a stick) of butter sit out for a while to soften.

3. Bring 1½ cups of water to a boil in a small saucepan (you will actually use only 1 cup, but some will evaporate).

4. Butter a 9-inch square glass baking dish.

5. Put 8 ounces pitted dried dates into the food processor and pulse until chopped up finely. Put in a small mixing bowl, pour 1 cup of the boiling water on them, and set aside.

7:15

6. In a medium mixing bowl, add the softened 4 tablespoons butter and ¾ cup sugar and beat with an electric hand mixer. Add 1 egg and mix well. Gradually add 2 cups flour, continuing to beat. Mix in 1 teaspoon baking soda, 1 teaspoon vanilla, and the date mixture.

7. Pour into the buttered dish and bake at 350 degrees. Set the timer for 30 minutes.

7:30

8. Rinse out the food processor. To make the rabbit, grate the 8 ounces cheddar cheese with a cheese grater or throw it in the food processor and pulse a few times. Melt 2 tablespoons butter in a medium saucepan over low heat. Add 2 tablespoons flour and ½ teaspoon dry mustard, stir with a wire whisk, and cook for 5 minutes.

7:45

9. Stir in 1 cup Guinness and cook for another 5 to 10 minutes. Add the cheese to the pan and stir in 2 tablespoons Worcestershire sauce and black pepper to taste. Cover and remove from heat.

After she arrives:

8:00

10. When the timer goes off, check to see if the cake is done. Press down gently on the middle (not hard enough to break the surface), then let go. If the cake springs back into shape, it's done. If not, give it 5 more minutes and check again. When done, remove the cake from the oven and set aside.

11. Take 2 pint glasses and slowly fill halfway with Bass, titling the glass so you don't get a head of foam. Very, very slowly, pour Guinness in to fill each glass. Do not jostle. You should have half dark liquid and half light. Serve. (You may want to practice this before she comes. Not bad as far as homework goes.)

12. Slice the pears. On a separate plate, arrange the walnuts and the sliced pears.

13. Put the pan of cheese back on the heat to warm it up. Toast 4 slices of bread, transfer to dinner plates, and spoon on the melted cheese. If you've got a toaster oven, stick them in for a minute or so until the cheese is bubbly on top.

14. When you're through with the first course, head into the kitchen to finish making the pudding. To make the toffee sauce: In a small saucepan melt a half stick of butter (4 tablespoons) over low heat. Add 6 tablespoons sugar and 3 tablespoons milk.

15. Cut the pudding into squares, set on plates, and pour on the hot toffee sauce. Serve with the whisky, either neat (no ice) or on the rocks, depending on how she likes it.

Bonus Points

Play a game of Scrabble while you sip whisky and have your pudding. If you're lucky, the wordplay will turn into foreplay.

Shakespeare on a Plate: A First Quarto Sampler

AMONTILLADO OR FINO SHERRY
ROMEO'S ROSEMARY CHICKEN
FALSTAFF'S SWEET POTATOES
JULIUS CAESAR SALAD
PALE ALE, CHARDONNAY, OR MERLOT

Doth not rosemary and Romeo begin both with a letter?
—Romeo and Juliet, act 2, scene 4, lines 206–7

After examining her young charge, Juliet's nurse properly diagnoses her sickness with this reference to ancient herbology. Rosemary was considered the herb of love and constancy, a symbol of undying affection and fidelity. Juliet looks "as pale as any clout in the versal[9] world," and the disease is love for her Romeo, so the nurse's comment says a lot about her knowledge of what these kids have been up to. Of course, rosemary wasn't always so innocent. In ancient Germany, young brides wore rosemary to guard against pregnancy, but perhaps we're getting ahead of ourselves.

Rosemary isn't the only part of this meal with sexual implications. Throughout the Middle Ages, potatoes were seen as an aphrodisiac, although that may have had more to do with the fact that they came from love-crazed Italy than any medicinal evidence.

Let the sky rain potatoes; let it thunder to the tune of
Green-sleeves, hail kissing-comfits, and snow eringoes; let
there come a tempest of provocation, I will shelter me here.
—The Merry Wives of Windsor, act 5, scene 5, lines 18–21

There were no white potatoes in Europe at the time, only the sweet potatoes featured here. Furthermore, contrary to Falstaff's witticism, it didn't rain either kind.

In Falstaff's honor, not only do we include potatoes in this meal, we also start off with a glass of sherry, the modern-day descendant of his favorite drink, sack. Sir John sometimes refers to "sherris sack," because much of the sack drunk in England came from the southern Spanish province of Jerez, of which *sherris* is a corruption. The word was shortened to *sherry* even during Shakespeare's time.

---

9. *Versal:* universal.

My salad days,
when I was green in judgment; cold in blood,
To say as I said then!

—Antony and Cleopatra, act 1, scene 5, lines 73–75

Cleopatra bemoans the loss of her youth, her salad days, in this mournful speech to Antony, the latest of the Roman statesmen who comes to conquer Egypt and its queen. Since those salad days were largely spent with Antony's predecessor, Julius Caesar, we thought it appropriate to use the salad that bears that emperor's name. Actually, if you want to be picky, *Caesar* was Julius's family name. Roman emperors after Julius also claimed the Caesar name, so it became a title of sorts, synonymous with *emperor*. While we're being picky, the salad isn't actually named after the emperor, it's named after a Mexican restaurateur—Caesar Cardini of Tijuana—who cooked it up when he was running short on all his normal salad supplies, but Geez Louise, can't we have a little artistic license here?

To Buy

3 tablespoons lemon juice (either bottled or from fresh lemons)

1 small bottle Worcestershire sauce (2 teaspoons)

1 whole roasting chicken

1 orange

1 bunch fresh rosemary

2 sweet potatoes

1 head romaine lettuce

1 small tub grated Parmesan cheese (½ cup)

Croutons

Staples

2 cloves garlic plus one entire garlic head

¼ teaspoon salt, plus more for sprinkling

¼ teaspoon pepper, plus more for sprinkling

¾ cup olive oil (extra virgin is best), plus some for rubbing on chicken

From the Liquor Store

Amontillado or fino sherry

Pale ale, chardonnay, or merlot

Before she arrives:

1. If you have pale ale or chardonnay, get it into the refrigerator to chill.

2. Mix up the Caesar salad dressing in a small bowl or large cup. Combine 3 tablespoons lemon juice, 2 minced garlic cloves, ¼ teaspoon salt, ¼ teaspoon pepper, 2 teaspoons Worcestershire sauce, and ¾ cup olive oil. Stir and set aside in the refrigerator.

6:30

3. Preheat the oven to 475 degrees. Wash and dry the chicken. Make sure you clean out the inner cavity. If the organs are inside the cavity, you can throw them away.

4. Roughly chop one head of garlic. You don't need to peel the individual cloves. Roughly chop the orange into about eight pieces, with the peel still on. Set aside four sprigs of rosemary and roughly chop up the rest. Combine all the chopped ingredients and stuff them into the inner cavity of the chicken.

5. Rub the chicken with olive oil and sprinkle it with salt and pepper. Place the chicken in a 9x13-inch glass baking dish, with the breast facing up. Take the other four sprigs of rosemary and stuff them in the elbows where the legs and wings meet the body.

7:00 (earlier if the chicken is more than 4 pounds)

6. Place the chicken in the oven for 15 minutes at 475 degrees, then turn the temperature down to 350 degrees and cook for about 20 minutes per pound. Unlike red meat, poultry should never be served rare, as it can contain bacteria that you don't really want to know about. In order to tell if the chicken is done, slice open the joint above the wing and see if the juice runs clear. If it isn't pink at all, then slice down into the breast and check the color. A completely cooked chicken is white all the way through. To be really safe, we recommend buying a meat thermometer and sticking it into the thickest part of the thigh. When it says 180 degrees, your chicken is done.

7:45

7. Wash and dry the sweet potatoes. Put the potatoes on the oven rack next to the chicken and bake for about 45 minutes.

8. Tear up enough romaine lettuce to fill two small plates. Throw the lettuce into a mixing bowl or large salad bowl.

After she arrives:

8:00

9. Start her off with a little glass of sherry.

10. Shake the dressing and pour it over the lettuce. Throw in ½ cup grated Parmesan cheese and toss. Serve the salad into two salad plates and throw a handful of croutons on top of each one. Serve.

11. Check the chicken and potatoes for doneness. The potatoes should give easily when you squeeze them. When the chicken and potatoes are done, slice the chicken off the bone and pile it on a plate or platter. Put one potato on each dinner plate and slice them open lengthwise. Bring the chicken platter and the two dinner plates to the table. Ask her if she would like dark meat (the drumsticks, thighs, and wings) or white meat (the breast). Serve her as she wishes.

12. Put on some classical music and say, "If music be the food of love, play on!"[10] OK, maybe you shouldn't say it out loud.

Bonus Points

Add a loaf of crusty French bread to the meal. Wrap it in foil and put it in the oven to warm. Slice and serve with butter.

10. *Twelfth Night,* act 1, scene 1, line 1.

The Progressive Girl

Moderation in all things, excess in nothing.

—Epicurus (342–270 B.C.)

Imagine that the Girl Next Door moved to the big city. Think of Meg Ryan in *When Harry Met Sally.* She's America's sweetheart with an urban sensibility. She's a post-Christian spiritualist, a pre-Monica Clintonite, and a dues-paying member of at least one social-change organization like NOW, Planned Parenthood, or the Sierra Club. You won't find her at an Earth First or PETA meeting, though. Those are the Granola Girl's stomping grounds. Progressive Girls want the world to be a better place, but they live out their politics in a moderate, left-of-center way. That's why you won't see any meals with red meat in this chapter. These are the Chicken and Fish Girls. These are the women who have Working Assets long-distance service or who volunteer for beach cleanups. Their tastes tend toward middle-of-the-roadism in music, film and arts, with a pronounced tendency toward artists with progressive agendas. When Natalie Maines of the Dixie Chicks stood onstage and stated her opposition to the war in Iraq, she opened up her fan club to the Progressive Girls.

On the other hand, you won't get a Progressive Girl to go to the mat on political, cultural, or artistic issues. Fact is, you may find it hard to get a rise out of her at all. Progressive Girls are just so darn easy to get along with. We were actually tempted to call them Moderate Girls, but that makes them sound a lot less interesting than they really are. They have strong personal feelings about their own behavior and the world at large, but they don't thrust those feelings on others. If you are going to date a Progressive Girl, the one sin you can commit is to be a chameleon. Molding your opinions to fit hers will lose her respect. One very positive thing you can do is offer her new experiences—the Progressive

Girl is fearless about trying new things. Whether it's pluralism, skydiving, or Asian peanut sauce, the Progressive Girl is always looking for new ideas.

Progressive Girls are hard to spot sometimes because of the lack of extremes in their lives. In fact, they share qualities with many of the other Girls. They like to see books in your apartment, like the Academic Girl does. They are confident and upwardly mobile in the workplace, like a Career Girl. Holidays are important to them, as they are to the Girl Next Door, and, because of their progressive mind-set, you will sometimes find them eating like Granola Girls. They even like to party with the Party Girls every now and then. If you do find a woman who has qualities of all the others, she's probably the Progressive Girl. The important thing to realize is that she doesn't put any of these things at the center of her life. She may dutifully shop at Whole Foods, but, when the urge hits for a Diet Coke, she'll make a pit stop at 7–Eleven without having a crisis of conscience. Christmas with family is important, until she gets a great deal on a vacation package in Belize.

If you are cooking for the Progressive Girl, keep it simple and casual. "We like good food," one Progressive Girl told us, "We just don't want to have to dress up to get it."

One useful tip: If you don't know what type of a Girl you are cooking for, you can cook the recipes for the Progressive Girl and you'll probably land on your feet.

Because so many of Meg Ryan's characters are Progressive Girls (although her personal life suggests that she may be more Indie), we have embraced her as the Progressive Girl poster child. All the recipes that you will find in this section are wound (a bit thinly in spots, we admit) around one of Meg's on-screen characters.

She Might Be a Progressive Girl If:

1. **She drives:** a small SUV but really wishes it got better mileage; once she can get a good hybrid, she will.

2. **She can talk for more than ten minutes about:** just about anything.

3. **She begins her sentences with:** "Susan Sarandon says . . ."

4. **She'd never:** pass up the chance for a new experience.

5. **She owns any of the following:** a water filter, a tabletop fountain, an acre of rain forest, a mutt from the pound.

Where You'll Find Her

In the suburbs of major cities, but also in urban areas. She's everywhere. She is the hardest one to spot because she lives in so many habitats. She will go to lectures on saving the world but also walk her dog in the park. She's always game for something new, so look for her in any type of community class, like cooking, scuba, or painting.

How to Spot Her

Elusive as she may be, she is the most common type and yet hardest to spot due to her lack of extreme qualities. No weird or supertrendy hairstyles (dreadlocks, updos, Indie Girl bobs), no piercings beyond the ears. If it's the weekend, she's in jeans. She's a Gap girl—typically in khakis, separates, casual sweaters—but she will resist being classified by one store. She's not wearing spiked heels, Doc Martens, or Birkenstocks. You'll find a comfortably dressed, sensibly shoed, lightly made up Girl with a soft, natural hairstyle. Ponytails are not uncommon.

Famous Progressive Girls

Meg Ryan in *When Harry Met Sally*, *Sleepless in Seattle*, *You've Got Mail*, *French Kiss*, and most other romantic comedies she has starred in, Renee Zellweger's character in *Jerry Maguire*, and Daphne on *Frasier*. Also Meryl Streep and Susan Sarandon.

Your Place

Because the Progressive Girl is so accepting of others, you can get away with almost anything, as long as the place is clean. If you want to get her attention, though, put some interest of yours on display, like a collection of something or a new painting that you've discovered. Eclecticism is good—having a collection of toy fire engines sitting next to a translation of Dante will catch the Progressive Girl's eye.

The Conversation

Keep your politics left of center but not too left. Like your place, your conversation should be eclectic. This Girl loves to travel, as well, so any talk of foreign places, whether you have been there or not, is a safe bet, as is any talk of home improvement. (Progressives are do-it-yourselfers). PGs also like to flip back and forth between large-scale issues and small talk, so opine about whether the United Kingdom should adopt the Euro, then mention this funny thing your nephew did.

The Coffee Table

Real Simple, Esquire, Harper's, Organic Style, plus travel-related or home-improvement books or magazines. Look for something that shows you have an interest in supporting something without being obsessive about it.

The Music

Sting, k.d. lang, Billy Joel, the Beatles, the Eagles, Paul Simon, Norah Jones, Tori Amos, Enya, Shawn Colvin, Tracy Chapman, and the Dixie Chicks are all good bets. Progressive Girls enjoy mainstream, melodic rock and pop, with an emphasis on any artist who has stood up to be counted in the fight for a better world.

The Drinks

The Progressive Girl will go with the flow on just about any drink you are serving, although it's best to start with the soft stuff. A good merlot or chardonnay will always please. For cocktails, she might like a daiquiri. If she doesn't drink, serve unsweetened iced tea (have a sugar bowl handy) or water with lemon.

The Shoes

If you are pretty sure she's Progressive, try going with no shoes at all. Meet her at the door in clean, pressed jeans, a stylish T-shirt (nothing with writing on it), and socks! If she's an Uptown Girl, you're hosed. But a true Progressive will appreciate the casualness and kick off her sandals, too. If you aren't ready to risk the no-shoes option, just stay away from extremes—no fancy basketball shoes, no high-priced Ferragamos, no Doc Marten combat boots. Casual and clean will do the job.

The Flowers

Roses, miniature roses, or daisies, but don't overdo it. Overdoing it is the quickest way to lose the Progressive Girl.

"Go to the Mattresses": Chicken and Artichoke Cacciatore

CHICKEN AND ARTICHOKE CACCIATORE
FRENCH BREAD
PEAS
CHARDONNAY OR MERLOT
ORANGE SORBET

Oh, get your mind out of the gutter. We're not talking about taking the Progressive Girl right to your mattress before she's even had dinner. We're talking about Tom Hanks encouraging Meg Ryan to take on the corporate conglomerate that is about to put her little bookshop out of business in *You've Got Mail.* Being a guy, he uses a line from *The Godfather.* Of course, he doesn't realize that he is encouraging her to attack *him,* because he is the president of that self-same corporation, but he has never actually met Meg—well, actually he has and just doesn't know it and . . . oh, see the movie.

In any case, the Progressive Girl is just the type to spend her energy saving a neighborhood children's bookstore in the face of a corporate onslaught. More than that, however, she wants to feel that her own life has meaning, that the efforts that she makes on a daily basis in some small way "help people to become the people that they want to become," as Meg's character says in the film. Her raging, activist boyfriend encourages her to "undo the Industrial Revolution," but he's more of a Granola-Academic type. Meg's character doesn't want to upset history, and she certainly doesn't wish ill on the corporate suits—heck, they seem like nice enough people—especially since she is falling in love with Hanks's corporate-guy character. She just wants some little kids to read books, and she is ready to go to the mattresses to do it. What a Progressive Girl.

In her honor, then, and in deference to the Italian Godfather, we present this Progressive Cacciatore. Like most Progressive Girl meals, it is a slightly classier version of the standard version. In this case, the artichokes give it that extra Progressive cachet. The best way to make this dish is with a cast-iron skillet, but if you don't have one, a large frying pan will do.

To Buy

2 chicken breast halves, boneless and skinless

¼ pound fresh mushrooms, sliced

1 (6-ounce) jar marinated artichoke hearts; do not drain

1 (8-ounce) can Italian stewed tomatoes; do not drain

1 teaspoon Italian seasoning

¼ cup dry cooking sherry

6 ounces angel-hair pasta

2 cups frozen peas

French sourdough or country French bread

1 carton orange sorbet

Staples

Flour (about ½ cup)

Salt (to taste)

Pepper (to taste)

1 tablespoon olive oil

1 clove garlic, minced

From the Liquor Store

Chardonnay or Merlot

Before she arrives:

6:45

1. Preheat oven to 350 degrees.

2. Pour about ½ cup flour onto a dinner plate and season it with a sprinkle of salt and pepper. Roll the chicken in the seasoned flour and set aside. Slice the mushrooms. (Some stores sell presliced fresh mushrooms, which would save you this step.)

3. In a large, oven-safe stockpot, heat 1 tablespoon olive oil. Add the chicken and lightly brown on both sides over medium-high heat—about 3 minutes a side. Add the artichoke hearts, stewed tomatoes, 1 minced clove of garlic, 1 teaspoon Italian seasoning, a sprinkle of pepper, and the mushrooms. Remove from heat.

7:15

4. Cover the stockpot, place it in a 350-degree oven, and bake for 1 hour.

5. Put 6 cups water in a medium saucepan over high heat. Once it boils, turn off the heat and let it sit. You are preheating the pasta water.

After she arrives:

8:00

6. Open the wine and pour glasses for both of you.

7. Bring the pasta water back to a boil. Add the angel-hair pasta and cook (following directions on package) until soft but not mushy (al dente).

8. Put the frozen peas in a soup bowl and cover with plastic wrap. Cook in the microwave for 3 minutes (or until hot). Remove plastic wrap and sprinkle a little salt and pepper over the top.

8:15

9. Add ¼ cup sherry to the stockpot in the oven, cover again, and bake an additional 10 minutes.

10. Stick the bread in the oven next to the chicken for the last 3 minutes to warm it up.

11. Drain the pasta and divide equally between two plates.

8:30

12. Serve the chicken over the bed of pasta with the bread and peas on the side.

13. Serve the sorbet for dessert.

Bonus Points

Before you put the bread in the oven, slice it open down the top. Spread garlic butter inside it, then close it up again, wrap it in foil, and pop it in the oven. For after-dinner entertainment, rent *You've Got Mail,* and bristle at corporate indifference to the plight of small businesses.

"What Is Tiramisu?": Chicken Piccata and Tiramisu

CHICKEN PICCATA
GREEN BEANS
NEW POTATOES
CHARDONNAY OR MERLOT
TIRAMISU
COFFEE

Remember that scene from *Sleepless in Seattle*? The one where Tom Hanks's character is trying to get back "out there," as in, back in the dating pool? He worries that he doesn't know what tiramisu is and in a panic says, "Some woman is gonna want me to do it to her and I'm not gonna know what it is!"

Well, if you, too, are wondering what the heck tiramisu is, here's your answer: Tiramisu is an Italian dessert, sort of like the dessert version of lasagna. It's essentially layers of mascarpone cheese and cookies soaked in coffee, topped off with a little chocolate. You won't find it on a dinner table in a small town in Nebraska. It's a big-city dessert, and yet simple to make—perfect for the Progressive Girl.

Similarly, chicken piccata is an everyday kind of dish—but much more sophisticated than fried chicken. And hey, it's got capers in it—sounds pretty impressive, doesn't it? Even so, it's really not difficult to make. We've added new potatoes and green beans—you might say that they are big-city versions of mashed potatoes and peas. Accompanied by a good chardonnay or merlot, this meal is light, classy, healthy, and tasty enough to please any Progressive Girl.

To Buy

½ pound good-quality coffee or espresso (decaf if you like)

2 large handfuls fresh green beans

8 ounces mascarpone cheese

1 package ladyfingers cookies

8 to 10 small new potatoes

1 lemon

2 boneless, skinless chicken breasts

1 small jar capers (1 tablespoon)

1 small container cocoa powder

Staples

3 tablespoons butter

Salt (to taste)

Pepper (to taste)

3 egg yolks

¼ cup sugar, plus some for the table

4 tablespoons olive oil, plus more for coating

½ cup flour

1 garlic clove

4 ounces (½ cup) chicken broth

Milk (for coffee with dessert)

From the Liquor Store

Chardonnay or merlot

Before she arrives:

5:00

1. If you've opted for chardonnay, put it in the fridge to chill.

2. Brew a very small pot of coffee. (You need only 2 cups. And, no, it's not to keep you awake—it's for the tiramisu.) Measure 2 cups brewed coffee and stick it in the fridge to cool.

3. Measure enough decaf coffee for a second small pot (to drink with dessert), only don't brew it yet, just get it ready to go in the coffeemaker. You can hit the "on" switch after you finish dinner.

5:30

4. Rinse and drain the green beans and cut or snap the ends off.

5. Put 1 inch of water into a small saucepan, put over medium-high heat, cover, and let it come to a boil.

6. Place the green beans into a steamer over the boiling water. Put a lid over the steamer. Let steam for about 5 minutes, stirring occasionally. They should be cooked, yet firm (*al dente*).

7. Transfer the green beans to a colander and rinse with cold water to stop them from cooking. Then transfer them to an oven-safe soup bowl, toss in a tablespoon of butter, and sprinkle a pinch of salt and pepper on top. Cover with foil and set aside.

8. To make the tiramisu: Separate the yolks from the whites of 3 eggs. Break each egg gently over a small mixing bowl, but capture the yolk in one of the halves of the shell. Gently pass the egg yolk back and forth between the shell halves, letting the white of the egg flow into the bowl. When nothing but yolk remains in the shells, dump it into a medium mixing bowl and throw the egg whites away. Wash and dry the small mixing bowl for use later.

9. Add ¼ cup sugar to the medium mixing bowl with the 3 egg yolks. Beat with an electric hand mixer until smooth. Then add the mascarpone cheese and stir with a wooden spoon just until it is incorporated. Set aside.

6:30

10. Get the cooled coffee out of the fridge.

11. One by one, dip the ladyfingers into the coffee and lay them flat in the bottom of a 9-inch square glass baking dish or a cake pan, making a single layer.

12. Spread half the mascarpone mixture over the ladyfingers.

13. Repeat with another layer of cookies dipped in coffee and then another layer of the mascarpone. Cover with foil or plastic wrap and stick in the fridge until ready to eat.

7:00

14. Rinse the potatoes, scrubbing with a brush (if you have one—otherwise, use your fingers), and drain. Place the potatoes in a medium saucepan and cover with water. Bring to a boil, cover, and reduce heat to medium. Set the timer for 30 to 40 minutes.

15. Slice the lemon in half and juice one half into a bowl. Take the other half of the lemon and, leaving the skin on, slice it thin. Set aside.

7:30

16. Preheat the oven to 200 degrees.

17. When the potatoes are done (you should be able to poke them easily with a fork, but not so much that they are mushy), drain them and toss in an oven-safe soup bowl with a tablespoon of butter, and some salt and pepper to taste. Cover with foil and set aside.

18. Measure ½ cup flour into the small mixing bowl and add a pinch of salt and pepper. Dredge chicken breasts in flour mixture. Shake to remove excess and set on a plate.

7:45

19. Heat a frying pan on medium and add 2 tablespoons olive oil. When the oil is hot, put the chicken breasts into the frying pan, and cook for about 3 minutes on each side, until lightly browned.

20. Put the chicken breasts on an oven-safe plate, cover with foil, and set them in the 200-degree oven. You aren't cooking the breasts, just keeping them warm until she arrives. Don't leave them there more than 15 to 20 minutes or they will dry out.

After she arrives:

8:00

21. Uncork the wine and pour.

22. Crush 1 garlic clove. Set aside.

23. Stick the bowl of potatoes and the bowl of green beans in the oven to warm them and remove the plate of chicken from the oven.

24. Put the chicken breasts back into the frying pan and add 2 tablespoons olive oil and 1 crushed garlic clove. Cook over medium heat for about 10 seconds. Add lemon slices and ½ cup chicken broth and increase the heat to high.

25. Scrape the pan with a wooden spoon or spatula to loosen the brown bits (the fancy term for this is "deglazing"). Turn the heat down and cook for about 3 to 4 minutes.

26. Add the bowl of lemon juice and 1 tablespoon capers (just the capers, not the liquid they come in) and cook for another minute.

27. Remove the frying pan from the heat and add 1 tablespoon butter, stirring until the butter melts. Spoon the sauce onto the chicken breasts and then transfer to dinner plates, adding the green beans and new potatoes. Serve immediately.

28. After dinner, set the coffee to brew. Take the tiramisu out of the fridge and lightly sprinkle some of the cocoa powder on top. (Yes, it's just decorative, but trust us—it's details like this that women notice.)

29. Slice and serve the tiramisu on plates with the coffee. Be sure to offer her milk and sugar with her coffee.

Bonus Points

If you want to make the tiramisu extrafancy, add a little shaved chocolate in addition to the cocoa powder. Just take a bar of semisweet chocolate and grate it with a cheese grater or vegetable peeler. You can also, of course, rent *Sleepless in Seattle* for a dose of cinematic romance.

"Pesto, the Quiche of the '80s": Pesto Swordfish over Capellini

PESTO SWORDFISH OVER CAPELLINI
JULIENNED VEGETABLES
CHARDONNAY
ANGEL FOOD CAKE WITH FRESH BERRIES AND REAL WHIPPED CREAM

Progressive Girls like to think that the way they live life is just a little bit better than the norm. A cut above, without being stuck up about it. While the Girl Next Door eats spaghetti with meatballs, the Progressive Girl dines on angel-hair pasta with pesto. Pesto is that green sauce that became so popular in the '80s. As Bruno Kirby's character says in *When Harry Met Sally,* "Pesto is the quiche of the '80s." Here it is twenty years later, though, and pesto is still going strong. It's practically a Progressive Girl staple. Chardonnay, also a Progressive Girl favorite, happens to go particularly well with pesto.

We've also included angel food cake with fresh berries, a lighter, slightly more sophisticated dessert than say, a chocolate cake or a Cool Whip pie. The fact that you are making the pesto and whipped cream from scratch will show her that you understand the "cut-above" idea and are not frightened off by the concept of "high-maintenance." Well, medium-high maintenance, anyway.

To Buy

1 package fresh berries—strawberries, raspberries, or blueberries

1 large bunch fresh basil (available in the produce section of most grocery stores—you will need 2 packed cups or 16 ounces)

¼ cup (4 ounces) pine nuts

¾ cup (6 ounces) freshly grated Parmesan cheese (not the powdered stuff in the green container)

2 swordfish steaks, about ½ pound each, cut 1 inch thick (if you can't get swordfish, you can substitute salmon)

1 zucchini

1 red or yellow bell pepper

1 8-ounce package capellini (angel-hair pasta)

1 store-bought angel food cake

1 pint heavy cream (1 cup)

Staples

3 cloves garlic

½ cup plus 2 tablespoons olive oil

1 tablespoon salt

Pepper (to taste)

1 tablespoon sugar

From the Liquor Store

Chardonnay

Before she arrives:

6:45

1. Chill the chardonnay in the fridge.

2. Rinse the berries, drain in a colander, transfer to a soup bowl, cover with plastic wrap, and refrigerate until needed.

3. Rinse the basil, break or cut off the stems, and spin in salad spinner or put on paper towels to drain. Measure out 2 well-packed cups.

4. Press or crush 2 cloves garlic. Put the garlic, basil, ¼ cup pine nuts, and ¾ cup Parmesan cheese into the food processor. Blend, slowly pouring ½ cup olive oil through the top opening, until it looks like a thick green paste. This is the pesto. Do not over-process. It should be mixed but still chunky.

7:30

5. Put the swordfish steaks in a 9x13-inch glass baking dish and spread the pesto very thickly on top. Flip the steaks over and cover the other side with pesto. Cover the baking dish with plastic wrap and put in the refrigerator.

6. Julienne the zucchini and bell pepper (that means cut them thin—¼ to ½ inch wide by 3 inches long) and set aside.

7:45

7. Put 1 tablespoon olive oil into a small saucepan and set it on medium heat. Press 1 clove garlic and add it to the oil. Throw in the julienned bell pepper (remove seeds) and zucchini and cook, stirring, for 5 minutes or so, just until tender.

8. When the vegetables are cooked, transfer them to a plate and cover them with another plate, inverted, to keep them warm.

After she arrives:

8:00

9. Set the oven on broil or, if the weather is nice, warm up the outdoor grill.

10. Uncork the chardonnay and pour.

11. Fill a medium saucepan halfway with water, add 1 tablespoon olive oil, cover, and bring to a boil. Add 1 tablespoon salt and 8 ounces (½ pound) angel-hair pasta. Stir the pasta, making sure it is completely submerged, then turn the heat down to medium.

12. Stir the pasta occasionally and cook for 4 to 6 minutes (check the directions on the box). Taste strands to check doneness. When the pasta is done, drain it in a colander under cool water (to keep it from cooking further) and set aside.

13. Take the fish out of the refrigerator, set on a baking sheet, and put in the oven, or if using an outside grill, put the fish directly on the grill rack. Grill or broil the fish for 4 to 6 minutes on each side. Do not overcook. It should be pink in the middle.

14. Put half the pasta on one serving plate and half on another plate. Arrange the vegetables next to the pasta. If necessary, reheat the pasta and veggies by sticking the plates in the microwave. Use a metal spatula to place the swordfish steak on top of the pasta. Sprinkle a little Parmesan cheese on top. Set the Parmesan cheese, along with the salt and pepper on the table.

15. After dinner, slice a couple pieces of the angel food cake and place them on serving plates. Pour 1 cup heavy cream into a mixing bowl and beat with an electric mixer until it's fluffy. Gradually add 1 tablespoon sugar and continue whipping until it gets firm and has soft peaks. Plop on top of the slices of cake, toss the berries on, and serve.

Bonus Points

Harry and Sally bond over *Casablanca,* one of the greatest romance pictures of all time, so rent the movie and discuss Ilsa's fateful choice between Rick, the handsome bartender, and Victor Laszlo, the brave freedom fighter. Duty or booty, you decide.

"I'll Have What She's Having": Salmon in Dill Sauce

SALMON IN DILL SAUCE
SAUTÉED SPINACH
BAKED POTATOES
CHARDONNAY
RASPBERRY LATTICE TART

Is there anyone alive who hasn't seen Meg Ryan's table-banging, head-thrashing, completely faked orgasm at the restaurant in *When Harry Met Sally?* It was Billy Crystal who came up with the droll punch line to Meg's public climax (Nora Ephron wrote the script), but the line itself was delivered by director Rob Reiner's mother playing a customer at a nearby table.

Meg's character, Sally Albright, is a Progressive Girl by the numbers. She moves to the big city not for fortune and fame but for new experiences and a chance to expand her life. She keeps her small-town morals, her nuclear-family priorities, and her deliberate innocence about male-female relationships. When goaded into picking up a karaoke microphone, she belts out an off-key version of "Surrey with the Fringe on Top" from the down-home musical *Oklahoma*. Far from accepting Harry's cynical notion that men and women can't be platonic friends, she insists that the two of them can break society's mold and move to a higher plane of existence. The fact that they do, eventually, fall in love does not in any way detract from her Progressive Girl ideas about how the world really should be.

One of our Progressive Girl friends recently pointed out a strange phenomenon that occurs when she eats out with other Progressive Girls. Once one of them orders the salmon, the rest say "Hmm, that sounds really good." Before you know it, they have all ordered the salmon. The rule holds true for most Progressive Girls—when in doubt, make salmon. It is the reliable stalwart, the NPR, the Meg Ryan romantic comedy, the Sting album. It is the safe choice that will always leave you in good standing.

It's worth putting the extra effort into the latticework for the tart. For some reason, this simple little detail impresses people to no end.

To Buy

1 cup ground almonds
1 small jar raspberry jam

2 baking potatoes

1 small jar mayonnaise (2 tablespoons)

1 jar Dijon mustard (2 tablespoons)

1 container dried dill weed (2¼ teaspoons)

1 small bunch fresh chives (1 cup chopped)

1 (8-ounce) bag baby spinach

¾ pound fillet of salmon

Small tub of sour cream

Staples

2 cups plus 2 tablespoons flour

½ cup plus ¾ cup sugar

3 sticks plus 3 tablespoons plus 2 teaspoons butter, plus some to serve at the table

3 eggs

About ½ cup milk

1 teaspoon plus ½ tablespoon olive oil

Sprinkle of salt

Sprinkle of pepper

Sprinkle of balsamic vinegar

From the Liquor Store

Definitely chardonnay. Besides the fact that it is perfect with this meal, it is the salmon of drinks for the Progressive Girl: always a safe choice.

Before she arrives:

6:30

1. Start with the crust for the tart. In a medium mixing bowl, combine 2 cups flour, ½ cup sugar, 2 sticks (16 tablespoons) cold butter, and 1 egg, in that order. Add milk slowly, very lightly kneading with your hands (make sure they're clean), until the dough holds together. *Don't* overknead. (You should still be able to see bits of butter—the key to a flaky crust.) Cover with plastic wrap and stick in the fridge.

2. For the filling, cream together 11 tablespoons butter (that's one whole stick plus 3 tablespoons) and ¾ cup sugar in a large mixing bowl. Beat in 2 eggs, then mix in 2 tablespoons flour and 1 cup ground almonds. You can do this in the food processor or with an electric mixer. Set aside.

7:00

3. Preheat oven to 350 degrees. Put aside ⅓ of the dough and press the remaining ⅔ into the bottom of a lightly greased pie pan. Spread a layer of raspberry jam over the dough. Cover with the almond filling. Roll out the remaining dough and cut into thin strips (about ½ inch thick). Arrange on top of the tart in a crisscross pattern, like a chain-link fence. Secure strips to the edges of the tart by pinching. Set the tart aside.

7:15

4. Wash the potatoes and poke them with a fork three or four times to allow the steam to escape. Put them directly on the oven rack and bake for 45 minutes to an hour, until they give when lightly squeezed.

7:30

5. Put the tart in the oven with the potatoes and bake for about 50 minutes or until the filling is set.

6. To make the dill sauce, combine 2 tablespoons mayonnaise, 2 tablespoons Dijon mustard, and 2 teaspoons dried dill (or dill weed) in a small bowl. Set aside.

7. Chop enough chives to make 1 cup and set them aside in a serving bowl as well.

8. Rinse the spinach and cut off the bottom inch or so of the stalk. Set aside.

After she arrives:

8:00

9. Offer her a glass of wine.

10. When the potatoes are done, take them out and wrap them in foil to keep them warm.

11. Drizzle 1 teaspoon olive oil over the salmon, then sprinkle ¼ teaspoon dill on top. Pour a little olive oil on the broiler pan and spread it across the pan to keep the fish from sticking. Put the fish fillets on the broiler and put them in the oven to broil while you concentrate on the vegetables.

12. Pour 2 cups water in a medium saucepan and bring to a boil. Drop in the basket steamer and fill it with the spinach. Don't worry if the spinach is overflowing the pan—it will be greatly reduced in a minute. Cram it down in the steamer and put the lid on top. Let it steam until it is limp—this should only take a few minutes.

13. Flip the fish over after 3 minutes. Check the center of the fish by opening it with a fork. The center should be slightly pink, but it should flake easily. If your fillet has a thin end, keep an eye on it. You may want to cut it off and set it aside on a plate if it gets done before the thick part. Remember, the fish will keep cooking all the way to the table.

14. When the fish fillets are done, put them on plates and spoon the dill sauce on top. Lay the spinach next to them along with the potatoes. Sprinkle a little balsamic vinegar over the spinach and put a tiny dab of butter (about 2 teaspoons) on top. Slice open the potatoes and serve the whole deal with butter, sour cream, and chives.

15. Check the tart before you sit down. When it is done, remove it from the oven and toss a piece of foil over it to keep it warm. When dinner is over, serve the tart.

Bonus Points

Serve vanilla ice cream with the tart, but serve it on the side, Sally Albright style. And if it isn't real ice cream, then nothing. Naturally you'll want to rent *When Harry Met Sally* to watch later—unless she's seen it a billion times, then nothing.

"Take Me to Bed or Lose Me Forever!": Lemon Shrimp Linguine

LEMON SHRIMP LINGUINE
GREEN SALAD WITH HEARTS OF PALM AND PINE NUTS
CHARDONNAY OR PINOT GRIGIO
FRUIT TART

Not many people remember that Meg Ryan played Goose's wife in *Top Gun*. Yes, it was her blast of sexual fervor that was the telltale precursor to his demise. While Meg's unbridled come-on to Goose of "Take me to bed or lose me forever" may seem more the mantra of a Party Girl, don't let your guard down. When properly fueled with future-oriented thinking and white-meat cooking, a Progressive girl will take your breath away.

This is a light, summery meal, useful for when the thermometer creeps upward and you've got a shaded deck to serve dinner on. Stock up on blue-and-green-checked cloth napkins and a breezeproof candleholder. Regardless of the weather, the Progressive Girl likes eating light, though; so don't just let the temperature determine when to serve this quintessential Progressive Girl meal.

The best way to serve this pasta is with a block of Parmigiana Regiano cheese and a grater. If you don't have a cheese grater, you can buy the preground Parmigiana Regiano at most stores. If you can't find Regiano, try to get the best quality Parmesan you can find. Avoid the green cardboard container of Parmesan, which, compared to Regiano or other good quality Parmesans, is as bland as the can it comes in. Trust us.

Look in the bakery section of your favorite grocery section for a fresh-baked tart (or pie). If you find yourself tartless, try the strawberries and cream from the "Chaucerian Feast" recipe in the Academic Girl chapter. Progressive Girls are first cousins to Academic Girls.

To Buy

1 big, juicy lemon

1 package or bunch fresh thyme

20 oil-cured kalamata olives (pitted and halved if you can find them)

1 pound cooked, peeled, and deveined shrimp

1 head or small bag red lettuce or mixed baby greens

1 (14-ounce) can or jar hearts of palm

1 small bag pine nuts (also called pignoli nuts)

1 pound dried or fresh linguine

8 ounces fresh Parmigiana Regiano cheese, whole or grated

1 premade fruit tart (or pie): cherry, peach, or apple (from the bakery section)

Staples

1 cup plus 2 tablespoons olive oil

1 clove garlic, minced

¼ cup balsamic vinegar

Sprinkle of salt, plus 1 tablespoon for the pasta

Sprinkle of pepper

From the Liquor Store

Chardonnay or pinot grigio

Before she arrives:

7:00

1. Chill the wine.

2. Rinse and "zest" 1 lemon with a zester. To zest basically means to scrape the peel against a zester or the fine-tooth side of a grater until you get a small pile of minced peel fragments. Set the pile of zest aside.

3. Slice the lemon and juice it into a small glass with a reamer or juicer—or squeeze it with your hand. Make sure you don't get any seeds into the juice. You should have about ¼ cup juice.

4. Combine zest and lemon juice in a small mixing or soup bowl and add ½ cup olive oil. Sprinkle in some salt and pepper. Set aside.

5. Rinse the thyme and pat dry. Pull off the leaves and chop fine. You can also pulse them (for a few seconds only) in the food processor.

6. Count out about 20 olives. Slice them in half and remove the pits. Again, this process is time-consuming but necessary. If you can find them already pitted and halved, get them.

7. Combine ½ cup thyme, 1 pound shrimp, the 20 olives, and 1 clove minced garlic in a medium mixing bowl.

7:30

8. Rinse the head of lettuce or bag of greens and either spin in a salad spinner or pat dry with paper towels. Tear into pieces into a large salad bowl.

9. Drain the hearts of palm and add to the salad. Sprinkle with a handful or two of pine nuts.

10. Using a whisk, mix together ¼ cup balsamic vinegar with ½ cup olive oil. Salt and pepper to taste. Set aside.

7:45

11. Preheat the oven to 200 degrees.

After she arrives:

8:00

12. Boil 6 to 8 cups water in a stockpot with 2 tablespoons olive oil. Stir in 1 tablespoon salt to the water. (It is important not to add the salt before the water boils because doing so will make the water take longer to heat. A whole tablespoon may seem like a lot of salt, but it does a lot to flavor the pasta. According to the Italians, you should cook your pasta in water as salty as the sea.)

13. Add the pasta and cook, stirring occasionally, until al dente (about 2 to 5 minutes, depending on whether you got fresh, frozen, or dried.) To test doneness, every once in a while, stick a fork in and pull out a noodle. Put it under the cold-water tap to cool it down, then sample. It should be tender but not mushy.

14. Drain pasta in a colander, then put it back in the stockpot. Add lemon mixture and toss. Add mixture of thyme, shrimp, olives, and garlic and then toss again.

15. Drizzle the dressing over the salad and set on the table. Serve the pasta with grated cheese on the side. As you leave the kitchen, slide the fruit tart into the oven. By the time you have finished dinner, it will be heated through.

Bonus Points

To add another flavor to the pasta, try adding 4 ounces of very thinly sliced prosciutto (a high-class Italian ham) to the pasta when you add the shrimp. Regardless of where the title of this one came from, you probably don't want to rent *Top Gun* for after-dinner entertainment. Never fear, however. Meg Ryan has a vast catalog of date-friendly flicks, including *Addicted to Love, Kate and Leopold,* and *French Kiss.*

The Indie Girl

It's no good pretending that any relationship has a future if your record collections disagree violently or if your favorite films wouldn't even speak to each other if they met at a party.

—Nick Hornby, High Fidelity

An Indie Girl's life is a Statement with a capital *S,* but unlike the Granola Girl, the statement is not political—it's artistic. Indie Girls consider themselves actresses in the movie of life. Your meal needs to be constructed like an independent film. If you're bringing her over for a date, you are playing a character in her movie. If you create a setting, props, and a soundtrack that are good enough to avoid the cutting-room floor, she's yours.

If you want to unlock the door to the Indie Girl, you must understand the concept of postmodernism. Indie Girls love anything postmodern. Postmodernism is a squirrelly term for a cultural movement: a post-1960s pop art reaction to our contemporary capitalist society. Yeah, that helps. OK, let's see if we can do a better job of explaining it . . .

The "PoMo" sensibility is ironic, cool, and eclectic. It's self-deprecating and self-referential. It defies traditional cultural values and blurs the distinction between highbrow and lowbrow. In other words, it's just as cool to watch opera on PBS (highbrow) as it is to watch *Behind the Music* on VH1 (lowbrow). It's also anything kitsch, something all Indie Girls love. *Kitsch* is a German word for "trash" or "junk," but it's come to mean things of lesser quality or in bad taste, or anything mass-produced. Be it those sad clown paintings, a Japanese candy wrapper collection, or Danielle Steel novels—the ironic humor of these items are not lost on this gal.

You can boil the Indie Girl down to two words: *cultural literacy.* Or how about these two: *media consumption.* As the Gourmet Girl loves food and all that goes with it, the Indie Girl loves media: books, movies, music, and art. The good news is you don't have to be rich, good-looking, or famous to win this girl's heart. The bad news is she will judge you based on your music choices, the books you read, and the films you watch.

She Might Be an Indie Girl If:

1. **She drives:** a classic car, a VW beetle, a Mini Cooper, or a Vespa scooter.

2. **She can talk for more than ten minutes about:** obscure pop culture.

3. **She begins her sentences with:** "It's like that *Simpsons* episode . . ."

4. **She'd never, *ever:*** drive a minivan.

5. **She owns any of the following:** TiVo, a mini-DV camera, an iPod, a pottery wheel, a serger, or a lava lamp.

Where You'll Find Her

You won't see this Girl at the mall. Look for her in art galleries, hanging out in dive bars, or at an independent movie theater's midnight showing of *Army of Darkness.* She might also be spotted DJing at an after-hours party, playing miniature golf, or singing karaoke.

How to Spot Her

Indie Girls are only native to the urban jungle. If you encounter one in the country, she's probably lost. Or visiting family, which, for an Indie Girl, is roughly the same thing. This woman does not get dressed—she dons a costume. Look for ironic thrift store clothing, which includes vintage T-shirts that say things like, "Virginia is for lovers." You may also see any of the following: body piercings and/or tattoos, checkerboard Vans, "bedhead" (hair that sort of sticks up all over), nerdy horn-rimmed glasses, black jelly "Madonna" bracelets from the '80s, a bike messenger bag, Pumas.

Famous Indie Girls

Parker Posey, Janeane Garofalo, Madonna (an Athletic/Indie hybrid), Winona Ryder, Drew Barrymore, Bjork, Liza Minnelli in *Cabaret,* Melanie Griffith in *Something Wild,* Ruth Gordon in *Harold and Maude,* Carrie Bradshaw on *Sex and the City.*

Your Place

Hopefully you live in a funky, artsy, underground part of town. In New York City, that would be the Meat Packing District or Williamsburg in Brooklyn; in San Francisco, the Mission or Bernal Heights; in LA, Echo Park or Silverlake. You say you live in the suburbs? Move. Just kidding. How about a kitschy trailer park? An artist's loft or converted theater would also work. Hang a Frank Kozik poster or leave an unfinished painting on an easel. Prominently display books by Dave Eggers, Haruki Murakami, Douglas Coupland, and Jacqueline Susann. Other stuff Indie Girls love: '70s shag carpeting, '50s furniture, lawn ornaments (gnomes and pink flamingos), and velvet Elvis paintings.

The Conversation

Quote David Sedaris. Even better, quote David Sedaris's sister, Amy, on her old TV show, *Strangers with Candy.* You say you don't know it? Time to do some research; you can get it on DVD. Be prepared for discussions on obscure foreign cinema, the underground art scene, or alternative music. If you don't know anything about these things, you can escape by talking about your own artistic pursuits. Say things like, "I don't follow the art scene. I prefer to remain a tabula rasa."

The Coffee Table

Go with an alternative or literary "zine" (FOUND or Dave Eggers's *McSweeney's*). Any magazine having to do with art (*Art Forum*), music (*Spin, Rolling Stone*), film (*Premiere, Film Threat*), literature (the *New York Times Book Review* or *Poets and Writers*), or enter-tainment (*Entertainment Weekly*) will also work. A copy of the *National Enquirer* shows your dark sense of humor.

The Music

ELO and Kiss won't cut it with the Uptown Girl, but they'll work great here, along with Beck, Tom Waits, Elvis Costello, Leonard Cohen, Badly Drawn Boy, and Yo La Tengo. You can't go wrong with classic alternative rock bands such as the Pixies, Radiohead, or Vel-vet Underground. You can also choose from any of the following genres: alt-country (Whiskeytown, Wilco, the Old 97's); retro country (Buck Owens, George Jones); electron-ica (Massive Attack, the Chemical Brothers); kitschy easy listening (Tom Jones, Burt Bacharach, Neil Diamond, the Carpenters); lounge and space-age pop (Esquivel, Herb

Alpert); punk (Dead Kennedys, Ramones, Sex Pistols); retro swing (Big Bad Voodoo Daddy, Squirrel Nut Zippers); Latin (Sergio Mendes, Manu Chao); or sound tracks to indie films (*Swingers*, *The Royal Tenenbaums*). *Warning: Avoid Top 40, or anything mainstream, at all costs. The Indie Girl will give you an automatic F for playing the Backstreet Boys.* Remember, the more obscure and eclectic, the better. This is an important category for this girl, so spend some time on the Web site www.allmusic.com and do your homework.

The Drinks

Artsy, kitschy, interesting drinks. Dirty Martys (martinis), Harvey Wallbangers, vodka gimlets, Maker's Mark. If you really want to wow the Indie Girl, serve drinks that have been featured in classic films, such as a zombie (*Breakfast at Tiffany's*) or a rusty nail (*The Lost Weekend*). As for wines, go with a bold, big red, like a cabernet, Chianti, zinfandel, Syrah/Shiraz, or a Spanish Rioja. (Merlots are tolerated by the Indie Girl, and she may drink white wines, but she typically prefers wine with some character. Remember—mediocrity is the bane of her existence!) The Indie Girl generally appreciates beer—but we're not talking Coors Light, folks. Go with anything microbrewed, Heffeweissen (with lemon wedge), or Guinness. Also: sake and single malt Scotch whisky.

The Shoes

Shoes by Adidas, Puma, Ben Sherman, Converse, Camper, or Diesel. Skateboarding shoes by Vision Streetwear or Vans. Doc Martens are always good, as are bowling shoes (especially vintage), or old-style '80s Creepers. While the Uptown Girl and the Career Girl will turn up their noses at a pair of flip-flops, the Indie Girl will dig 'em. Here's what *not* to wear: anything with a tassel. Docksiders or cross trainers will get you flushed, pronto. Like everything else with the Indie Girl, get out of the mainstream and show a little style.

The Flowers

Gerber daisies in a bouquet of bright colors—hot pink, blazing orange, and purple.

Monsoon Wedding: Bollywood Curry Chicken

CURRY CHICKEN

DAL MAKHANI (MADRAS LENTILS)

ALOO BHAJI (SILMA POTATOES)

BASMATI RICE

CHUTNEY

NAN

KINGFISHER OR GEWÜRTZTRAMINER

MANGO SHERBET

In a world where male directors far outnumber females, Mira Nair has directed a string of indie successes that any male director would be proud of: *Salaam, Bombay!, Mississippi Masala, Kama Sutra,* and the brilliant *Monsoon Wedding.* Nair, a Harvard graduate, is a pioneer in the United States as well as in her native India, where she is confronting a culture that is in many ways still oppressive to women. Many of her films deal with sexual politics and women's opportunities to make their own choices instead of blindly following tradition. *Monsoon Wedding* (2001), for example, explored issues such as arranged marriages and incest.

Besides its subject matter, the film *Monsoon Wedding* is also interesting because of its "Bollywood" influences—for example, the way song and dance are worked into the plot. *Bollywood* is the name for the Indian film industry, and it's the largest in the world (the *B* stands for the city of Bombay, which is now called Mumbai—we know, confusing). If you've ever watched one of those soap-opera-ish Indian music videos with all the bright colors and the dancing, where the girl is being courted by her suitor—that's "Bollywood."

This is one of the easiest meals to cook for the Indie Girl, since everything is out of a box or a jar. However, it doesn't taste like it. TastyBite brand Indian foods are available at many stores, including Trader Joe's and Whole Foods. If you can't find them, go to the company's Web site: www.tastybite.com.

To Buy

1 bag basmati rice (1 cup dry)

2 russet potatoes

1 pound boneless, skinless chicken breasts

1 bag frozen peas (½ cup)

1 (10-ounce) jar curry sauce (available at Trader Joe's or an Indian food store)

1 package nan (an Indian bread available at Trader Joe's or an Indian food store—you can also substitute pita bread)

1 box TastyBite Instant India Silma Potatoes

1 box TastyBite Instant India Madras Lentils (TastyBite has other side dishes—you can substitute any of them)

1 jar chutney

1 container mango sherbet

Staples

½ teaspoon salt

½ onion

1 tablespoon olive oil

From the Liquor Store

Kingfisher (Indian) or another kind of beer. If you want to go with wine, serve gewürtztraminer (see wine primer chapter in Part One).

Before she arrives:

5:30

1. Chill the beer or wine.

2. In a medium saucepan on high heat, bring 1½ cups water to a boil.

3. Put 1 cup rice into a small mixing bowl, and add some water. Stir the rice around with your hands, drain, and rinse again and again until the water is no longer cloudy. (This will make fluffier, less sticky rice by removing a lot of the starch.) Drain and add to the boiling water. Add ½ teaspoon salt.

6:00

4. Let the saucepan of rice return to a boil, then turn heat down to low, cover, and let cook without stirring for 15 minutes or until all water is absorbed.

6:30

5. Fill a stockpot ¼ full with water, cover, and bring it to a boil.

6. Peel the potatoes with a vegetable peeler and cut them into large bite-size pieces.

7. Add the potatoes to the pot of boiling water, cover, and cook for 15 minutes. Remove from heat, drain in a colander, and set aside.

7:15

8. Cut the chicken breasts into large bite-size pieces.

9. Chop up ½ an onion.

7:30

10. To a frying pan add 1 tablespoon olive oil and the chopped onion. Cook on medium heat, stirring occasionally, until onion is translucent.

11. Add the chicken pieces. Add the boiled cubed potatoes and ½ cup of the frozen peas. Dump the jar of curry into the pan. Stir to cover everything in the curry. If you like, you can add a bit of water to make the sauce less thick.

7:45

12. Cover and cook on medium heat for 10 to 15 minutes (or until chicken and potatoes are cooked), stirring occasionally. Cover and remove from heat until ready to serve.

13. Preheat the oven to 350 degrees.

After she arrives:

8:00

14. First of all, fetch her a drink.

15. Put the nan on a baking sheet and put into the oven for 10 minutes—just to warm it.

16. Empty the pouches of potatoes and lentils into separate microwave-safe bowls and put the bowls into the microwave. Cook them each for 1 to 2 minutes.

17. Serve everything on plates. You can serve the chutney in a bowl on the side or directly on the plates.

18. After dinner, serve a few scoops of the mango ice cream in bowls or on plates.

Bonus Points

If you really want to make your Indie Girl feel like she's dining in Mumbai, hang Christmas lights along the walls and put out tea lights. You could also hang garlands of marigolds, the Indian wedding flower. String marigold blossoms like you would popcorn or cranberries on a Christmas tree, or you could use pots of marigolds. (Watch the movie for inspiration; that scene at the end where the guy is sitting outside his beloved's door, candles everywhere, holding the heart filled with marigolds—that is enough to make any woman, but especially an Indie Girl, faint.) You can also play the *Monsoon Wedding* sound track or rent the film (not both—overkill). Both the CD and the DVD are very lush, romantic, and sexy.

[easy]
Tampopo: Spaghetti Western Udon Soup

UDON SOUP WITH SHRIMP AND VEGETABLES
HOT SAKE AND/OR JAPANESE BEER
ICE CREAM MOCHI

The late Juzo Itami, who died in 1997, was one of the greatest Japanese directors of all time. A true independent filmmaker, he raised the money for all of his films himself, and his friends and family starred in them. Arguably his greatest masterpiece was *Tampopo* (1986), a comedy about the connection between sex and food. The story follows a female owner of a noodle shop who is struggling to discover the most perfect recipe for soup, as well as a couple of juicy subplots, including the ongoing sexual adventures of a gangster and his girlfriend.

It also pays homage to the spaghetti western, like *Fistful of Dollars* and *The Good, the Bad and the Ugly.* There were actually close to 600 westerns made in Europe between 1960 and 1975. Because they were mostly financed by Italians, they were dubbed "spaghetti westerns." *Tampopo,* chock-full of pop culture references, also parodies the films *Rocky* and *Tom Jones,* as well as samurai movies.

Although the noodles featured in *Tampopo* were actually ramen noodles, we've decided to go with udon. Ramen in America has become associated with cheap food you eat in college, unlike in Japan, where it is quite a different thing. Udon noodles are basically thicker and fatter. Udon is to ramen what linguine is to angel hair. In any case, many people in the United States are not familiar with udon—and, remember, Indie Girls are impressed by obscurity.

To Buy

1 large bunch spinach

1 zucchini or yellow squash

6 frozen, peeled and deveined, cooked jumbo shrimp

1 (12-ounce) package dry Japanese udon noodles (can also use soba if you can't find udon)

1 bottle soy sauce (2 tablespoons, plus more for sprinkling)

1 bottle mirin (cooking rice wine available at Asian grocery stores) (1 tablespoon)

1 container white sesame seeds

1 box ice cream mochi (available at many grocery stores, including Trader Joe's and Whole Foods, and also at Asian food stores)

Staples

16 ounces chicken broth

From the Liquor Store

1 large bottle of sake, Japanese rice wine (pronounced "SAH-kay")

Kirin, Sapporo, or other Japanese beer

Before she arrives:

7:15

1. Fill a stockpot halfway with water and put it on the stove over high heat. Cover and bring to a rolling boil.

2. Set the colander in the sink. Rinse the spinach very well, rubbing lightly with your hands to remove all traces of sand. Remove the stems from the spinach and discard them.

3. Rinse the zucchini or squash and cut into ½-inch-thick slices.

7:30

4. In a medium saucepan, add a few inches of water and bring to a boil. Set a metal steamer on top of the saucepan.

5. Put the shrimp and squash into the steamer for 3 to 4 minutes. Then toss the spinach into the boiling water for 30 seconds. (If you don't have a steamer, you can also boil the vegetables.)

6. Immediately transfer the squash and spinach to the colander and flush with cold water. Transfer to a small mixing bowl and set aside. Rinse out the medium saucepan so it can be used later.

7. Add the udon to the stockpot of boiling water and let cook for about 10 minutes (or until *al dente*), stirring with a wooden spoon.

8. When the udon is finished cooking, drain in a colander, flush with cool water, and set aside.

After she arrives:

8:00

9. Heat some of the sake for 15 to 30 seconds in the microwave. (If you don't have a sake set, heat it up in a coffee mug and serve in shot glasses.) Serve her some sake and, if she wants some, cold beer.

10. Put a medium saucepan on high heat and add the 16 ounces (2 cups) of chicken broth, 1 cup water, 2 tablespoons soy sauce, and 1 tablespoon mirin. Bring to a boil and remove from the heat.

11. Divide the udon into 2 soup bowls. Arrange the shrimp, squash, and spinach on top of the noodles. Cover noodles, shrimp, and vegetables with the hot broth. Sprinkle a handful of sesame seeds on top. Make sure you have soy sauce on the table.

12. After dinner, pile the ice cream mochi (available in vanilla, chocolate, green tea, and other flavors) in an attractive display on a serving dish for dessert.

Bonus Points

Buy a sake set, chopsticks, and extralarge bowls for serving the soup. Rent the movie *Tampopo*. It is not only appetizing but also very sexy.

Eat Drink Man Woman: Shrimp and Fortune Cookies

SHRIMP WRAPPED IN LETTUCE
TWO KINDS OF VEGETABLES
RICE
TSING TAO OR GEWÜRZTRAMINER
FORTUNE COOKIES AND PLUM WINE

You know the famous Chinese director, Ang Lee? *The Incredible Hulk; The Ice Storm; Crouching Tiger, Hidden Dragon; Sense and Sensibility?* Yeah, he directed all those. But before he went Hollywood, he directed a cool, indie date flick called *Eat Drink Man Woman.* And it's a classic. Not only is it a great little art house picture, but it's all about food and romance.

We've concocted a delicious (if we do say so ourselves) meal based on that fabulous film. Your Indie Girl will enjoy eating the shrimp wrapped in lettuce because it's so ethnic. Plus eating with your hands is so sexy. In the film, there's a recipe called Four Kinds of Vegetables, which we have reduced to two. (We did promise to get you through the express lane.)

We added fortune cookies, which are not actually from China. They were invented in San Francisco, but we just couldn't resist the high charm factor of making up fortunes for the Indie Girl. Sounds hard? It isn't! They're super easy to make and way impressive.

To Buy

1 bottle almond extract (½ teaspoon)

1 cup (8 ounces) white rice

1 head iceberg lettuce

½ pound raw shrimp, peeled and deveined (ask at the fish counter)

1 box cornstarch (½ tablespoon plus ½ teaspoon)

1 bottle Chinese chile oil (2 tablespoons)

1 bottle peanut oil (1 tablespoon)

1 bottle soy sauce (1½ tablespoons)

½ pound black or shiitake mushrooms

2 heads baby bok choy

Staples

2 ½ tablespoons butter, plus enough to grease a baking sheet

2 egg whites

½ cup sugar

½ cup flour

¼ teaspoon plus a pinch of salt and more to taste

1 ½ tablespoons milk

½ onion

½ tablespoon chicken broth

Pepper to taste

From the Liquor Store

Tsing Tao beer (Chinese beer). If she doesn't like beer, you can also serve wine; we
recommend gewürtzraminer (see wine primer in Part One).

Plum Wine (available at Asian grocery stores and many liquor stores)

One day before she arrives:

1. Now's your chance to get a little creative. We hope you have a computer. If not, you
can write out the fortune cookies by hand (just make it legible.) OK, so open your
word processing program and come up with 6 cute fortunes (that's how many cookies
this recipe yields). What? You can't think of any? OK, we'll give you a few:

NOT ONLY CAN THIS GUY COOK, BUT HE'S A GENIUS . . .
(That's assuming she will add the obligatory "in bed" to the end of the fortune.
If she doesn't know that joke, you can explain it to her.)

YOU ARE MORE BEAUTIFUL THAN BRITNEY SPEARS, CAMERON DIAZ,
AND JENNIFER LOPEZ ALL ROLLED INTO ONE.
(This one may be too long to fit on a fortune cookie. You'll have to make the font very tiny.)

ANCIENT CHINESE SECRET: YOU'RE A TOTAL FOX.

If you're feeling really crafty, add the Lucky Lottery Numbers to the back. Like this:

LUCKY NUMBERS: 7, 14, 21, 22, 32, 45

Put different numbers on the back of each fortune, of course—just don't ask us how to get the numbers on the back to line up with the fortunes on the front—we'll leave that up to you word-processing software whizzes.

2. Set your font so that each fortune can be cut into 2x½-inch strips. Print and cut, trying to cut it as straight as you can (we realize you probably don't have a paper cutter).

3. OK, now on to the actual baking. Preheat the oven to 400 degrees.

4. Lightly butter a baking sheet.

5. Separate the whites from the yolks of 2 eggs: Break each egg gently over a small mixing bowl, but capture the yolk in one of the halves of the shell. Gently pass the egg yolk back and forth between the shell halves, letting the white of the egg flow into the bowl. When nothing but yolk remains in the shells, throw the yolks and shells away. Set the bowl of egg whites aside.

6. In a microwave-safe bowl, melt the 2½ tablespoons butter in the microwave; set aside.

7. In a medium mixing bowl, use an electric mixer to beat together the 2 egg whites and ½ cup sugar for 30 seconds. Mix in ½ cup flour and a pinch of salt, then the melted butter, 1½ tablespoons milk, and ½ teaspoon almond extract.

8. Drop 1 tablespoon of batter onto the buttered baking sheet. Spread it in a circular motion with the back of the spoon until the batter is 3 to 4 inches in diameter and ⅛ inch thick. You can fit two cookies on a baking sheet.

9. Bake for 3–5 minutes, just until the edges are light brown.

10. Using a thin metal spatula, remove one cookie and place it on a dinner plate or clean cutting board. Very quickly place a fortune in the center of the cookie and lightly fold it in half, pinching the edges together. Quickly fold in half again, pushing in the middle of the cookie and drawing the points together. This may take some practice, but you will get the hang of it.

11. Set each fortune cookie into a shot glass or a coffee mug so it will hold its shape while it cools. Repeat this process until the cookie batter is gone.

12. When cooled, put in a bowl, cover with plastic wrap, and set aside. You should end up with 6 fortune cookies (or less—but you really only need 2).

The day of the date, before she arrives:

5:30

13. Chill the beer and wine.

14. Add 1 cup rice to a large mixing bowl. In the sink, add water and swirl with your hands. Drain and repeat until the water is no longer cloudy.

15. In a medium saucepan over high heat, add the rice and 1 cup water. Cover and bring to a boil. Reduce heat to low, keep it covered, and let it cook for 15 minutes or until done. Add salt to taste, transfer to a soup bowl, cover with plastic wrap, and set aside until ready to serve. Rinse out the large mixing bowl.

6:15

16. Wash the lettuce and peel off the leaves, keeping them whole. Drain on paper towels or run through salad spinner. Wrap in paper towels and put in the fridge until ready to use.

6:30

17. Cut the tails off the shrimp and discard the tails.

18. Mince the shrimp and put into the large mixing bowl.

19. Add ½ teaspoon cornstarch, ¼ teaspoon salt, and ⅛ teaspoon water, and mix together with a wooden spoon. Let it sit for 10 minutes.

7:00

20. Mince ½ of an onion.

21. In a frying pan over medium heat, add 1 tablespoon chile oil.

22. Add the shrimp and cook 1 to 3 minutes, just until it turns pink. Remove the shrimp from the pan, transfer to a medium mixing bowl, and set aside.

7:15

23. Add 1 tablespoon peanut oil to the frying pan. Add the minced onion and cook for 2 to 3 minutes.

24. Put the shrimp back into the frying pan and add ½ tablespoon soy sauce and ½ tablespoon chicken broth. Mix well and add salt and pepper to taste. Transfer back to the medium mixing bowl, cover with plastic wrap, and set aside until ready to serve.

7:30

25. Wash the mushrooms. If they are big, slice them.

26. Wash the bok choy, tearing each leaf off.

7:45

27. Add ½ tablespoon chile oil to the frying pan and then add the mushrooms. Add ½ tablespoon soy sauce and cook for 1 minute.

28. Add ½ tablespoon cornstarch and ¼ teaspoon water. Cook for another 1 to 3 minutes, until the mushrooms are soft. Transfer to a small mixing bowl and cover with plastic wrap until ready to serve.

29. Add ½ tablespoon chile oil to the frying pan. Add the bok choy and ½ tablespoon soy sauce. Cook just until wilted, about 1 minute. Transfer to a soup bowl and cover until ready to serve.

After she arrives:

8:00

30. Offer her a beer or glass of wine.

31. If necessary, toss the veggies in the pan for a quick reheat. You can nuke the shrimp and the rice in the microwave for a minute or so.

32. Serve the lettuce on a plate and the shrimp in the soup bowl. Arrange the bok choy and mushrooms on two dinner plates. Serve the rice on the side in a soup bowl. Eat the shrimp by spooning it onto the lettuce leaves and rolling them up like burritos.

33. After dinner, bring out the fortune cookies and plum wine (served in wineglasses).

Bonus Points

Rent *Eat Drink Man Woman,* of course. If she has seen it, your Indie Girl will not mind seeing it again—it's probably been a while. And besides, it's a sweet little story about people falling in love. If the fortune cookies don't get her, the movie most definitely will.

Amélie: Le Fabuleux Dîner d'Amélie Poulain

FIRST COURSE (APPETIZER):
COUNTRY PÂTÉ (PRONOUNCED "PAH-TAY")
FRENCH BAGUETTE ("BAH-GET")
APERITIF: MAURESQUE ("MORE-RESK")

SECOND COURSE (ENTREE):
ROAST CHICKEN WITH POTATOES
ENDIVE AU GRATIN A LA DEUX MOULINS ("ON-DEEV OH GRAH-TEN A-LA DEW MOO-LAHN")
WINE: SANCERRE OR VOUVRAY ("SAHN-SEHR" OR "VOO-VRAY")

THIRD COURSE (DESSERT):
AMÉLIE'S FAMOUS PLUM CAKE
DIGESTIF: MUSCAT ("MOO-SKAHT")

Jean-Pierre Jeunet's film *Amélie,* or *Le Fabuleux Destin d'Amélie Poulain* (*The Fabulous Destiny of Amélie Poulain;* 2000) features Audrey Tatou as Amélie, the quintessential Indie Girl. After returning a lost cache of boyhood toys to its rightful owner, this Parisian loner-tomboy-hipster-waitress goes on a quest to brighten the lives of strangers, one at a time, through a series of artfully designed encounters. Any time you find someone living her life as an art project, you've found an Indie Girl. If that weren't enough to tip you off, Amélie goes and falls in love with a "found object artist." This guy makes scrapbooks from photos he finds on the floor of train station photo booths. Who would love a guy like that? An Indie Girl, that's who.

The dishes in this meal are taken straight from the movie: the Mauresque, the Sunday Roast Chicken, Endive au Gratin (courtesy of Les Deux Moulins, the cafe where Amélie works), and, of course, Amélie's Famous Plum Cake. We've modified them to limit the ingredients, *naturellement.* Endive au Gratin is just endive (a kind of lettuce) baked with cheese and béchamel (which is a cream sauce).

Oh, and by the way, if you haven't yet seen *Amélie,* then *dépêche-toi* (hurry up)! Go straight to your local video store or add it to your Netflix queue. No joke, this is one of the great cinematic masterpieces.

PS: Always give the woman the oysters from the chicken—it's the best part. (If you don't know where the oysters are, that's another reason to rent the movie.)

To Buy

1 whole roasting chicken (called a fryer)

3 medium Yukon Gold potatoes (can substitute white or red—but don't use baking potatoes)

1 container nutmeg (small amount, to taste)

3 fresh plums (plums are in season in the summer—if you can't find fresh plums, you can substitute any stone fruit, such as nectarines or peaches or apricots; frozen are OK if you absolutely have to, but they won't look as pretty or as fresh)

1 container baking powder (*not* baking soda) (½ teaspoon)

2 large heads Belgian endive (most grocery stores carry this)

4 ounces fresh ground Parmesan cheese

1 French baguette

1 container goose liver or duck pâté (available at gourmet shops)

Decaf coffee

Staples

Olive oil

8 tablespoons (1 stick) butter, plus a little extra

1¾ cups plus 1½ tablespoons flour

Salt and pepper to taste

1½ cups milk, divided

¾ cup plus 2 tablespoons sugar

2 eggs

From the Liquor Store

1 bottle Pernod or Ricard (anise liqueur)

1 bottle Toriani almond (orgeat) syrup

1 bottle white French table wine (for the chicken)

1 bottle Vouvray or Sancerre (French white wine)

1 bottle muscat (French dessert wine)

Before she arrives:

5:30

1. Stick the wines in the fridge to chill.

2. Preheat oven to 450 degrees. (Note: You are going to have a lot of things in the oven; make sure you arrange the racks in such a way that you have enough room for the chicken, the endive, and the plum cake.)

3. Scoop out of the insides of chicken and remove excess fat. Rinse off the whole thing inside and out. Salt liberally inside and out. Douse the whole thing with olive oil.

5:45

4. Rinse the potatoes and quarter them.

5. Put a little bit of water in the bottom of a 9x13-inch glass baking dish. Add ¼ bottle of the white table wine.

6. Put chicken in the pan (breast side up) and stick the quartered potatoes all around the sides of the chicken. Put pan into the oven for about 10 minutes.

7. Reduce heat to 350 degrees and set the timer to let it cook for about an hour or more. When you are nearing the end, cut the chicken open in parts with a knife to see that it is cooked all the way through. Ideally, if you have a baster, you can baste it every so often, although this is not necessary.

6:15

8. Now for the Endive au Gratin. First you need to make béchamel (that's pronounced "bay-sha-MEL"): In a small saucepan on low heat, melt 2 tablespoons butter.

9. Using a wire whisk, mix in 1½ tablespoons flour, and add salt, pepper, and nutmeg to taste. Cook for 1 to 2 minutes.

10. Continue to simmer, slowly adding 1 cup milk, stirring constantly. Cover and set the sauce aside until you are ready to use.

6:45

11. To make the plum cake: Rinse the plums and slice them in half, removing the pits but leaving the skin on. Put them in a small mixing bowl, cover with 2 tablespoons sugar, toss, and set aside.

7:00

12. With an electric hand mixer, mix together 6 tablespoons butter, ¾ cup sugar, and 2 eggs in a medium mixing bowl. Add ½ cup milk, 1¾ cups flour, and ½ teaspoon baking powder and beat until well blended but not overmixed.

7:15

13. Butter a 9-inch square baking dish. Pour batter into pan and arrange the plums on top. They will sink into the cake as it cooks. Bake at 350 degrees for 1 hour.

7:30

14. Rinse and dry the endive. Remove the outer leaves if necessary.

15. Butter the bottom and sides of a loaf pan, and put the endive in.

16. Pour enough of the béchamel to just cover the endive.

17. Sprinkle the Parmesan cheese on top, and add salt and pepper. Bake for 30 to 40 minutes or until the endive is fork tender and brown on top. (If the cheese and sauce begin to brown too soon, carefully cover the dish with aluminum foil.)

7:45

18. Slice up the baguette and open the pâté and arrange on a platter.

After she arrives:

8:00

First course:

19. Offer her some pâté and bread and a Mauresque. To make the Mauresque, just take a couple of wineglasses, add a finger (about a half-inch) of the Pernod (or Ricard) and a finger of the almond syrup, and stir in a little water to taste. Fill with ice.

Second course:

20. When the endive and the cake are done, take them out of the oven and cover with foil to keep them warm. (You will know the cake is ready if a toothpick or knife inserted in the middle comes out clean.) Use a knife to check if the chicken is done—if it is still pink inside, it's not done yet. Continue to check the chicken until it's done. When you are ready, carve pieces from the chicken with a chef's knife. Ask your guest if she wants a wing or a breast or a drumstick. Serve the endive alongside the chicken on dinner plates, with the chilled bottle of Vouvray or Sancerre.

Third course:

21. For dessert, serve the cake warm with some decaf coffee and a glass of Muscat.

Bonus Points

Serve cornichons (fancy little French pickles) with the bread and pâté. You can also serve either a green salad or steamed artichokes with the entree, and vanilla ice cream with the cake if you like. Definitely play the *Amélie* sound track or watch the DVD (not both, though). If you're going to watch the DVD, and you want a little French mood music for later (when the lights are low), put on some romantic old stuff like Charles Trenet, Edith Piaf, or Mistinguette. *Voilà!*

Like Water for Chocolate: Chiles en Nogada and Chocolate Flan

CHILES EN NOGADA (STUFFED POBLANO PEPPERS)
MEXICAN MARTINIS AND/OR MICHELADA NEGRAS
CHOCOLATE FLAN

Laura Esquivel's 1990 novel and 1992 movie, *Like Water for Chocolate,* included a recipe for Chiles en Nogada: spicy poblano chiles stuffed with a sweet meat mixture topped with a creamy walnut sauce and garnished with parsley and pomegranate seeds. The white sauce, green parsley, and red pomegranate seeds are meant to symbolize the Mexican flag.

Chiles en Nogada are not easy to find outside of Mexico, and the obscurity will surely impress the Indie Girl. This is the hardest Indie Girl meal to prepare (and one of the hardest menus in the book), but it is so stunning and sexy, it is definitely worth the extra effort. Yes, you have to start a day in advance, but this is the kind of meal she will never forget. Be forewarned, pomegranates are a fertility symbol in Mexico, and in the story, this dish is a strong aphrodisiac. It was served at a wedding, and after tasting it, all the guests couldn't get out of there fast enough so they could go have sex.

We have reduced the number of ingredients substantially—but it still comes out fantastic. The combination of tastes—hot pepper with salty pork, sweet pears and raisins, and the cool walnut cream sauce—is complex and interesting. Serve with potent Mexican martinis (a margarita/dirty martini hybrid) and/or refreshing Michelada Negras (Mexican beer and lime juice over ice). Finish with the delectable chocolate flan, and your Indie Girl will be fanning herself—and not just from the heat of the peppers.

To Buy

1 bar or package semisweet chocolate (2 ounces)

20 walnuts

1 pear (can substitute apple) (using only half)

1 box raisins (2 tablespoons)

1 small container ground cinnamon (½ teaspoon plus ⅛ teaspoon)

1 pound boneless pork

2 poblano peppers (also called pasilla peppers—found in most grocery stores these days, but you may have to go to a Mexican market or specialty store)

1 small container sour cream (4 ounces or ½ cup)

1 bunch Italian flat leaf parsley or cilantro

1 pomegranate (pomegranates are available in most gourmet grocery stores—if you can't find them, you can substitute fresh raspberries; if those are unavailable, buy frozen raspberries, just make sure you give them enough time to defrost)

Staples

1 egg plus 3 egg yolks

1 cup plus 1 tablespoon milk

1 cup sugar, plus a teaspoon or two extra

1 clove garlic

¼ onion

1 tablespoon olive oil

Salt (to taste)

Pepper (to taste)

From the Liquor Store

1 6-pack Negra Modelo (Mexican) beer

1 bottle good-quality tequila

1 jar martini olives—preferably jalapeño-stuffed

1 bottle Cointreau (can substitute triple sec if you want to save money)

1 bottle Rose's lime juice (fresh is better but not necessary)

1 bag ice

1 container margarita salt

The day before she arrives:

1. To make the chocolate flan: Preheat the oven to 350 degrees.

2. Separate the 3 egg yolks by cracking the eggs in two over the sink or trash can. Pass the yolk back and forth between the two shell halves, allowing the egg white to fall into the sink or can. Drop the egg yolks into the food processor and discard the eggshells. Now add 1 whole egg (including the yolk and the white, but not the shell!) to the processor.

3. In a microwave-safe bowl, melt 2 ounces semisweet chocolate and ¼ cup water. Stir and set aside to cool for about 1 minute.

4. Add 1 cup milk and ½ cup sugar to the food processor with the eggs. Pulse until thoroughly mixed. Add the melted chocolate and pulse some more until mixed.

5. In a small saucepan over medium heat, add ½ cup sugar and stir constantly with a wooden spoon. When sugar begins to melt (it will take a few minutes), reduce heat and continue stirring until sugar has all melted into a liquid and is a very light brown color (this is called caramelizing).

6. Working quickly, pour the caramelized sugar into a loaf pan, tilting the dish to completely cover the bottom with the liquid. The caramelized sugar liquid will harden quickly on the bottom of the loaf pan.

7. Pour the melted chocolate mixture over the caramelized sugar in the loaf pan. Set aside.

8. Fill a 9x13-inch glass baking dish halfway with hot water. Gently place the loaf pan in the middle of the 9x13-inch baking dish. Put the glass baking dish with the loaf pan in the oven and set the timer to bake for about an hour. When the flan is done baking (check by sticking a butter knife down the side of the loaf pan—when it comes out clean, it is done), remove both pans from the oven and set on a trivet or an oven mitt to cool for half an hour.

9. Remove the loaf pan with flan from the baking dish. Cover the flan with plastic wrap and let it cool in the fridge overnight.

The day of the date, before she arrives:

3:30

10. To make the Chiles en Nogada: Fill a small saucepan halfway with water and bring to a boil.

11. Add the walnuts and boil them for 5 minutes.

12. Take the walnuts off the heat and flush them in cool water in a colander.

4:00

13. Now comes the worst part of this recipe: Peel the skins off the walnuts. Yes, you heard that right. Just trust us—it's a necessary step. If you leave the skin on, you will be able to taste it in the sauce, which won't fly. Here's how to do it: Using your index finger and thumb, rub the walnut until the skin comes off. (Not difficult, just tedious.)

4:30

14. Take half the skinned walnuts and put them in the food processor, along with half a pear (minus stem, seeds, and core—keep the skin on), 2 tablespoons raisins, and ½ teaspoon ground cinnamon. Blend until it becomes a paste.

4:45

15. Cut the pork into small cubes and set aside.

5:00

16. Crush 1 clove garlic and chop up the ¼ onion and add to a frying pan with 1 table-spoon olive oil. Set over medium heat, stir occasionally, and cook until the onions and garlic are translucent, making sure not to let them turn brown.

17. Add the cubed pork to the pan. Cook the pork until it is brown.

18. Drain off the fat (into an old milk carton or coffee can) and add the pear-walnut mixture from the food processor to the pan with the pork. Cook for another 5 minutes or so, stirring with a wooden spoon. Add a little salt and pepper to taste. Remove from heat.

5:45

19. Roast the poblano peppers in the broiler or directly on the gas stove burners, turning them with a fork (or tongs if you have some) until they are blackened in spots all over—about 5 minutes. (Note: wear rubber gloves when handling peppers, or just be careful not to touch your eyes while handling chiles, especially the seeds. Wash your hands with soap afterwards.)

20. After the peppers have cooled slightly, transfer them to a brown paper bag (or, if you can't find a paper bag, roll in some paper towels) and set aside.

6:15

21. Rinse out the food processor and add the rest of the walnuts. Chop until finely ground.

22. Add 1 tablespoon milk, ½ cup sour cream, ½ teaspoon lime juice, and ⅛ teaspoon ground cinnamon.

23. Process and add pinches of sugar until it is tastes slightly sweet—a teaspoon or two.

24. Put the walnut sauce in the fridge to chill until you are ready to serve dinner.

6:45

25. Remove the peppers from the bag. Rub off loose skin with your hands (wear gloves if you can, and keep your hands away from your face).

26. Cut the peppers in half with a chef's knife, making a slit vertically down the side of each pepper. Remove and discard the seeds, but leave the stem end intact. Preheat the oven to 350 degrees.

7:15

27. Spoon the meat filling into the pepper halves. Put into a 9x13-inch glass baking dish and transfer to the oven. Set the timer to bake for 20 minutes.

7:30

28. Chop a couple of handfuls of parsley very finely. You can do this by hand or in the food processor. Set aside.

29. Cut open the pomegranate, remove the seeds, and put it in a soup bowl. Set the parsley and pomegranate seeds aside.

30. Chill a couple of martini glasses (you can use wineglasses)—just stick them in the freezer.

31. Remove *Chiles en Nogada* from the oven and cover with foil to keep warm until ready to serve.

After she arrives:

8:00

32. Make her a drink. Ask her if she'd like to start with a Mexican martini or a Michelada Negra. For the Mexican martinis: Take out the martini glasses and salt the rims with the margarita salt. In a martini shaker, mix together 3 ounces tequila, 1 ounce Cointreau or triple sec, 1 tablespoon lime juice, 1 tablespoon olive juice, 1 teaspoon sugar, and 2 tablespoons water. Add ice and shake at least 30 times. (If you don't have a shaker, you can make a stirred martini.) Garnish with olives. To make the Michelada Negras: Salt the rims of 2 pint glasses, add ice, fill them halfway with Negra Modelo beer, and add about 1 tablespoon lime juice to each glass. Stir. If you like, you can make it even spicier with a dash of Tabasco and some Worcestershire sauce.

33. To serve the Chiles en Nogada, place one on each dinner plate. Pour a little walnut cream sauce on top, and lightly decorate with chopped parsley and pomegranate seeds.

34. When you're ready for dessert, take the flan out of the fridge and slide a spatula or knife around the sides of the loaf pan to loosen it. Cover with a larger plate and invert carefully onto the plate.

Bonus Points

On the side, you can serve rice, black beans, and warm tortillas. For music, go with the Gipsy Kings or the sound track from the movie *Frida* or the *Buena Vista Social Club.* You can serve decaf coffee or dessert sherry with the flan.

The Granola Girl

She's cooking salad for breakfast She's got tofu the size of Texas

—Beck song, "Nitemare Hippy Girl"

Face it. You're going to have to eat tofu for this girl. But don't freak out. It's just bean curd. And, it doesn't taste bad. In fact, tofu doesn't really taste like anything. It has the chameleon-like quality of taking on the flavor of whatever you mix it with; kind of like that spineless, sidekick friend who used to follow you around in high school, mindlessly adopting your opinions. Bad quality for a friend, good quality for a protein.

Plan on going vegetarian but be aware, vegetarians come in different stripes. There are lacto-vegetarians, who will eat dairy, and lacto-ovos, who include eggs in their diet. Pesco-vegetarians allow fish, a choice that is common in Asian cultures, while pollo-vegetarians tolerate poultry. A vegan will not eat meat, fish, eggs, or any kind of dairy. Nor will she eat or use any product that was produced by an animal, including wool, leather, and honey (the bees are oppressed).

Then there is the macrobiotic eater, who attempts to live a nutritional life that is fully in rhythm with the principles of yin and yang. Yin is light and upward, yang is heavier and more grounded, and all foods are one or the other. Macro Girls are prone to search for the balance between these powers, so their diet is not too extreme in any sense. They eat seasonally, regionally, and organically, and they don't eat nightshade vegetables, such as tomatoes, spinach, or eggplant, unless they are in season. They mostly eat grains and veggies, plus sea vegetables, light pickles, chutneys, and salads. It may sound a bit wacky, but many macros report near-miraculous recoveries from disease, so they have a dedicated and growing following.

There are also those who follow the raw food diet. They only eat foods that are raw, and we're not talking sashimi (although, logically, raw fish is raw, isn't it?). They eat lots of raw fruits and vegetables, sprouts, tofu, seaweed, and "superfoods" like blue-green algae and spirulina. If you think raw food is radical, try being a fruitarian. These Girls don't even eat plants—just fruit, because they think it is cruel to cut the plant, while fruit trees willingly give sustenance.

There are also breatharians. Yes, you guessed it. Breatharians don't eat food at all. They subsist on air and light. (Well, if you read the small type on their Web site, they do eat. They say they don't actually have to eat, but they just do it for the pleasure.) So how do they get sustenance? They shine flashlights into their mouths, of course. Breatharians also believe in aliens who are currently orbiting the earth on the *Starship Marigold.* (Note: The authors of *Cooking to Hook Up* do not advocate the dating of breatharians.)

Regardless of what particular type of diet she follows, remember that eating, like everything else in a Granola Girl's life, is a political statement. Most of the food we buy is full of stuff we don't want to know about—hormones, antibiotics, pesticides, etc.—and Granola Girls are trying to clean up their act. A true Granola Girl lives the maxim: *Think Globally, Act Locally.*

She Might Be a Granola Girl If:

1. **She drives:** a VW bus, a bicycle, or an electric car, or uses public transportation.
2. **She can talk for more than ten minutes about:** hemp.
3. **She begins her sentences with:** "Ralph Nader says . . ."
4. **She'd never:** vote Republican.
5. **She owns any of the following:** a smudge stick, ear candles, a tongue scraper, a compost bin, Dr. Bronner's soap (bulk size).

Where You'll Find Her

Health food stores, political protests, yoga studios, New Age bookstores, major state universities, and liberal arts colleges.

How to Spot Her

Whether in jeans, hiking shorts, or a sundress, the Granola Girl wears all-natural fabrics, such as cotton or hemp. You won't see any leather or fur on this Girl. The Granola Girl's wardrobe is comfortable and casual. Tie-dyed skirts or peasant dresses are common, and if she's not wearing her Birkenstock sandals or Tevas, she is probably barefoot. Her hair is usually long, possibly beaded and/or dreadlocked. She wears essential oils like patchouli and is often braless.

Famous Granola Girls

Jane Fonda in her pre–Ted Turner days and TV characters Dharma of *Dharma & Greg* and Phoebe on *Friends.* Vegan celebs include Alicia Silverstone, Brandy, and Fiona Apple. Gwyneth Paltrow and Geri Halliwell are strictly macrobiotic.

Your Place

Unlike the Uptown Girl, living in a posh neighborhood can actually work against you here. You don't want to be seen as "the Man," a capitalist tool of the oppressor. She wants to know that you live among the people, so a down-and-out neighborhood with a funky coffee shop is recommended. A clothing-optional co-op is even better. Or a yurt in New Mexico. At the very least, get yourself a Bob Marley poster and burn some Nag Champa (that's incense).

The Conversation

Don't discuss politics unless you're leaning to the left. Don't discuss religion unless you've had an out-of-body experience. Don't discuss sex unless you can define the word *tantric.* For safety's sake, stick with folk music, astrology, and why we're better off without television.

The Coffee Table

Mother Jones, New Age, Vegetarian Times, Utne Reader, Adbusters, Z Magazine.

The Music

Think ethnic. Look for the Gipsy Kings, Ladysmith Black Mambazo, Erykah Badu, or the equivalent. Classic folk music, such as Woody Guthrie or Carole King, is as good as the modern stuff, like Norah Jones or David Wilcox. There's always reggae, and you can never go wrong with the Dead (or the more modern Phish). You're also safe with New Age music or nature recordings, such as the sound of rain or humpback whales.

The Drinks

Many Granola Girls like to drink, but they always drink responsibly. In other words, they don't support giant multinational corporations that own breweries: for example, Atria Group, Inc., owns Philip Morris Companies, Inc., which owns Miller Brewing Company. The problem with these multinational corporations is that they keep buying each other up and getting bigger and bigger. So big, in fact, that they are larger than nations. And since they are multinational . . . well, you can see the problem. When corporations are larger than nations, they somehow end up making decisions about how the world should be run. Granola Girls are aware of all this, and they'd rather support small, independent microbreweries. As far as wine goes, serve organic, which can be procured at large health food stores (you should be shopping there anyway for the Granola Girl). If she doesn't drink, be prepared with nonalcoholic cider or fruit juice (again, organic is best). Whether she drinks or not, always have good-quality filtered or spring water on hand. Tap water won't cut it with the Granola set.

The Shoes

Birkenstocks are de riguer, with or without socks. Depending on the occasion and climate, you might opt for Tevas, mucklucks, or hiking boots. Barefoot is never wrong.

The Flowers

Go with sunflowers or wildflowers.

Resources

If you are hanging out with the Granola Girl, you are going to need to get involved. Study up on some of the groups we have listed here—we've included URLs so you can educate yourself and, in turn, impress your Granola Girl.

Environment

Earth First

www.earthfirst.org

These are the people who tie themselves to trees to prevent the clear-cutting of forests (it's called "tree sitting"). The front line of the environmental movement.

Green Party

www.gp.org

The only political party, as far as the Granola Girl is concerned.

Greenpeace

www.greenpeace.org/international_en

International organization of environmental activists.

Rainforest Action Network

www.ran.org

Protecting Earth's rainforests.

Animal Rights

Animal Liberation Front

www.animalliberationfront.com

The equivalent of Earth First for animals. These are the folks who rescue animals from laboratories.

Farm Sanctuary

www.farmsanctuary.org

Campaigning to stop factory farming and animal cruelty.

PETA

www.peta.org

People for the Ethical Treatment of Animals; the largest animal rights organization in the world.

Politics

Ralph Nader

www.nader.org

He's *the man:* longtime environmental and consumer rights activist who challenges large multinational corporations.

Essential Action

www.essential.org

Founded in 1982 by Ralph Nader.

Noam Chomsky

www.chomsky.info

A libertarian socialist—one of the leading forces of the American left.

Food

Macrobiotic

www.kushiinstiute.org

The source for info about macrobiotics.

Raw Foods

www.living-foods.com

Want to know more about why you should eat raw foods? It's all here.

Shopping

Diamond Organics

www.diamondorganics.com

Online resource for organic foods; overnight delivery in the United States.

Dr. Bronner's Magic Soaps

www.drbronner.com

Not tested on animals, and they use hemp oil in the soap.

Eco Wine

www.ecowine.com

Organic French wine. Ships overnight in the United States.

Real Goods

www.realgoods.com

"Products for an ecologically sustainable future." Lots of info on solar power and renewable resources.

Whole Foods Market

www.wholefoods.com

Whole Foods Market is the world's largest retailer of natural and organic foods, with more than 155 stores throughout North America and the United Kingdom.

Macrobiotic: Magic Marinated Mushrooms

MARINATED PORTOBELLO MUSHROOMS
NOODLE, LETTUCE, AND CARROT SALAD
ORGANIC WINE
FRUIT KANTEN

A macrobiotic diet is all about striking balances—between "expansive" and "contractive" food, acid and alkaline, yin and yang, and so on. If things work out between the two of you, we would suggest picking up a book on the subject and getting some serious education about this very healthy lifestyle. While you're sussing out the situation, though, the following meal should get you through the first dinner. The portobello mushroom is one of the most common varieties that you will find in a normal grocery store—it resembles a brown Frisbee, 4 to 6 inches across, and it tastes like a vegetarian steak. Umeboshi plums and agar-agar flakes may take a little searching, but you can find them at better grocery stores. Failing that, try a natural foods or Japanese grocery store.

Make sure that the fruit you buy is in season. Macro Girls, whenever possible, eat foods that are grown in the area they inhabit and in season. If your body is in Minnesota, it gets confused when you feed it Chilean grapes in February, dig? Also, whenever possible, buy organic. These days, you can even get organic pasta.

If you want to get fancy with the dessert, consider buying a set of jelly molds.

Note: This meal is also vegan.

To Buy

¾ cup fruit in season (strawberries, cherries, blackberries, blueberries, peaches, pears, apples, raisins, etc.)

1 container agar-agar flakes (2 tablespoons)

1 jar fruit juice (cranberry, cranberry-raspberry, apple, grape, etc.) (2 cups)

1 to 2 packages whole-wheat ribbon noodles or udon noodles (4 cups)

1 bunch scallions (1 tablespoon chopped)

2 to 3 umeboshi plums, pitted

1 container organic, roasted tahini (2 to 3 tablespoons)

4 huge portobello mushrooms

1 bunch organic leaf lettuce (2 cups small pieces)

3 medium-size carrots (¼ cup grated)

Staples

1 teaspoon grated onion

¼ cup olive oil

2 tablespoons balsamic vinegar

Pepper (to taste)

From the Liquor Store (or Whole Foods)

Organic wine

Filtered or spring water

Before she arrives:

6:30

1. Even in the world of macrobiotics, it's good to start with dessert. Chop up ½ cup of whatever fruit you have chosen. In a medium saucepan, combine the agar-agar flakes, the chopped fruit, and 2 cups fruit juice, and bring to a boil. Pour quickly into 2 small bowls or jelly molds. Put them in the refrigerator so they can set. Yes, you have just made macrobiotic Jell-O.

7:00

2. Cook the noodles, following the package directions. Make sure you take them off the stove before they even think about getting mushy. Rinse them in cool water and put them in the refrigerator.

7:30

3. Grate 1 teaspoon onion and chop 1 tablespoon scallions. Mix together with the ume-boshi plums and 2 to 3 tablespoons tahini in a small bowl to make the dressing. Put it in the fridge.

7:45

4. Mix together ¼ cup olive oil and 2 tablespoons balsamic vinegar in a small dish. Put the mushrooms in a 9x13-inch glass baking dish and pour the oil and vinegar mixture over them. Let them soak for about 10 minutes. Portobellos are like little sponges, so they will soak that liquid right up.

After she arrives:

5. Offer her a drink.

6. Put a frying pan over medium heat and sauté the mushrooms for 2 minutes on each side.

7. Tear lettuce into small pieces until you have 2 cups. Grate enough carrot to make ¼ cup. Mix together the cooked, cool noodles, lettuce, and carrots. Pour the dressing over the top and toss. Arrange the salad on two plates, then put a mushroom (or 2, if they are small) on each plate.

8. Bring the pepper to the table and invite her to season the salad herself. Macrobiotic eaters are particularly careful about spices.

9. When you're done with the main course, bring out the agar-agar dessert. Make sure to tell her that it is *not* animal gelatin. Otherwise, you may have to peel her off the ceiling when she sees it.

Bonus Points

Sprinkle sesame seeds on top of the mushrooms. Many macro meals include a soup, and you can easily add one at the top of the meal. You can make a simple miso soup by heating 4 cups vegetable broth and adding 1 cup tofu squares, 1 tablespoon miso paste, and 3 to 4 chopped scallions. Miso is a macrobiotic staple, so serving it is always in good taste.

Eco-Friendly: Crop Rotation Casserole

CROP ROTATION CASSEROLE
ORGANIC WINE OR FILTERED SPRING WATER
FRUIT COBBLER

Most people tend to eat the same thing over and over. Americans eat lots of eggs, orange juice, bread, peanut butter, and hamburgers. Most of the vegetables we eat are potatoes (the average American eats one medium potato a day, or 110 pounds per year), and most of those are french fries. Our lettuce is iceberg, our bread is from wheat, and most of our protein is from cows. Not that there's anything wrong with that. Except that there is.

Why? In a word: monocultures. When you grow the same food over and over again (such as wheat for bread, potatoes for french fries, or one variety of lettuce), the soil becomes depleted of minerals. Not only is depleted soil bad for growing healthy crops, but it also encourages pests. Bugs and sickness tend to be specific to a particular kind of plant. If you're growing only one type of plant, and the bug for that particular plant shows up, you are sunk. This is the reason why computer viruses spread so quickly. Since most of the computers in the world run one operating system, Windows, they can all be brought to their knees by a single piece of computer code.(This fact is only distantly related to cooking, but you can never go wrong with a Granola Girl if you get in a dig at a multinational corporation like Microsoft.)

Organic farmers not only rotate their crops, creating healthier soil that requires fewer pesticides, but also grow various kinds of plants, bringing diversity to the environment. In tribute to organic farming, we've created a menu that is designed so you can swap out the ingredients and use them interchangeably. Just like rotating crops! Depending on your mood, you could make a millet-lentil-tofu-zucchini-kale casserole and a peach cobbler, or a quinoa-adzuki-tempeh-eggplant-Swiss chard casserole and pear cobbler. Imagine the possibilities! You can have a different meal for every day of the week! Then again, let's not get too carried away . . . after all, man cannot live on casserole and cobbler alone.

So, impress your Granola Girl—and help save the environment—with this casserole made of alternative grains and not-so-common veggies. And yes, it's entirely vegan! (Of course!) Just make sure you go organic with everything—even the sugar and flour if you can. This Girl is committed to the cause, and the last thing she wants to do is eat any pesticides.

To Buy:

1 cup of *one* of the following uncooked organic grains: amaranth, barley, buckwheat, bulgur, kamut ("kah-MOOT"), millet ("MILL-it"), or quinoa ("KEEN-wah")

1 of the following organic vegetables: acorn squash, butternut squash, eggplant, spaghetti squash, or 1 pound carrots, zucchini, or yellow squash

1 bunch of *one* of the following organic leafy greens: kale, spinach, Swiss chard, or collard greens

1 cup (8 ounces) of *one* of the following organic soy product: tempeh, tofu, or TSP (texturized soy protein)

1 can of *one* of the following organic beans: black, garbanzo, navy, lentil, great northern, or adzuki beans (if you can't find beans in a can, you can buy them dry—just follow the instructions on the package and cook them before you add them to the casserole)

6 of *one* of the following organic fruits: peaches, apples, or pears

1 box organic cornstarch (1 tablespoon)

1 box organic baking powder (*not* baking soda) (1½ teaspoons)

1 small container organic vegetable shortening (3 tablespoons)

1 carton soy milk (½ cup)

Staples

A sprinkle of salt and pepper

½ cup plus 1 tablespoon organic sugar

1 cup organic flour

From the Liquor Store

Organic wine and/or filtered or spring water

Before she arrives:

6:30

1. Preheat the oven to 350 degrees.

2. Rinse the grain in cold water in a colander. In a medium saucepan, add 1 cup grain and the corresponding amount of water from the chart on the next page. You can also substitute organic vegetable broth for the water, to make it more flavorful.

Grain	Water to Add	Cooking Time
Amaranth	3 cups	25 minutes
Barley	4 cups	35 minutes
Buckwheat	3 cups	20 minutes
Bulgur	2 cups	15 minutes
Kamut	3½ cups	1 hour
Millet	4 cups	25 minutes
Quinoa	2 cups	15 minutes

Vegetable	How to Prepare	Microwave Instructions
Acorn Squash	Halve squash, discard seeds. Place cut-side down on a plate and put in microwave.	5–10 minutes. Scrape out squash with fork.
Butternut Squash	Prick with a fork and stick in microwave.	5–10 minutes. Scrape out squash with fork.
Eggplant	Rinse, cut up into bite-size chunks, and put in microwave in a dish.	4–5 minutes.
Spaghetti Squash	Cut lengthwise, remove seeds. Put one of the halves in the microwave, covered with plastic wrap, cut-side up in a dish with ¼ cup water.	10–15 minutes. With fork, comb out the strands (looks like spaghetti).
Carrots	Rinse and cut into ½-inch slices (discard ends). Put in microwave.	3–5 minutes.
Yellow squash	Rinse and cut into ½-inch slices (discard ends). Put in microwave.	3–5 minutes.
Zucchini	Rinse and cut into ½-inch slices (discard ends). Put in microwave.	3–5 minutes

3. Bring the water to a boil, then lower the heat, cover, and simmer the grain for the proper cooking time.

4. When the grain is done, remove from heat and add 1½ cup's worth (different grains yield different amounts after they are cooked) to a 9x13-inch glass baking dish. Sprinkle on a little salt and pepper. Set aside. Wash and dry the medium saucepan for use later.

5. Rinse the vegetables and greens thoroughly, especially the greens because they can be a bit sandy—then remove stems and ends (and, in the case of eggplant, seeds).

6. To prepare the vegetable, all you have to do is follow the preparation and cooking instructions listed in the "Veggie-Table" on the opposite page.

7. When the vegetable is cooked, layer it over the cooked grains in the baking dish.

8. Put about 2 cups water in the medium saucepan and bring to a boil. Place the basket steamer in the pan over the boiling water, then toss the greens into the steamer. Cover the saucepan and let the greens steam until they are limp. Add greens to the casserole. Sprinkle a little more salt and pepper on top. Rinse out saucepan.

9. Use the following chart to make the soy layer. Layer the cooked soy over the greens.

Soy Product	How to Prepare
Tempeh	Cook in water or a flavored broth for 10–15 minutes before using.
Tofu	Mash and stir-fry in a little olive oil for 10–15 minutes.
TSP	Rehydrate 1 cup TSP granules by pouring 1 cup boiling water over it and allow it to sit for a few minutes.

10. Layer the beans on top. Sprinkle on a little more salt and pepper.

7:30

11. Put the casserole into the oven and cook for 30 minutes.

12. Rinse the fruit and slice into bite-size pieces, removing any pits, cores, or stems. Toss them into the medium-size saucepan over medium heat, and gently stir in ½ cup sugar and 1 tablespoon cornstarch. Cook until the fruit gets soft and the juice starts to boil. Pour into a 9-inch square glass baking dish and stick in the oven beside the casserole to keep warm.

13. In the food processor, mix 1 cup flour, 1 tablespoon sugar, 1½ teaspoons baking powder, ½ teaspoon salt, and 3 tablespoons organic shortening. Process until it has the consistency of fine crumbs. Add ½ cup soy milk and pulse to incorporate. Take the hot fruit out of the oven and drop spoonfuls of the dough mixture randomly all over the top. Bake about 25 to 30 minutes.

After she arrives:

8:00

14. Offer her a drink and serve the casserole. After the cobbler comes out of the oven, keep it warm by covering it with foil, and serve whenever you're ready for it.

Bonus Points

This casserole is really improved with a dash of soy sauce. Serve organic, wheat-free tamari soy sauce for best effect. For an extraspecial touch, serve vanilla soy milk (or rice milk) ice cream (such as Tofutti, Rice Dream, or Soy Delicious) with the cobbler.

[easy]
Raw Lust: Sprout Salad and Wheatgrass Shots

SPROUT SALAD
WHEATGRASS SHOTS
SLICED PEACHES

This menu is for that breed of Granola Girl who eats only raw food. That means nothing cooked. Before you get all whipped up about how ridiculous a raw-food diet is, think about it: Before the whole *Quest for Fire* thing, primitive man had nowhere to cook his meager dinner of roots and berries. Raw-food salad was the only thing on the menu. So you can hardly call this a fad diet.

Fortunately for that meager analogy, the rationale for a raw-food diet goes a lot further, and it actually has a physiological basis. The real issue here is enzymes. Raw foods contain enzymes, and cooking destroys them. Enzymes are catalysts in the body that aid digestion, arguably the body's single most important function. Without proper digestion, it really doesn't matter what you put in your system. Enzymes break down the nutrients and make them available to the organs in your body.

Raw food may sound unappetizing, but this salad is actually quite delicious. And, it's one of the most effortless recipes in the book. After all, there's no cooking involved! Note that everything must be organic. This is nonnegotiable. There really is no point in eating a bunch of healthy living enzymes if you're going to annihilate them with pesticides. Go to your local health food store—you'll find everything you need.

One last thing: Don't try to get fancy and serve something on the side, like bread. Remember, bread is cooked! See how easy it is to get tripped up? Just stick with what's on the page, and you'll be fine. This meal also works for the vegan Granola Girl, but not the macrobiotic.

To Buy

3 organic peaches (can substitute oranges or apples)

1 head organic green or red leaf lettuce

2 organic tomatoes

2 organic carrots

1 container organic sprouts—daikon, sunflower, or alfalfa

4 tablespoons (2 ounces) *each* of 3 of the following: raw sunflower seeds, flaxseeds, sprouted lentils, sprouted mung beans, sprouted garbanzos, sprouted kamut, etc. (take a look around the health food store and pick whatever strikes your fancy)

1 bottle organic ginger-vinaigrette dressing

1 small container (enough for 2 "shots") wheatgrass juice (available fresh at Whole Foods, Jamba Juice, or health food stores)

Before she arrives:

7:00

1. Rinse the peaches and set aside.

2. Rinse the green or red leaf lettuce and tear into large pieces.

3. Spin lettuce pieces in a salad spinner or just lay on paper towel to dry.

4. Transfer the lettuce pieces into a large mixing bowl.

5. Rinse the tomatoes, cut them into quarters, and add them to the bowl.

7:30

6. Cut the ends off the carrots.

7. Using a vegetable peeler, peel the skin off the carrots and discard.

8. Grate the carrots with a cheese grater or food processor and add them to the bowl, along with 2 handfuls each of the daikon or alfalfa sprouts and all the other sprouts and seeds.

After she arrives:

8:00

9. Toss everything with a couple tablespoons of the dressing (to taste).

10. Serve immediately with shots of wheatgrass.

11. After dinner, cut the peaches (or other fruit) into quarters and arrange decoratively on plates or in bowls.

Bonus Points

Serve filtered water to drink. If you like, drizzle a little honey over the peaches. Not if she's a vegan, though. Remember, the bees are oppressed.

Lacto-Ovo: Greekin' Out

SPANAKOPITA
HUMMUS
TABOULI
ORGANIC WINE OR MICROBREWERY BEER
BAKLAVA

For some reason, the Greeks seem to be one of the least stressed-out people in the world, despite the fact that Greece has been the site of some of the most cataclysmic events of the last five thousand years. Just in the last hundred, the Greeks have had two world wars, a massive civil war, and no end of revolving-door governments. It could be the fact that most of Greece is spread out over an idyllic archipelago, with sapphire-blue water and glistening white beaches. Or it might be the soporific effect of ouzo, the national drink. We think, however, that it has something to do with their diet. Light on meats, heavy on greens, fish, and olive oil, the Greek diet is something that Americans eat at restorative spas and "natural food" restaurants. Whatever it is, the following meal will do your heart good, both physically and spiritually.

This meal satisfies the needs of the lacto-ovo vegetarian, who eats milk and eggs in addition to standard vegetarian fare. Everything should be at your grocery store, with the exception of the baklava, an outrageously good Greek dessert that is essentially layers of paper-thin pastry stuck together with honey. Look for a Greek deli or restaurant where you can pick it up premade. It's worth the extra trip.

To Buy

1 (16-ounce) bag frozen spinach

1 package or bunch fresh mint *or* fresh dill

½ pound (8 ounces) feta cheese

2 lemons (the second one is just for the ouzo)

1 can olive oil spray

½ pound phyllo dough

1 (16-ounce) can garbanzo beans, drained

1 small jar tahini (⅓ cup)

½ pound tabouli

4 squares baklava

Staples

1 small onion

4 tablespoons olive oil, divided

1¼ teaspoons salt

A sprinkle of black pepper

2 eggs

2 cloves minced or pressed garlic

From the Liquor Store

Go with an organic wine or a microbrew beer. If your Granola Girl is in a celebra-tory mood, you might want to try the Greek national firewater, ouzo. Serve it with a slice of lemon. Down the shot, bite into the lemon, and shout "Hupa!"

Before she arrives:

6:00

1. Preheat the oven to 350 degrees.

2. To make the spanakopita, thaw the spinach (you can do it in the microwave) and drain well. Toss it on a dish towel and squeeze out the excess water. This will leave a stain on the towel that might be permanent, so don't use the ones your mother gave you for Christmas.

6:30

3. Chop 1 small onion finely and sauté it in 1 tablespoon olive oil until transparent. Add it to the spinach in a large mixing bowl, along with ¾ cup chopped mint (or dill), ½ pound feta cheese, ¼ teaspoon salt, a sprinkle of pepper, 2 eggs, 3 tablespoons olive oil, and the juice of ½ the lemon.

7:00

4. Spray the bottom of a 9x13-inch glass baking pan with the olive oil spray and begin layering the sheets of phyllo dough in the bottom. If the phyllo dough is longer than the pan, cut each piece in half before layering it in the pan. Do *not* fold them. After you lay each sheet down, spray it lightly with oil. This will help keep the layers from stick-ing together while baking, leaving you a flaky crust.

5. When you have half the dough in the pan, scoop the spinach mixture on top and spread evenly. Using the same technique as in step 4, lay the other half of the phyllo dough on top, spraying oil between each layer.

6. Bake for 45 minutes or until golden brown.

7:30

7. While the spanakopita is in the oven, make the hummus. Drain the can of garbanzo beans. Put them in a blender or food processor with ⅓ cup tahini, 1 teaspoon salt, 2 cloves minced garlic, and the juice of the other half of the lemon. Blend until very smooth and pour out into a soup bowl or small serving bowl. Drizzle some olive oil over it before serving.

After she arrives:

8:00

8. When the spanakopita comes out of the oven, cut a square for yourself and one for the lady. Serve it on plates with a small mound of tabouli and a dollop of hummus. Serve more tabouli and hummus on the side. Offer her the organic wine or a microbrew.

9. After dinner, a couple of squares of baklava on a small plate will guarantee a sweet finish to this Mediterranean feast.

Bonus Points

Add a pinch of paprika and/or a teaspoon of fresh chopped parsley to the hummus.

Vegan Thanksgiving: Tofurkey Dinner

TOFURKEY
BAKED SWEET POTATOES
CRANBERRY SAUCE
ORGANIC WINE
TOFU PUMPKIN PIE

It sucks being a vegan on Thanksgiving. Imagine what it must feel like, on a holiday cele-brating the harvest, and abundance, to be limited to only side dishes. If she's a vegan due to her sensitivity to animal rights, then the last thing she wants to do is have to sit at a big table glorifying a slaughtered bird. It's hard enough being a vegan the rest of the year, but at Thanksgiving, it's particularly difficult.

If your Granola Girl is a vegan, this meal will show her that you feel her pain. Don't think that you can make this one only on the fourth Thursday of November, though. It's a superb dinner for any Granola Girl on any day of the year.

Note that we call for a specific brand of stuffing mix. You can use other brands, but make sure that (1) it doesn't have any animal products and (2) you don't have to add any-thing other than butter and water or vegetable broth. And while we're discussing butter, remember that your staple butter will need to be vegan butter, made especially from soy instead of milk. One alternative, called Earth Balance, can be found at most health food stores. Also, try to go organic with all your ingredients, if you can.

It's best to get the pie done ahead of time, because you will need to let it cool.

To Buy

2 (10–12-ounce) packages of soft tofu

1 (16-ounce) can of pumpkin pie filling (get the kind that is completely premixed)

1 small box saltine crackers

1 box cornmeal (¼ cup)

1 container seasoning of your choice (we like Herbes de Provence, but any
   all-in-one poultry seasoning will work) (1 teaspoon plus ½ teaspoon)

2 sweet potatoes

1 bag Pepperidge Farm Corn Bread Stuffing

1 small can cranberries or cranberry sauce

8 large mushrooms (2 cups chopped)

1 small bottle soy sauce (1 tablespoon)

Staples

¾ cup plus 2 tablespoons flour plus more for kneading

¾ cup plus 1 teaspoon sugar

1 teaspoon salt

Pinch of pepper

Vegetable broth (amount depends on stuffing mix)

Vegan butter (¾ cup plus extra for stuffing mix; keep chilled)

1 onion (1 cup finely chopped)

½ cup very cold water (chilled in the fridge)

From the Liquor Store

Organic wine and/or filtered water

One day before she arrives (if possible):

1. Preheat the oven to 350 degrees.

2. Start with the pie crust. In a medium mixing bowl, measure ¾ cup flour, ½ teaspoon salt, and 1 teaspoon sugar. Add ¾ cup chilled vegan butter and mix together with your hands until the flour has coated all the butter and the clumps of butter are the size of peas. Add ½ cup chilled water and roll the dough with your hands just until it holds together. (Do not overknead—this will create a hard, dense crust instead of a light, tender, flaky crust.) Drop the dough on a flour-covered countertop or large cutting board. Using the rolling pin, lightly roll it out to a circle big enough to drape over your pie pan. Press it gently down into the pan and prick the bottom with a fork (otherwise it will bubble up). Bake at 350 degrees for about 15 minutes.

3. Cut open the corner of 1 package of tofu and let the water drain out. Then blend the drained tofu in a food processor until smooth.

4. In a medium mixing bowl, combine the can of pumpkin filling with ¾ cup sugar. Add the tofu from the food processor. Pour the mixture into the pie shell and bake for 15 minutes.

5. Increase oven temperature to 375 degrees and bake for another 40 minutes. When the pie comes out of the oven, cover with foil and set it out on the counter on a trivet to cool. (If you don't have a trivet, set it on an oven mitt so you don't burn the counter.)

The day of the date, before she arrives:

7:15

6. Preheat the oven to 375 degrees.

7. Drain the other package of tofu.

8. In a small mixing bowl, mix together 5 saltine crackers, ¼ cup cornmeal, 1 teaspoon seasoning, ½ teaspoon salt, a pinch of pepper, and the drained tofu. Mix well. Pay attention to the consistency. It should hold together in a loose ball.

7:30

9. Poke holes in two sweet potatoes and place them in the 375-degree oven for 45 minutes.

10. Back to the tofurkey. Following the instructions on the stuffing mix, combine vegetable broth, butter, and the stuffing mix in a medium mixing bowl.

11. Get out the loaf pan. Scoop half the tofu mixture into the bottom of the pan and smooth it out flat. Lay all the stuffing mix on top of that to make a second layer. Finally, scoop the remaining tofu mix on top for the third layer.

7:45

12. When the timer for the potatoes says 30 minutes, pop the tofurkey in the oven with them.

13. Open the can of cranberries or cranberry sauce and put it in a small serving bowl.

14. Chop up 1 cup worth of onion and 2 cups of mushrooms and set aside.

After she arrives:

8:00

15. Offer her a glass of (organic) wine.

16. Time to do the gravy. Heat ½ cup water and 1 tablespoon soy sauce in a small saucepan. Add the mushrooms and onions. Cook over medium-high heat for 10 minutes, stirring often.

17. Dissolve 2 tablespoons flour in 2 cups water and add it to the mushroom mixture while stirring. Add ½ teaspoon of the same seasoning as the tofurkey. Reduce the heat to low and let the gravy thicken, stirring often.

18. Check the potatoes and the tofurkey. The former should give when you press on them, and the latter should be crisp and golden brown.

19. When the mushroom mixture is the consistency of, well . . . gravy, serve it in a small bowl next to the piping hot tofurkey, the sweet potatoes, and the cranberries or cranberry sauce. If this meal doesn't launch her into vegan heaven, she should probably start eating meat.

Bonus Points

If you want to put in a little extra effort on the pumpkin pie, buy the filling that contains only pumpkin, without any other ingredients. Then cream the can of pureed pumpkin with ¾ cup sugar. Add ½ teaspoon salt, 1 teaspoon ground cinnamon, ½ teaspoon ground ginger, ¼ teaspoon ground cloves, and the tofu from the food processor. These things always taste better when you mix them up at home. You will need to add ground cinnamon, ground ginger, and ground cloves to the grocery list.

The Career Girl

I have a head for business and a bod for sin.

—Tess McGill in **Working Girl**

You don't need to be a rocket scientist to hit a home run with the Career Girl. However, it wouldn't hurt to be an EVP, SVP, or CEO of a Fortune 500 consortium. Bottom line: You can achieve synergy with the Career Girl by strategically leveraging your core competencies in order to deliver value-added, win-win solutions. At the end of the day, the Career Girl appreciates a proactive, results-driven approach. What you need, my friend, is an operational game plan.

If the paragraph above leaves you feeling a little out of the loop, here's the English translation: You don't have to be brilliant to deeply impress the Career Girl, but it wouldn't hurt to be a senior executive at a large, successful company. In simple terms, you can build a common bond with the Career Girl by focusing attention on your own basic talents in order to show her how a relationship with you could be a good thing for everybody. Once everything is said and done, the Career Girl is looking for a guy who is upwardly mobile, forward-looking, and, above all, isn't just letting life happen to him. So, you can't just let this date happen to you, either.

Now, let's get down to brass tacks. To the Career Girl, cooking skills are less important than your potential success quotient. In fact, culinary ignorance may be a selling point. Just like a healthy tan means you've got the dough to spend Christmas in Fiji, an empty refrigerator means you're eating out and expensing it. While the Career Girl does require you to spend some bucks on the food, what's more important is that you understand the politics of power dining.

Career Girls understand that there are a finite number of hours in the day, and every moment she spends doing something is a moment that she will never have again. Thus, she is careful with how she parcels out those precious slots in her Day-Timer, and she may want to spend her evening with you being productive. We're not talking about painting the house, we're talking about being productive on a personal level—building a relationship that is going somewhere. Did you ever read *The Seven Habits of Highly Effective People* by Stephen Covey? Now would be a good time.

Covey points out that each of us, by making choices about how we spend our time, basically creates the life we have. This principle doesn't hold true just at the office—it defines every moment of our life. So, rule number one with the Career Girl: Don't waste her time.

The Career Girl's food should be upscale, but not labor-intensive for the eater. No ribs, no lobster, no king crab—not even chicken on the bone. We know one Career Girl who recruited her date to peel her shrimp for her. Disassembling food is too much work, and it detracts from the work she really *wants* to do, which is getting to know her date. She isn't lazy—just the opposite, in fact—she is just efficient. She is here to check you out, to see if you deserve a button on her speed dial. She is looking for success, whether now or in the future. Career Girls give credit for hard work, even if it hasn't paid off in your bank account yet.

Career Girls are sometimes so busy that they will skip the meal altogether. For that Girl, we've included one meal that isn't a meal at all, just dessert.

She Might Be a Career Girl If:

1. **She drives:** a BMW, Acura, or Mercedes.
2. **She can talk for more than ten minutes about:** her company's stock valuation.
3. **She begins her sentences with:** "My financial advisor says . . ."
4. **She'd never:** pass up lunch with the CEO.
5. **She owns any of the following:** the latest and fanciest cell phone with a headset, a laptop, a Franklin Covey planner (with the convenient inner pocket for a PDA).

Where You'll Find Her

In weekend MBA classes, 6:00 A.M. aerobics classes, at the Starbucks on her way to work in the morning, networking during happy hour at upscale wine bars. However, you will not find her out late on a "school night."

How to Spot Her

The Career Girl always looks buttoned up. Her hair is styled and highlighted; her shoes match her bag. Even if it's the weekend and she's in khakis and cotton, she will look smart—presentable enough for a client meeting. And she'll probably have one—even if it's on the golf course or for an informal lunch. Career Girls don't mix business and pleasure—business is pleasure.

Famous Career Girls

Miranda on *Sex and the City,* Mary Tyler Moore on *The Mary Tyler Moore Show,* Holly Hunter in *Broadcast News,* Candace Bergen in *Murphy Brown.* Rachel on *Friends* used to be an Uptown Girl, but after she got her high-powered job at Ralph Lauren, she evolved into a Career Girl.

Your Place

Two things will impress this Girl: (1) cleanliness and (2) status symbols. Being "clean" means picked up, straightened, vacuumed, and Endusted. You want to give her the impression that you have a housekeeper. Regarding status symbols, Career Girls are highly attuned to them so you should nonchalantly display any of the following: a set of Henckel knives, a Mont Blanc fountain pen, a fancy entertainment system. You must have "adult" furniture that looks like you put some thought (and some cash) into it—no bean-bags, no futons, and no Ikea. The furniture must be matching. Manly pieces with leather or wrought iron are a good choice. If it is all from one particular style, such as arts and crafts or all Danish modern, all the better. The decor should be all about creature comfort and luxury—as much as you can afford. If you are still on the way up and don't have the requisite bucks, don't worry. Concentrate on a few high-class items. She would rather see a sparsely furnished pad with a few high-quality things than a full set of cheap stuff.

The Conversation

Obviously what will impress this girl is what you do, what you've accomplished. You say you haven't accomplished anything? Focus on your ambition. Show her you're angling for the corner office, and she'll be on board by close of business.

The Coffee Table

You can't go wrong with the bible: the *Wall Street Journal*, that is. (Rough it up a little to make it look like you actually read it.) Or you can go with the three *F*s: *Fortune*, *Forbes*, and *Fast Company*.

The Music

Stay mainstream: male-fronted contemporary rock bands like R.E.M., Counting Crows, Dave Matthews, Sting. You can also go with boxed sets and "best of" compilations—Career Girls like proven formulas.

The Drinks

She generally likes masculine drinks that say "executive," such as a Seven & Seven or a vodka tonic. Make sure your vodka is of high quality: Stoli, Absolut, Ketel One, Belvedere, Chopin. For wines, she is very similar to the Progressive Girl—think simple, unassuming, and mainstream (read: merlot and chardonnay). If she's into wine at all, she probably reads "Tastings," the wine column in the *Wall Street Journal* (by Dorothy J. Gaiter and John Brecher). For nondrinkers, serve fancy European mineral water, sparkling or non. Definitely not from the tap.

The Shoes

Stay away from the Foot Locker and head to Nordstrom. Spend the money on a professional shoeshine. There's a reason they call it "well-heeled."

The Flowers

Go to a high-end florist in one of the trendier parts of town and have them put something together for you. Have it delivered to her office, preferably the day of the dinner. If you don't have time for that, pick up a very simple but classy bouquet of tulips.

Maximizing Your ROI: Low-Investment, High-Yield Sushi

EDAMAME (PRONOUNCED "EH-DUH-MA-MAY")

SUSHI

HOT SAKE ("SAH-KAY," NOT "SAH-KEE")

JAPANESE BEER

ORANGES

In case you haven't been in an office lately—maybe you're one of those artsy types—ROI is short for "return on investment." Sushi is incredibly impressive, yet it's very easy to make, so it's an easy way to maximize your return with the Career Girl.

The most important thing is to get really fresh fish. Go to a higher-end grocery store or Japanese market and get the freshest fish you can; it should not smell at all fishy—it should have no smell at all. Then make good, sticky sushi rice. Neither of these things is particularly difficult, if you know what you are doing. Don't worry; we'll get you up to speed.

Edamame is the Japanese word for green soybeans, eaten as a snack or appetizer. Tip: Do not eat the outside skin. Just break it open and eat the beans inside of the pod. For dessert we have included the traditional oranges, although we'll spare you the task of cutting them into fancy shapes, the way better sushi restaurants do.

To Buy

1 package sushi rice (Japanese short-grain white rice) (1 cup)

1 bottle Japanese rice vinegar (2 tablespoons)

½ pound of 3 kinds of fresh sushi-grade fish: salmon, yellowtail, swordfish, or tuna

1 package frozen edamame (still in pods)

1 box kosher salt (coarse salt)

1 tube wasabi

1 jar pickled ginger

1 container soy sauce

2 oranges

Staples

1½ tablespoons sugar

1 teaspoon plus 1 tablespoon salt

From the Liquor Store

1 bottle sake

Kirin, Sapporo, or other Japanese beer

Before she arrives:

5:30

1. Put 1 cup rice in a large mixing bowl and place the bowl in the sink. Rinse the rice with cold water, swirling and rubbing the rice with your fingers. You will see a white starch being released, which will make the water look cloudy. Pour out the cloudy water and continue rinsing until the water looks clear. Transfer the rice into a fine-meshed colander to drain. Rinse out the bowl.

2. Put the rice into a medium-size saucepan and add 1¼ cups cool water and 1 teaspoon salt. Cover the pan of rice and let it sit for 30 minutes. Rinse the colander.

6:15

3. Put the saucepan of rice on the stove on very low heat and cook for 15 minutes. Do not remove the lid. (If it starts to boil over, turn the heat town slightly.)

4. While the rice is cooking, get out a small saucepan, add 2 tablespoons rice vinegar, 1½ tablespoons sugar, and 1 tablespoon salt, and cook over medium heat just until the sugar dissolves. Do not boil. Remove the vinegar mixture from the heat, pour into another bowl, and set aside to cool.

5. Remove the saucepan of rice from the heat and set aside on a trivet or on top of an oven mitt, still not removing the lid, for at least 15 more minutes.

6:45

6. Transfer the rice into the large mixing bowl and pour a little of the cooled vinegar mixture onto it. Fold the vinegar mixture into the rice with a wooden spoon, just enough to incorporate the vinegar mixture. Do not stir—just very lightly fold it in. Continue lightly folding in the vinegar mixture little by little until the rice is sticky but not wet. You might not need to add all the vinegar mixture. Cover the bowl of rice with a damp towel. Wash the saucepan you cooked the rice in—you will need it for the edamame.

7. Empty the package of frozen edamame into the colander, rinse with cool water, drain, and transfer to a medium mixing bowl. Pour a couple handfuls of the coarse kosher salt onto the beans and massage onto the pods with your fingers, making sure to cover all of them. Set the bowl aside.

8. Get out a very sharp knife and a very clean cutting board. Cut the fish fillets into 3x1½-inch pieces, each ¼ inch thick. Transfer fish onto a plate, cover with plastic wrap, and stick in the fridge.

7:30

9. Fill the medium-size saucepan halfway with water. Bring to boil over high heat.

7:45

10. When the water is boiling, add the salt-covered edamame and cook for about 5 minutes. Immediately transfer the edamame to the colander and briefly flush with cold water, then drain. Transfer the edamame to a serving bowl. Sprinkle on more of the kosher salt and stir it in.

After she arrives:

8:00

11. Heat a small amount of sake for 15 to 30 seconds in the microwave (if you don't have a sake set, you can use shot glasses). Serve her some sake and a bowl of edamame while you make sushi. (Offer a second bowl to put the empty pods in.) You can also give her a cold beer if she wants one.

12. As she sips her sake and nibbles on edamame, let her watch while you prepare the sushi. Take some rice and mold it with your hands into oblong blocks just large enough for the slices of fish to sit on. With your finger, wet each block with water (so the rice will stick). Dot each rice block with one small dab of wasabi, then stick the fish slices on top.

13. Arrange the sushi on a fancy tray with a small heap of pickled ginger and some wasabi paste on the side. Make sure there is soy sauce on the table, and you might want to offer her a small plate so she can mix her wasabi and soy sauce.

14. After dinner, slice the oranges lengthwise for dessert. (You don't have to peel them.)

Bonus Points

Buy a fancy sake set and porcelain chopsticks.

[easy]

Bottom-Line Priorities: Just Dessert

NEW YORK CHEESECAKE WITH RASPBERRY COMPOTE,
FRESH RASPBERRIES, AND MINT
BENEDICTINE AND BRANDY
DECAF COFFEE

Busy, busy, busy, that Career Girl. As that Career Girl guru, Tony Robbins, says, "Action is the foundational key to all success," so it may be tough to get yourself into her Palm Pilot without a merger to discuss. Her evenings may be booked up with business dinners, seminars, or client meetings. For that matter, she may just be working late, trying to clear those last few to-dos off her list. Never fear, though. If you want to get onto the Career Girl's calendar, you can still make a date for a late-night soiree by inviting her over "just for dessert." But what a dessert! This concoction is light enough that it won't disturb her sleep and the coffee is decaf. Perfect for the Girl who has a 6:00 A.M. workout before her 7:00 A.M. conference call. And that's on a Sunday.

You should be able to find the springform pan at a good grocery store. You can use a standard pie pan, but you won't get that statuesque cheesecake that will really catch her eye. The Benedictine liqueur doesn't come cheap, either, but trust us: It's a wise long-term investment strategy.

To Buy

1 box graham crackers

1 springform cake pan

5 (8-ounce) packages cream cheese (yes, 5—that's not a typo)

1 bottle vanilla extract (1 tablespoon)

1 can evaporated milk (1 cup)

1 box cornstarch (3 tablespoons)

1 pint fresh raspberries

Decaf coffee

1 bunch mint leaves

Staples

3 tablespoons plus 2 cups sugar

3 tablespoons butter

3 tablespoons flour

3 eggs

From the Liquor Store

Benedictine liqueur

Brandy

Before she arrives:

The cheesecake needs to cool for at least 2 hours before eating, so the best thing to do is make it the night before. If you are making it the day of the date, however, follow the times listed here for a 9:30 P.M. soiree.

5:45

1. Preheat the oven to 350 degrees.

2. Crush enough graham crackers to make 1 cup. Mix together with 3 tablespoons sugar and 3 tablespoons butter. Press onto the bottom of the springform pan. Do not put any of the crust mixture on the sides. Bake the crust for 10 minutes. Let it cool for at least 15 minutes. Leave the oven on at 350 degrees.

6:00

3. While the crust is cooling, mix the 5 (8-ounce) packages cream cheese, 1 cup sugar, 3 tablespoons flour, and 1 tablespoon vanilla with the electric mixer on medium speed until well blended. Add 3 eggs, one at a time, mixing on low speed after each one. Pour in 1 cup evaporated milk and mix until smooth. Pour the mixture over the graham cracker crust.

6:15

4. Bake the cheesecake for 1 hour and 5 minutes to 1 hour and 10 minutes, or until the center is almost set. Gently run a knife around the edge of the cake to loosen it from the side. Let it cool before trying to release the springform pan. Leave the cake on the bottom of the pan and chill until it's ready to serve.

6:30

5. Blend 1 cup sugar and 3 tablespoons cornstarch in a small saucepan. Stir in ⅓ cup water. Reserve about 12 raspberries and stir the rest into the pan. Cook, stirring constantly, until the mixture (now called a compote) thickens and boils. Boil and stir for 1 minute. Take it off the stove, cover, and put it in the refrigerator.

After she arrives:

9:30

6. Have the coffeemaker set to brew, then hit the switch when she arrives.

7. Take the raspberry compote out of the refrigerator and pop it in the microwave for about 30 seconds. Pour a small pool of it in the center of two dessert plates. Slice off a wedge of cheesecake and place it in the center of the compote pool. Place three raspberries on top with a sprig of the smallest mint leaves you can find in the bunch.

8. For her drink, mix 1 ounce brandy with 1 ounce Benedictine liqueur and stir gently. Best glass to use here is a cordial glass, but a brandy snifter will work, too. Bring the dessert to the table with the drinks, then coffee once she has finished. Now that's the way to get a permanent spot on her "priority" list.

Bonus Points

Any time you can get *the best*, it's a good thing for dating the Career Girl. In this case, it's decaffeinated Kona coffee, imported fresh from Hawaii.

[easy]

Midtown Power Dining: Ahi, Shrimp, Scallops, and Vegetables on a Bed of Baby Greens

AHI, SHRIMP, SCALLOPS, AND VEGETABLES ON A BED OF BABY GREENS
CRUSTY BREAD
FUME BLANC OR SAUVIGNON BLANC
HÄAGEN-DAZS OR GODIVA ICE CREAM

This is a very easy, yet extremely impressive entree salad, the kind of thing you would order at one of those upscale midtown Manhattan joints with single-word names. The kind of places where senior management types and high-level muckety-mucks eat. Serve with a loaf of crusty bread and a crisp white wine. This is a perfect meal for spring or summertime, since it's not heavy. While most Career Girls would be perfectly happy with a chardonnay, a fumé blanc or sauvignon blanc is preferable. This salad is very flavorful and deserves a wine with a lighter touch than your average chardonnay.

For dessert, we were going to tell you to make homemade caramelized lemon tarts, but then we decided to lay off. You'll get a lot of mileage out of this entree, so we'll let you skate with some high-quality ice cream. And when we say "high-quality," we mean don't buy regular ice cream. Since she's the Career Girl, she'll appreciate that you went to the trouble to get the good stuff: Häagen-Dazs or Godiva.

To Buy

1 yellow, red, or orange bell pepper (not green)

2 hothouse or plum tomatoes

½ pound green beans

1 bag fancy gourmet lettuce (baby greens)

½ pound sashimi-grade tuna

4 Alaskan sea scallops (not bay scallops)

6 frozen, peeled and deveined, cooked jumbo shrimp

1 loaf crusty bread

12 pitted kalamata (black) olives

1 pint Häagen-Dazs or Godiva ice cream (pick your flavor)

Staples

½ cup olive oil

¼ cup balsamic vinegar

1 garlic clove

Salt (to taste)

Pepper (to taste)

Butter (for the bread)

From the Liquor Store

Good quality fumé blanc or sauvignon blanc white wine (see wine primer chapter in Part One)

Before she arrives:

6:45

1. Chill the wine.

2. Rinse the pepper and tomatoes and drain in a colander. Rinse the green beans, and then snap off the ends and discard them. Rinse the lettuce and put in salad spinner (or otherwise pat dry with paper towels).

7:00

3. Make the dressing: Using a wire whisk, mix ½ cup olive oil and ¼ cup balsamic vinegar in a large mixing bowl. Crush 1 garlic clove and add it to the mix. Salt and pepper to taste.

7:15

4. Put the tuna, scallops, and shrimp into the mixing bowl with the dressing. Stir them around and set aside to let them marinate. Preheat the oven to 350 degrees.

5. Fill a medium saucepan halfway with water, cover, and set on high heat to bring to a boil.

7:30

6. While you are waiting for the water to boil, julienne (*julienne* is a fancy word for cutting into long, thin strips, like matchsticks) the pepper and quarter the tomatoes.

7. Put the green beans in the boiling water, cover, and cook for 4 to 5 minutes. They should still be crisp. Drain green beans in a colander and flush with cold water (this will stop them from cooking, and it will make them stay bright green).

8. Lay the tuna, scallops, and shrimp in a 9x13-inch glass baking dish, put in the oven, and cook for 2 to 3 minutes. Turn the tuna, scallops, and shrimp over and cook for 2 to 3 more minutes. Remove from oven and set them on a plate (to stop from cooking). Leave the oven on; you'll need to warm the bread.

After she arrives:

8:00

9. Pour her a glass of wine.

10. Stick the bread on a baking sheet and put it into the oven to warm for about 10 minutes.

11. On 2 plates, divide and artfully arrange the lettuce, then the pepper, the tomatoes, the green beans, and the kalamata olives. Drizzle with some of the dressing.

12. Slice the tuna into 1-inch slices. Arrange the tuna, scallops, and shrimp, again, artfully, on top of your salads.

13. Drizzle a little bit of the remaining dressing over the fish and vegetables. (It's OK if it isn't hot when you serve it.)

14. Take the bread out of the oven, slice it with a serrated bread knife, and serve in a basket (put a dishcloth or cloth napkin over it to keep it warm). Have butter on the table for the bread—or put olive oil on small plates. Make sure you have salt and a pepper grinder on the table for the salad.

15. After you are finished with the salad, serve the ice cream in small bowls or, if you want to get fancy, in martini glasses.

Bonus Points

Serve upmarket cookies with the ice cream—either gourmet cookies like Brent & Sam's, or imported European cookies such as Bahlsen or Leibniz. (You can find all these at most grocery stores.) You can also serve the ice cream with decaf coffee or some port wine.

[easy]

Achieving Synergy: Spinach, Raspberry, and Goat Cheese Salad

SPINACH, RASPBERRY, AND GOAT CHEESE SALAD
DINNER ROLLS
FROZEN YOGURT
CHARDONNAY

Any time several parts of an organization blend together seamlessly, each of them bringing something useful to the table, without any roadblocks to shareholder profitability, that's called synergy. Actually, corporate pundits talk about two kinds of synergy: horizontal and vertical. In the business world, vertical synergy means that the boss's goals are in tune with the frontline worker, while horizontal synergy means that different divisions of the same company are supporting each other. When it's time to cook for a hookup, though, working on vertical synergy may earn you the horizontal version later.

We think that you and the Career Girl will agree that this friendly merger of spinach, raspberry, and goat cheese leverages core assets without creating prohibitive liabilities. The macadamia nuts and beets are value-added options that show off your flexibility in a turbulent dating market. No question about it, synergy adds value to any kind of strategic partnership.

To Buy

1 medium-size avocado

1 small jar of macadamia nuts (1 cup chopped)

1 bunch cilantro leaves (¼ cup chopped)

1 large bunch or bag spinach leaves (6 cups)

1 (4-ounce) can sliced beets

1 small bottle raspberry vinegar (¼ cup)

1 small jar seedless raspberry jam (1 tablespoon)

2 ounces goat cheese

Brown-and-serve dinner rolls (look for dough that has been rolled into small loaves but not yet baked)

1 tub of vanilla frozen yogurt

Staples

½ cup olive oil

Salt

Pepper

From the Liquor Store

A top-notch chardonnay (see the wine primer chapter in Part One)

Before she arrives:

7:00

1. Put the chardonnay in the refrigerator to chill.

7:15

2. Cut the avocado in half around the pit. Bury the blade of your knife into the avocado pit and twist it out. Cut the avocado in quarters and remove the skin, then chop it into bite-size pieces.

3. Chop the macadamia nuts until you have 1 cup.

4. Rinse the cilantro and chop until you have ¼ cup. Drain the water from the can of beets.

5. Rinse and dry the spinach. In a large mixing bowl, combine the spinach, the beets, the 1 cup chopped macadamia nuts, the avocado, and the ¼ cup chopped cilantro.

7:45

6. In a small mixing bowl, mix ½ cup olive oil, ¼ cup raspberry vinegar, 1 tablespoon jam, and a sprinkle each of salt and pepper.

After she arrives:

8:00

7. Pour her a glass of wine.

8. Pour the dressing over the salad and toss gently.

9. Follow the directions for the brown-and-serve rolls. When the rolls are ready, divide the salad onto 2 plates and garnish with dollops of goat cheese.

10. Serve the frozen yogurt for dessert.

Bonus Points

Offer chocolate syrup and walnuts to top the frozen yogurt.

Getting to the Top: Trump Tower of Polenta and Pork Tenderloin

TOWER OF POLENTA AND ROSEMARY GARLIC PORK TENDERLOIN
CARAMELIZED ONIONS AND GRILLED BABY VEGETABLES ON A BED OF ARUGULA
RED ZINFANDEL, SYRAH/SHIRAZ, OR CABERNET
FLOURLESS CHOCOLATE CAKE
PORT

The Career Girl is fond of towers. Not only are they de rigeur in the fancy restaurants she frequents, but the tower is a symbol of success.

Take the skyscraper. In the early part of the twentieth century, there was a war being waged between superpower moguls who owned Manhattan skyscrapers. First there was the Metropolitan Life Building, erected in 1909, which stood 50 stories and 700 feet tall. In 1913 it was followed by the Woolworth Building, also known as "the Cathedral of Commerce," standing at 57 stories and 792 feet tall. Walter Chrysler got in the game and started constructing the Chrysler Building, refusing to reveal the height until the 1928 groundbreaking.

Meanwhile, John Jacob Raskob, former VP of General Motors, had come up with the idea for the Empire State Building. Raskob and Chrysler were literally racing neck and neck, floor by floor. The plans for the Empire State would have put it at a whopping 77 stories tall, which Raskob thought would make it the world's tallest building. Unfortunately, Chrysler beat him by 3 stories. Raskob, not to be outdone, tacked on 8 more stories, bringing the Empire State Building to an unprecedented 85 stories.

We're getting exhausted just writing about it. It's all just so competitive (not to mention phallic). Nonetheless, tall buildings symbolize power and prestige. It's no wonder the Career Girl likes to eat her food in a vertical fashion. This pork medallion tower may require a bit more effort than some of the other meals, but trust us, it will show the Career Girl that you're playing to win. And for dessert, the flourless chocolate cake has all the panache of a soufflé without the headaches.

To Buy

16 ounces (1 pound) semisweet chocolate (chips or bar)

1 springform pan (available at most grocery stores; if you can't find one, substitute a 9-inch square baking dish)

3 kinds of baby vegetables (3 of each): baby carrots (with the greens on), baby bell peppers, baby zucchini, baby cauliflower, etc. (if you can't find baby vegetables, substitute regular red and yellow bell peppers, carrots, zucchini, etc., and cut them into thin strips)

1 tube ready-made polenta

1 bunch arugula

1 bunch fresh rosemary

1 pound pork tenderloin

1 package bamboo skewers

1 small bag powdered (confectioner's) sugar

Staples

8 ounces (2 sticks) butter, plus a little more for greasing pan

8 eggs

¼ cup sugar

1 white onion

4 garlic cloves, divided

8 tablespoons olive oil, divided, plus dash

Salt

Pepper

4 tablespoons balsamic vinegar, divided, plus dash

From the Liquor Store

Good quality red zinfandel, Syrah or Shiraz, or cabernet (see wine primer chapter in Part One)

Good quality port wine (see wine primer chapter)

Before she arrives:

5:00

1. Preheat oven to 350 degrees.

2. Take some butter and grease the bottom and sides of the springform pan.

3. Put the chocolate and 8 ounces (2 sticks) butter into a microwave-safe (nonmetal) bowl and put it into the microwave on high for 1 to 2 minutes, until barely melted. Do not overcook.

5:15

4. Add 8 eggs to a large mixing bowl, and beat with an electric hand mixer for about 5 minutes. Add ¼ cup sugar and mix until blended.

5. With a wooden spoon, fold in half the chocolate/butter mixture, stirring very lightly just to incorporate. Add the other half, stirring lightly until the mixture is uniform in color.

6. Pour the cake batter into the buttered springform pan (or 9-inch square baking dish) and bake at 350 degrees. Set the timer for 20 minutes.

5:30

7. Peel the white onion and slice into half-inch slices. Rinse the baby vegetables and cut off the ends if need be. Set aside.

8. Take out the tube of polenta, cut into 1-inch-thick slices, and set aside.

5:45

9. Take 2 large handfuls of arugula (enough for 2 people) and rinse and dry with either paper towels or run through the salad spinner. Transfer to a medium mixing bowl and stick in the fridge until you are ready to use.

10. When the cake is done, take it out of the oven and put it on the counter (or, if the room is hot, in the fridge) to cool. It should have a brownielike crust on top.

6:00

11. On to the pork. Peel and smash 2 garlic cloves and put in a bowl.

12. Rinse the rosemary and pull off the spikey leaves from the stems. Discard the stems. Finely chop enough of the leaves to make 2 to 3 tablespoons' worth. (Be sure to reserve a few nice long branches of rosemary—you will need them for the garnish.) Add the rosemary to the bowl of garlic and mix.

13. Put the pork loin into a 9x13-inch glass baking dish (or on a baking sheet). Rub 4 tablespoons olive oil into the pork (on both sides). Then rub in the rosemary-garlic mixture. Salt and pepper (freshly ground) on both sides.

14. Put the pork into the 350-degree oven and set the timer for 30 minutes.

6:30

15. While the pork is cooking, place a medium saucepan over medium to high heat and add 2 tablespoons olive oil and 2 tablespoons balsamic vinegar. When it is good and hot, add the onion rings. Don't worry about keeping them intact. Stir them around and cook for about 10 to 15 minutes. Salt and pepper to taste and set aside on a plate.

6:45

16. In the same medium saucepan, add another 2 tablespoons olive oil and 2 tablespoons balsamic vinegar. When it's hot, throw in your baby vegetables. If you are using carrots or cauliflower, put them in first, because they take longer to cook than, say, bell peppers. Cook the vegetables for 10 to 15 minutes, until wilted and browned.

7:00

17. By now the pork should be done. Take it out of the oven and turn the oven down to 200 degrees. The pork should still be very pink on the inside. Transfer it to a cutting board to let it rest for 5 to 10 minutes. Transfer the vegetables you just grilled to the baking dish you cooked the pork in and set aside.

18. Take the mixing bowl with the arugula and add a dash of olive oil, a dash of balsamic vinegar, and a little salt and pepper, and mix with your hands or a spoon.

7:15

19. Now it is time to build the tower. Slice the pork into 1-inch-thick pieces. Take the first piece of pork and jam a bamboo skewer through the center and twirl it around so you have a good solid hole.

20. Get out 2 oven-safe dinner plates. Remove the pork you skewered from the skewer and place it on the dinner plate. Put a layer of polenta on the first piece of pork. On top of that, add another piece of pork (again, jamming in the center with the skewer). Keep adding layers of polenta and pork. You should have 3 layers; repeat on the second plate.

21. Take a stalk of rosemary and very gently but firmly jam it down through the center of each tower (going through the premade holes) as far down as you can. You're going to have to be very delicate, because it's easy to topple the tower. When finished, set the plates with the towers on them aside.

7:45

22. Just before she arrives, stick the baking dish with the grilled vegetables and the plates with the towers into the warm oven for about 10 to 15 minutes (no longer, because they will dry out).

After she arrives:

8:00

23. Offer her a glass of wine.

24. Take the baking dish and plates out of the oven. Make beds of arugula next to the towers. Arrange the warmed vegetables on top of the arugula. Serve with the red wine.

25. After dinner, offer her a glass of port (serve in wineglasses) and head into the kitchen to get the cake ready. Release the cake onto a large plate or platter. Lightly sprinkle powdered sugar on top with your fingers.

26. Serve slices of the chocolate cake with the port wine.

Bonus Points

If it isn't a school night, suggest a movie to go with dessert: the classic Career Girl movie, *Working Girl,* with Melanie Griffith and Harrison Ford. If she happens to be a Career/Indie hybrid, here's an obscure yet brilliant choice: Barbara Stanwyck in the 1933 film *Baby Face.* A gem of precode cinema (meaning before the censors cracked down), it's the story of an ambitious young woman who literally sleeps her way to the top of one of those New York skyscrapers we were talking about. Look for the cameo of John Wayne (one of his very first roles!) as a lowly mail clerk she leaves in her wake.

The Uptown Girl

I've been rich and I've been poor. Rich is better.

—Sophie Tucker

If her last name is a household word, like Disney or Kellogg, chances are she's an Uptown Girl with a trust fund the size of Texas. But it isn't wealth that defines the Uptown Girl, it's breeding and decorum (unless she's a Party/Uptown hybrid like those *Wild On* royals or the aristobrat child of a celebrity). A true Uptown Girl has Park Avenue taste and the manners of Emily Post, at least when Mummy is watching. Uptown Girls have generally been raised with a sense that they were put here to do something more important, and that's why they live with the kind of privilege that they do. Noblesse oblige is a very real concept to her, and her family may have some high expectations, both of her and of any young man who wants to date her. These kinds of expectations are why Uptown Girls occasionally catch a cab and slum around with Downtown Boys. After all, they have to blow off steam somehow. Ultimately, however, history has shown that these adventures come to an end, and, like Dorothy returning to Kansas, the wayward Uptown Girl comes home to roost.

There is also the Uptown Girl wannabe; the woman who already feels the noblesse oblige even before the noblesse (and the cash that goes with it) is bestowed upon her. This is the woman who needs you to support her in the style to which she plans to become accustomed. Often, this sense of divine destiny appears in women of great beauty who have been attended at every step by hopeful suitors, but it also appears in some women for no apparent reason. Perhaps she was a princess in a former life and is unwilling to give up the crown. In any case, you will know her if you meet her by the way she appraises other women's jewelry, pauses to let you open the door, and comfortably gives orders to bellmen in expensive hotel lobbies. Some women are just born to be rich, sooner or later.

The Uptown Girl is a challenge—one that requires a little more, well, money. Menus in this chapter are going to cost you more than the others because you will need a few premium ingredients to get this Girl's attention (read: oysters, caviar, and very expensive Champagne). If this is really the type of girl that you are after, you're probably used to this already. If you don't have the budget to support her tastes, we would suggest becoming a musician. Seems like those guys can always get women to buy them groceries.

One important thing to note is that the Uptown Girl will not necessarily notice if you are spending money on her. She has had money spent on her for her whole life—it's a natural state. While a Career Girl may be impressed with a show of affluence, the Uptown Girl has seen it all from birth, and your Rolex, your leather sofa, and your butler will simply fit into her vision of how people should live. Doesn't everybody have those? She will note their absence more than their presence.

She Might Be an Uptown Girl If:

1. **She drives:** a Jaguar, a Porsche, or a Rolls-Royce, or a limo with a driver and tinted, bulletproof windows.

2. **She can talk for more than ten minutes about:** being a debutante.

3. **She begins her sentences with:** "When we were on Martha's Vineyard . . ."

4. **She'd never:** fly coach.

5. **She owns any of the following:** an exotic toy breed dog (which she carries in a Burberry bag), Waterford crystal, anything from Tiffany's, real pearls.

Where You'll Find Her

Upper-crust cocktail parties, shopping at Nordies (that's Nordstrom to you and me) or Bergdorf Goodman, or dining at four-star restaurants. You may also see her at the symphony or a charity benefit or show-jumping at equestrian events.

How to Spot Her

The Uptown Girl is always stylishly dressed. Look for cashmere sweater twinsets, Chanel and Ralph Lauren everything, and an "updo." Yes, that's a hairstyle.

Famous Uptown Girls

Charlotte York on *Sex and the City* is the quintessential Uptown Girl. Also Karen Walker on *Will and Grace* (Party/Uptown hybrid). Other Uptown Girls include royals like the legendary Grace Kelly, her princess daughters Caroline and Stephanie, or the gorgeous Zara Phillips. There are also the pseudoroyals: heiresses like Aristotle Onassis's granddaughter Athina Roussel and Paris and Nicky Hilton (Party/Uptown). And any of the Kennedys.

Your Place

If you are going to invite her over, you'd better inhabit a pretty nice part of town. "I better walk you to the bus stop 'cause you never know around here" just ain't gonna cut it. Better to have a studio uptown than a three-bedroom in the 'hood. If there is barbed wire within a mile, you're in trouble. If you don't live in a nice neighborhood, move. If that isn't a possibility, consider borrowing a house or apartment from an investment banker friend. (Be sure to change the family photos.) As for decor, real antiques go a long way with the Uptown Girl—armoires, highboys, Oriental rugs. The kind of stuff people get the big bucks for on *Antiques Roadshow*. She'll feel right at home with a crystal chandelier, real silver flatware, and fancy stuff like wainscoting and crown molding.

The Conversation

Uptown Girls appreciate a man with means and money, but they have a soft spot for an ambitious upstart, so talk about your plans and your goals. Make it sound concrete. Show a grasp of international finance and exotic travel. It's OK if you haven't been there yet. Vague plans are good enough, particularly if they are presented with panache and a smattering of the local language.

The Coffee Table

Cover with magazines from the money-and-leisure set: the *Robb Report*, *CondéNast Traveler*, *Town & Country*, *Travel & Leisure*, *Vanity Fair*, the *New Yorker*.

The Music

Better to stay conservative. Try classic jazz (nothing too atonal, so put that Mahavishnu Orchestra back on the shelf). Try Miles Davis, John Coltrane, or Ella Fitzgerald. It's also safe to go with members of the Rat Pack, Tony Bennett, and, of course, the Chairman of the Board (Frank Sinatra—you should know stuff like this.) Classical music also works with the Uptown Girl. Be sure to go with something light and uplifting, such as Mozart or Vivaldi's "Four Seasons." Stay away from experimental modern stuff like Stravinsky. And no Pearl Jam or Bjork, even as a joke. She won't get it.

The Drinks

You're gonna have to fork over some cash for the good stuff. Check out *Wine Spectator* for high-quality (and high-priced) picks. As usual, it's all about the dollar signs with the Uptown Girl. It's not good enough to buy Champagne—you will need the Dom Perignon, the Louis Roederer, if not the Krug's Clos du Mesnil (that last one is about $350 a bottle).

The Shoes

Loafers from a high-quality department store, like the aforementioned Nordies. Make sure the name holds up. Hush Puppies won't work here. We're talking Gucci, Prada, Versace, people. A pair of Versace loafers can run you $600—a little more than you'll need to spend on the Champagne, but not much more.

The Flowers

Carnations and daisies would be a huge mistake with this girl. As *Sex and the City's* Charlotte once said, "They're filler flowers." Think elegant, sophisticated, rare. Uptown Girls, like the temperamental hothouse flowers they are, love orchids. You can also go with the classic dozen long-stem red roses, delivered in the box. Calla lilies are also very elegant.

[easy]

Dinner on the Yacht in the French Riviera: Champagne, Caviar, and Lobster

FIRST COURSE:
BELUGA CAVIAR CANAPÉS
DOM PERIGNON OR LOUIS ROEDERER CHAMPAGNE

SECOND COURSE:
LOBSTER TAILS WITH A LEMON BUTTER SAUCE
ASPARAGUS WITH HOLLANDAISE SAUCE
MORE CHAMPAGNE, BABY!

THIRD COURSE:
CHOCOLATE TRUFFLES FROM LA MAISON DU CHOCOLAT
HENNESSEY COGNAC PARADIS, OR COURVOISIER XO IMPERIALE

Nothing says luxury like Champagne and caviar. Throw a little lobster into the mix, and you're practically on a yacht. In Monte Carlo, darling. And French chocolates? Beyond swank. This menu is so Cary Grant. So Grace Kelly. It's Liz Taylor and Richard Burton . . . before they started drinking so damn much and things got ugly.

In case you were wondering, beluga caviar is basically fish eggs from the beluga sturgeon, one of the oldest fish in the world. Believe it or not, the beluga has been around since the dinosaurs. Now that's what we call *old money.* (Ouch, that one hurt.) It ain't cheap, either. Beluga's gonna cost you upwards of $100 per ounce.

Same goes for the Champagne. We specifically call for Dom Perignon or Louis Roederer for a reason. The reason: The Uptown Girl will get a raging headache from cheap Champagne. And raging headache equals no nooky. So be prepared to spend anywhere from $50 up to $300 on the bottle of Champagne alone. Hey, we warned you the Uptown Girl was expensive!

Same goes for the Cognac. Remember, she's used to the good stuff. If she isn't, you can bet that she wants to be. A bottle of Paradis will run you at least $250. The Courvoisier, $150. If you go with something else, expect to spend at least $100. Pinching pennies is never a good idea with the Uptown Girl. Whatever you do, make sure the Champagne is cleared away before you bring out the chocolate. Champagne and chocolate do not go together. We're talking *serious* faux pas.

One last thing about the beverages: Proper glassware is required. Call Crate & Barrel—they can set you up. You don't have to have real crystal, although that wouldn't hurt. As long as you get a couple of proper Champagne glasses and some brandy snifters, you're golden. And while you're shopping for glassware, pick up a couple of little finger bowls for the lemon butter sauce.

As far as the chocolate goes, Hershey's ain't gonna cut it with this girl. Chocolate from La Maison du Chocolat is simply the most expensive chocolate in the world, and with good reason. You may need a moment of silence after you taste it. Maison has stores in New York City, Tokyo, and Paris. Actually, all the chocolate is made in Paris and flown to NYC and Tokyo every morning. Your second-best bet is Godiva. A box of chocolate truffles from La Maison du Chocolat will run you around $50, whereas you can get a box from Godiva for half that. You can buy online from either store—you'll just have to pay extra for shipping.

The good news is this is the easiest of all the Uptown Girl meals. Just sixteen simple steps, not including taking out the loan to pay for it. Once you get back from the bank, the actual preparation is a snap. You may not be able to buy happiness, but culinary rapture is well within reach of every millionaire.

To Buy

2 lemons

1 loaf cocktail bread (those cute little loaves of bread you can find in the fancy cheese section)

1 container crème fraîche

1 jar grade-one beluga caviar

2 fresh lobster tails

1 bunch asparagus

1 box chocolate truffles from La Maison du Chocolate or Godiva

Staples

16 ounces (2 sticks) unsalted butter

3 egg yolks

2 tablespoons salt, plus extra to taste

Pepper (to taste)

From the Liquor Store

1 to 2 bottles Dom Perignon or Louis Roederer champagne

1 bottle Hennessey Cognac Paradis, or Courvoisier XO Imperiale

Special Equipment

2 finger bowls

Before she arrives:

7:00

1. Put the Champagne in the fridge to chill.

2. To make the hollandaise sauce, put 4 ounces (1 stick) of butter in a microwave-safe bowl in the microwave and heat on high just until it melts (watch it closely).

3. Separate the yolks from the whites of 3 eggs: Break each egg gently over a small bowl, but capture the yolk in one of the halves of the shell. Gently pass the egg yolk back and forth between the shell halves, letting the white of the egg flow into the bowl. When nothing but yolk remains in the shells, dump it into a metal mixing bowl and throw the egg whites away.

4. Cut one of the lemons in half. Squeeze the lemon halves, extracting 2 tablespoons of the juice. With a wire whisk, mix in the 2 tablespoons fresh lemon juice. Put the bowl on top of a medium saucepan of boiling water (this is why you need a metal mixing bowl).

5. Turn the heat down to medium. Slowly add the melted butter in a steady stream, whisking as you go. Salt and pepper to taste. Remove from heat and transfer to a microwave-safe bowl (you're going to reheat it later).

7:30

6. Rinse the asparagus in a colander. Chop a half-inch off the nonspear ends and set aside.

7. Arrange the bread slices onto a serving platter. Spoon a dollop of crème fraîche on each one, and then top each one with a little caviar.

After she arrives:

8:00

First course:

8. Get out a stockpot, fill it halfway with water, cover, and set on the stove on high to boil. Take the medium saucepan you used before, rinse and fill it halfway with water. Cover and set on high to boil.

9. Pop the Champagne and serve the canapés.

Second course:

10. Pour her another glass of Champagne and excuse yourself for a moment. Do not let her help. The stockpot of water should be boiling by now. Add 2 tablespoons salt, drop the lobster tails in, and let them cook for 10 to 15 minutes.

11. While the lobsters are cooking, steam or boil the asparagus in the medium saucepan of water for 5 to 10 minutes, just until they are al dente.

12. When the lobster tails are done, transfer to a cutting board and slice them down the back with a sharp knife.

13. Remove the asparagus from the heat, transfer to a colander, and flush with cold water (this will stop them from cooking and keep them bright green).

14. Heat up the hollandaise sauce (you can do it in the microwave or on the stove) and in another microwave-safe bowl, melt 8 tablespoons (4 ounces or 1 stick) butter.

15. Serve the lobster tails on dinner plates with lemon wedges and small bowls of the melted butter on the side. (If you don't have little bowls, you can just drizzle some of the butter directly on the lobster tails, but it's not as fancy and we don't really recommend it.)

Third course:

16. Pour a couple of snifters of brandy and get out the box of chocolates. You could put them out on a fancy platter, but then she wouldn't see the box—and that would defeat the purpose, now, wouldn't it?

Bonus Points

What? You don't have a yacht? Darling, how *do* you manage? Seriously, you can make this meal sans yacht. It's just as elegant on land as at sea. Jettison those everyday dishes and flatware you bought at Target and replace them with some good-looking formal china (you only need two place settings) and formal flatware, a white linen tablecloth and matching napkins, and some silver candlesticks and silver serving platters. Try Neiman Marcus, Saks Fifth Avenue, Nordstrom, or Williams-Sonoma—shop online and have it delivered. Then just lower the lights, light the candles, and put on some jazz standards (perhaps a little Ella Fitzgerald or Sarah Vaughn), and she will completely forget she's dry-docked and stateside.

By the way, if you are thinking ahead toward breakfast, set any extra hollandaise sauce aside in the refrigerator. You can reheat it in the morning for Eggs Benedict.

Sinatra at the Sands: Martinis, Oysters, and Filet Mignon

FIRST COURSE:

OYSTERS ON THE HALF SHELL

VODKA MARTINIS

SECOND COURSE:

GREEN SALAD

FILET MIGNON

TWICE-BAKED POTATOES

RED BORDEAUX

THIRD COURSE:

BANANAS FOSTER

COGNAC

This menu is old school. The kind of thing you'd eat in the '60s in Vegas, watching Sinatra at the Sands Hotel, the 500-room circular tower known as "A Place in the Sun." Those were the ring-a-ding-ding Rat Pack years, Old Blue Eyes at the Copa Room, with his buddies Dino, Sammy, and Joey. You know that movie, *Ocean's Eleven,* with Brad Pitt and George Clooney? Well, that was a remake. This was the real thing.

You're going to have to cash in some chips, though, because French Bordeaux can go for $1,000 per bottle. You don't have to spend anywhere near that much, though, if you're not a high roller. You can get a decent one for as little as $50 to $60, if you are willing to bet on a long shot. We recommend spending a little more to be on the safe side.

Oh, and PS: Serving a martini in anything other than an actual martini glass is a major letdown. With this drink, it's all or nothing. If you don't have any, go out and buy a couple of authentic martini glasses. Not to mention decent wineglasses and brandy snifters for the Cognac. We're going to assume that you have a martini shaker. If you are lacking this essential bachelor calling card, go get one quick and we won't tell nobody.

This is an extremely easy menu, except for the shucking of the oysters, which takes a bit of work, as well as some special equipment. While we don't normally require special equipment for the Uptown Girl, for this menu it is essential that you buy a shucking knife and a shucking glove. You can get these things at any housewares store and many grocery stores. You may think you don't need the glove, but do without and you could end up in the emergency room. If you can't find a shucking glove, you can use a heavy-duty gardening glove (like the rubberized kind people wear for working with roses). You could opt to skip the oyster course entirely, but remember, oysters are an aphrodisiac, so we think the extra work of shucking is worth it.

The odds are good that between the steak and the oysters, you'll be on a winning streak, and you're sure to hit the jackpot with the Bananas Foster. Just make sure you use standard dark rum—no 151 rum unless you want to risk setting the kitchen on fire. You may start out as strangers in the night, but shell out the requisite clams (and shuck those oysters), and chances are, the Uptown Girl will be working her wicked witchcraft on you. And, if luck be a lady, or the lady is a tramp (sorry, couldn't resist that one), you'll be under that old devil moon, makin' whoopee in the wee small hours of the morning, the summer wind blowing in your hair.

To Buy

2 (8-ounce) filet mignon steaks

2 large russet (baking) potatoes

12 fresh oysters in shells

1 bag crushed ice

2 lemons

1 bag baby greens

1 small container sour cream (2 tablespoons)

3 bananas

1 container cinnamon (¼ teaspoon)

1 pint vanilla ice cream

Staples

5 cloves garlic

½ cup plus 3 tablespoons balsamic vinegar

½ cup olive oil

½ teaspoon salt, plus some to taste

Pepper (to taste)

5 tablespoons butter, divided

¼ cup milk

½ cup sugar

From the Liquor Store

1 bottle good-quality vodka (Grey Goose, Belvedere, or Ketel One)

1 bottle good-quality red French Bordeaux (see the wine primer chapter in Part One)

1 bottle good-quality cognac (see the wine primer chapter)

1 bottle dry vermouth

1 jar good-quality olives

1 package toothpicks or cocktail spears

1 small bottle banana liqueur

1 small bottle dark rum (*not* 151 rum)

Special Equipment

Oyster shucking knife

Oyster shucking glove (or heavy-duty rubberized gardening gloves)

Brandy snifters

Before she arrives:

5:30

1. Preheat the oven to 400 degrees.

2. Marinate the steaks: Crush 2 cloves garlic. In a Ziplock or other resealable plastic bag, add ½ cup balsamic vinegar, ¼ cup olive oil, the 2 crushed garlic cloves, ½ teaspoon salt, and fresh ground pepper. Seal the bag and mush the marinade around on the steaks with your hands. Set aside.

5:45

3. Rinse and scrub the potatoes with a brush or your hands. Dry with a dish towel.

4. Transfer the potatoes to a baking sheet, prick them all over with a fork, and stick them in the oven. Set the timer for 1 hour.

6:00

5. Here's how to shuck the oysters: Hold the oyster in the palm of your gloved hand and shove the knife in at the hinge between the top and bottom shell. Sometimes you have to work a while to find an opening. Run the knife along the hinge to pry the shells apart. Be careful not to lose any of the juice (known as the liquor). Pry the top shell off and discard. Slide the knife under the oyster to free it from the shell. Cut the 2 lemons into wedges.

6. Arrange the oysters and lemon wedges on a platter or tray full of crushed ice. If you have those little oyster forks, that's great—but it's not necessary. You can just serve it with regular forks. Keep it chilled (in the fridge) until your date arrives.

6:45

7. Take the potatoes out of the oven. Let them cool for 5 to 10 minutes.

8. While you're waiting for the potatoes to cool, rinse the baby greens, spin in salad spinner or just let drain in colander, and put into a couple of salad bowls. Stick them in the fridge until later.

9. Crush 3 cloves garlic. Set aside.

7:00

10. Slice the potatoes in half lengthwise and scoop out the insides. Set the potato-skin shells aside.

11. Transfer potato insides to the food processor. Add 2 tablespoons butter and ¼ cup milk. Pulse until well blended. Add salt and pepper to taste.

7:15

12. Scoop the blended potatoes back into the shells and put back into the oven on a baking sheet. Set the timer for 20 minutes. Wash and dry processor bowl.

13. To make the salad dressing, pour 3 tablespoons balsamic vinegar into the food processor. Slowly drizzle in ¼ cup olive oil. Add the 3 crushed cloves of garlic, and salt and pepper to taste. Process well, pour into a small mixing bowl, cover with plastic wrap, and refrigerate.

7:45

14. Take the twice-baked potatoes out of the oven, cover with foil, and set aside. Turn the oven down to 200 degrees.

After she arrives:

8:00

First course:

15. Time to mix the martinis. Take out a couple of martini glasses and fill with ice and water to chill them. In a martini shaker, add ice, 5 parts vodka, and 1 part dry vermouth. (Notice that we are not making those trendy modern superdry martinis with barely any vermouth like everyone seems to think is so chic these days—this is the old-style real vodka martini. Actually, if it were a real old-style martini, it'd be made

with gin—but everyone seems to like vodka these days, so we're going with that.) If she likes it "dirty," you can add a dash of olive juice. Shake over your shoulder, using both hands, at least 30 times. Dump the ice water out of the glasses and pour the martinis, garnishing with an olive or two on a spear. Serve the martinis with the plate of oysters.

Second course:

16. After the first course is complete, excuse yourself and go into the kitchen. Your date may offer to help. If she wants to watch, that's fine—but by no means should you allow her to do anything. Tell her to relax and finish her martini—you'll just be a few minutes. First things first: Stick the twice-baked potatoes back in the oven to warm them.

17. Uncork the red, set out a couple of wineglasses, and dress the salads.

18. On a baking sheet, broil the filets mignons for 3 to 4 minutes on each side.

19. Put the filets on dinner plates with the twice-baked potatoes. Put a tablespoon of sour cream on the twice-baked potatoes. Serve bowls of salad on the side. To really make the Uptown Girl feel at home, bring out the pepper grinder and ask her if she'd like fresh pepper on her steak or salad.

Third course:

20. Once you've finished with the second course, pour another glass of wine for your Uptown Girl and invite her to watch you make dessert. Get the ice cream out of the freezer and let it soften a bit on the counter.

21. Peel the bananas, then slice them lengthwise, and then halve them.

22. In a frying pan, melt 3 tablespoons butter over medium heat. Add ½ cup sugar and stir until dissolved. Add the bananas and cook for 2 to 3 minutes, turning to brown on both sides.

23. Add 2 tablespoons banana liqueur, 3 tablespoons dark rum, and ¼ teaspoon cinnamon. Measure one more tablespoon rum, and very carefully, as close as you can to the frying pan, set a match to it. Use it to ignite the alcohol in the pan. Shake the pan a bit, so that the bananas get covered with the flaming sauce, until the flame dies out.

24. Scoop the ice cream into bowls and lay some of the bananas on top. Spoon the sauce from the pan over that. Serve with the Cognac in brandy snifters.

Bonus Points

Pick up a few CDs: *The Rat Pack Live at the Sands*, *The Summit: In Concert*, and *Eee-0-11*. Put them on shuffle and she'll feel like she's back in Vegas in the '60s.

[food: easy]
[behavior: hard]

Afternoon Tea at the Savoy: Finger Sandwiches and Scones

CUCUMBER SANDWICHES
SCONES
LEMON COOKIES
TEA

The Savoy is actually a string of hotels around the world, but the true original is the Savoy, a ritzy Uptown Girl haven in London that advertises its afternoon tea as "the Most Civilised Part of the Day," and they do spell it with an *s*. Guess it's more civilized that way.

Afternoon tea is considered a "low tea," as opposed to a "high tea," because it is eaten around a low tea table, as opposed to a higher dinner table. Afternoon tea is the afternoon snack of the landed gentry, served around four o'clock. High tea is more of a workingman's meal, with much more substantial food. Lengthy books have been written on the ins and outs of tea etiquette, and some of it is actually important, so here in a nutshell are the particulars:

1. Send an invitation. Certain particulars should be called out in advance to avoid messy embarrassments. These include whether this is an afternoon tea or a high tea, whether the tea is outside or in (she will need to know if she should wear a hat), and whether or not you wish her to bring a favorite teacup (not an uncommon tradition, brought forward from Edwardian times, when porcelain was costly).

2. Linen napkins are preferable, but good-quality, small, cloth or paper ones will suffice.

3. Serve tea with milk, not cream. Cream is too heavy and will mask the taste of the tea. There is actually a meal known as a "cream tea," which is the regional meal of Devonshire and West England, but that's another animal entirely.

4. Tea is served either of two ways: in three courses (savories like the cucumber sandwiches, scones, then sweets) or on a three-tiered platter (savories on the bottom, scones in the middle, sweets on top). You can find such platters at high-class department stores, like Nordstrom or Saks. Neiman Marcus has them by mail order, naturally.

5. Lift the teacup by its handle, pinching it between index finger and thumb. Contrary to what you've heard, it is not necessary to thrust the pinkie out when drinking. If it wanders out on its own, you are still within the bounds of acceptable behavior, but special effort is not required in this respect.

6. Take a deep breath. OK, what follows is a dreadfully incomplete list of what you may *not* do during tea:

- Don't serve large chunks of lemon. Tiny wedges or slices are preferable.

- Don't clink your teaspoon against the side of your cup whilst stirring. As a matter of fact, you shouldn't be stirring at all. According to *Tea Travels: Etiquette Faux Pas and Other Misconceptions about Afternoon Tea* by Ellen Easton, you should place your teaspoon at the six o'clock position and softly fold the liquid toward the twelve o'clock position two or three times.

- Don't leave your spoon in your cup.

- Don't use tea bags. Loose tea is preferred.

- Don't drink tea while standing without holding the saucer under the cup. If you sit on a sofa or armchair, hold the saucer on your knee with the left hand while raising the cup with your right. Political correctness has yet to appear amongst the teatime crowd, so this obvious discrimination against left-handed people has yet to be challenged.

- Don't apply butter or jam to your scone directly from the serving dish. Spoon it on your plate first, then apply it to the scone from there. Dipping your entire scone in the jelly dish is to be avoided at all costs.

- Don't swirl the tea in the cup, slurp your tea, talk with your mouth full, sip your tea before swallowing your food, or peer at others over the top of your cup whilst drinking. Lower your eyes and look into your cup when you raise it to your lips.

- Don't take big bites. Teatime is a time for thoughtful conversation, so taking small bites will allow you to chime in with your witty thought before the opportunity for brilliance has passed.

- Don't put dirty dishes back on the tea table, use your napkin as a handkerchief, or grab your teacup like a coffee mug, with your fingers stuck through the handle.

- Don't smoke. It pollutes the tea. Besides, this is America. No one of delicate breeding smokes anymore.

Some etiquette rules are open to discussion and sometimes to fearsome debate. The raging controversy over whether to drop one's napkin in the chair or place it to the left of one's plate when leaving the table has ended many a close friendship. One can only imagine the marriages that have foundered over whether one should slice a scone completely in half or break off a bite-size morsel before buttering. The bottom line is probably that you should behave as your mother always wished you would when visiting your grandmother. Beyond that, imitate Merchant Ivory films or Jane Austen novels and you will probably survive.

Having said all that, let's get started on the recipes. Tea is traditionally served at 4:00 P.M., so the times for this recipe are oriented toward that. Adjust the times earlier or later as appropriate.

To Buy

¼ cup plus 1⅓ cups powdered sugar

2 lemons (⅓ teaspoon lemon zest, ½ teaspoon lemon zest, plus 2 tablespoons lemon juice, plus wedges for the tea service)

1 small bottle vanilla (¼ teaspoon)

1 small box cornstarch (½ cup)

1 box baking powder (*not* baking soda) (2 tablespoons)

1 small bottle corn oil (2 tablespoons)

Bread (fresh, sliced white bread from the bakery)

1 cucumber

Whole tea leaves—not tea bags (best to get a selection of black, green, and herbal)

1 jar fruit preserves

Staples

13 tablespoons butter, plus a little more for the bread

3⅔ cups flour

½ cup sugar

1 teaspoon salt

1 cup milk, perhaps a little more

Special Equipment

Teapot

Tea ball

Wire rack

Before she arrives:

In this case, you basically do everything but pour the tea before she arrives.

1:30

1. Take the butter out of the refrigerator so it can soften.

2. Preheat the oven to 350 degrees and start the cookies. In a large mixing bowl, beat 11 tablespoons (1 stick plus 3 tablespoons) butter until creamy. Add ¼ cup powdered sugar and keep stirring until fully mixed and a little fluffy. Add ⅓ teaspoon lemon zest (you get zest from a lemon by scraping the peel with a zester or fine tooth grater), ¼ teaspoon vanilla, ⅔ cup flour, and ½ cup cornstarch and beat well.

3. Roll the cookie dough into 1-inch balls. Place onto an ungreased baking sheet and bake for 15 minutes until they are light brown. While they are baking, stir up the frosting. Combine 2 tablespoons butter, ½ teaspoon lemon zest, 2 tablespoons lemon juice, and 1⅓ cups powdered sugar in a small mixing bowl. Stir until well mixed.

4. Remove the cookies from the oven and cool them on a wire rack or paper towels. When cool, spread the frosting on them.

5. Boost the oven temperature to 400 degrees.

3:00

6. To prepare the scones, mix 3 cups flour, ½ cup sugar, 2 tablespoons baking powder, 1 teaspoon salt, 2 tablespoons corn oil, and 1 cup milk in a medium mixing bowl, adding the milk last. The batter should be a little gooey, so you may need to add a shade more milk, perhaps 2 to 3 tablespoons.

7. Shape the dough into four mounds on an oiled baking sheet. This is best done by scooping a third of the batter into your hands, shaping it into a rough ball, and dumping it onto the sheet. Dip a sharp knife into some flour and press it down into each scone twice, making a "+" sign.

8. Bake 15 to 20 minutes. They should be golden brown, but not burned on the bottom. If you are not ready to eat by the time they come out, cover them with a dish towel to keep in the heat.

3:30

9. While the scones are cooking, cut the crusts off of eight pieces of bread. Lightly butter four of them. Put a thin layer of cucumber on each piece of bread and put an unbuttered piece on top. Cut the sandwiches into halves or quarters.

10. If you've dropped the cash for the three-tiered serving tray, then load it up with—from top to bottom—the cookies, the scones, and the cucumber sandwiches. Otherwise, use three separate plates.

After she arrives:

4:00

11. Ask her what type of tea she prefers. Boil the water for the tea and place the loose tea leaves she has chosen in a tea ball in a teapot. Set out the food tray(s), butter, preserves, milk, sugar, and lemon slices. Pour the boiling water over the tea and let it steep for about 3 minutes. Pour the tea into the cups. Offer sandwiches. Converse.

Bonus Points

Use a fluted cutter to cut the cucumber sandwiches into little shapes. Add ½ cup of dried cranberries to the scones.

A Meal Fit for a Queen (and a Duke): Beef Wellington and Cherries Jubilee

FIRST COURSE:
BEEF WELLINGTON
BRUSSELS SPROUTS
BORDEAUX OR BURGUNDY

SECOND COURSE:
CHERRIES JUBILEE
COGNAC

You might find a trashy tabloid magazine with Prince Harry on the cover stashed away in an Uptown Girl's boudoir, as Uptown Girls have a fascination with, and deep, abiding respect for royalty. Even though they themselves may not have royal blood, they still consider themselves worthy of hobnobbing with the title-and-tiara crowd. Grant your Uptown Girl the royal peerage she deserves by cooking up a meal fit for a queen (and a duke).

A little history: When the Duke of Wellington returned to England as a hero after defeating Napoleon at Waterloo in 1815, his nation's chefs named his favorite dish after him. It is essentially a fillet of beef smothered with mushrooms and foie gras and wrapped in flaky French pastry. The celebration of Queen Victoria's diamond jubilee in 1897 was another occasion that called for something extra special. Hence, cherries jubilee was born: cherries and brandy, flaming, spooned over ice cream.

Duke, meet Queen.

To Buy

4 ounces white mushrooms

10 brussels sprouts

½ ounce black truffles

1 sheet (½ package) frozen puff pastry (in the freezer section of most grocery stores)

1 fillet of beef, preferably filet mignon (2–3 pounds—you will have leftovers)

2 ounces foie gras or liver pâté

1 pint vanilla ice cream

1 can pitted cherries in heavy syrup

Staples

1 onion

4 tablespoons olive oil

4 tablespoons (½ stick) butter

Salt (to taste)

Pepper (to taste)

1 egg yolk

1¼ cup chicken broth

Several pinches of flour

From the Liquor Store

Bordeaux or Burgundy (see wine primer chapter in Part One)

Good-quality brandy (see wine primer chapter)

Before she arrives:

5:00

1. Finely chop one onion. Set aside.

2. Rinse and thinly slice the mushrooms. Set aside.

3. Rinse brussels sprouts and cut the bottoms off. Set aside.

4. Chop the ½ ounce black truffles and set aside.

5:45

5. Preheat the oven to 425 degrees. Put the fillet of beef in a 9x13-inch glass baking dish. With your hands, massage the fillet all over with 1 tablespoon olive oil and then 2 tablespoons (¼ stick) of butter.

6. Get out a medium saucepan and add 1 tablespoon butter. Add ½ of the chopped onions and sauté until soft, 5 to 10 minutes. Add the mushrooms. Add salt and pepper to taste. Cook about 5 minutes more until mushrooms are soft. Transfer to a soup bowl and set aside to cool. Wash and dry the medium saucepan for use later.

7. Take 1 sheet of frozen puff pastry out of the freezer and set on the counter to thaw for about 30 minutes.

6:15

8. Transfer the fillet (in the baking dish) to the oven and set the timer for 10 to 15 minutes, or until browned.

9. Remove the fillet from the oven and transfer to a cutting board. Turn the oven down to 400 degrees. Pour the drippings from the baking dish into a soup bowl and set aside.

10. Unfold the pastry sheet on a floured surface. Using a rolling pin, roll the pastry sheet out into a rectangle a little longer and a little wider than the fillet.

11. With a butter knife, spread the 2 ounces foie gras on the pastry, within 1 inch of the edges.

12. Spread the mushroom-onion mixture on top of that.

6:45

13. Place the fillet in the middle of the pastry. Fold the edges of the pastry over the fillet. Press the edges together to seal. Transfer to glass baking dish, seam-side down.

14. Separate the yolk from the white of 1 egg: Break the egg gently over a small mixing bowl, but capture the yolk in one of the halves of the shell. Gently pass the egg yolk back and forth between the shell halves, letting the white of the egg flow into the bowl. When nothing but yolk remains in the shell, dump it into a medium mixing bowl and throw the egg white away.

15. In the bowl with the egg yolk, mix in 1 teaspoon of water. With your fingers (or with a pastry brush if you have one), brush the yolk-water mixture onto the puff pastry (this is called an egg wash). Set aside (if your kitchen is warm, put it in the fridge) while you make the sauce.

7:00

16. To make the sauce: In a small saucepan, add 3 tablespoons olive oil and the rest of the onion. Cook over medium heat for about 5 to 10 minutes, or until the onion is soft.

17. Stir in the pan juices and 1 cup chicken broth.

18. Uncork the red wine and add ½ cup to the sauce.

19. Sprinkle in small pinches of flour and stir until sauce thickens into a gravy. Add another ¼ cup chicken broth and then keep stirring in pinches of flour until it is thick and gravy-like.

20. Stir in the chopped black truffles and cook for a few more minutes. Season with salt and pepper to taste. Remove from heat, pour into a small serving bowl, cover, and set aside until ready to serve. Wash and dry the small saucepan for use later.

7:45

21. Stick the fillet into the oven and set the timer to bake at 400 degrees for 20 to 25 minutes (don't overcook because you want the beef to be rare to medium-rare in the center).

22. In a medium saucepan, add the brussels sprouts and just enough water to cover them. Cover with a lid and cook on medium heat until just fork-tender, about 5 to 10 minutes. Drain in a colander. Transfer back to saucepan, add 1 tablespoon butter, and salt and pepper to taste. Cover and set aside.

After she arrives:

8:00

23. Pour her a glass of wine.

24. Take the beef Wellington out of the oven, and set it on a cutting board to rest for 5 minutes. Reserve any pan juices.

25. Warm up the sauce on the stove and the brussels sprouts in the microwave (or also on the stove).

26. Slice the beef Wellington into 1-inch slices. Arrange 3 to 4 slices on each of two plates. Cover with the sauce, and serve the brussels sprouts on the side.

27. After dinner, pour a couple of snifters of brandy and invite your date into the kitchen to watch you make the cherries jubilee. Take the ice cream out of the freezer to let it soften a bit.

28. Pour the can of cherries into a small saucepan and set on medium heat.

29. Stir in ½ cup brandy to the saucepan, and cook for about 1 minute, just to heat through.

30. Take 1 teaspoon brandy and light a match to it, then use that to set the whole thing on fire. Stir the cherries until the flame burns out.

31. Scoop the ice cream into two bowls, and then spoon the cherry mixture on top.

Bonus Points

This is the perfect meal to make for a birthday dinner. And during dessert you can give her your gift: tickets for a little two-week jaunt to Europe and back on the new *Queen Mary 2*. Don't try to pass off a Carnival cruise on her—that's the equivalent of staying at the Holiday Inn. While those kinds of things are fine for the great unwashed, the Uptown Girl would rather stay home and have a root canal.

At the Villa in Avignon: Coq au Vin and Tarte Tatin

FIRST COURSE:
COQ AU VIN (PRONOUNCED "coco VAN")
HARICOTS VERTS ("ah-ree-coh VARE")
BAGUETTE ("bah-GET")
BURGUNDY, CÔTES DU RHÔNE ("COAT dew RONE")

SECOND COURSE:
TARTE TATIN ("TART tah-TAN")
COGNAC ("CONE-nyack") OR ARMAGNAC ("ARM-ugh-NYACK")

This meal sounds super posh but it really isn't. Actually, it's what you might call a "rustic" meal. It's just a little bit of home-cookin' from the country—the French countryside. Coq au vin is just a fancy name for rooster cooked in wine. (Roosters are hard to find these days, so most people use chicken.) *Haricots verts?* A slightly skinnier green bean. And tarte tatin is just plain old apple pie, baked upside down (a long story involving a French cook forgetting to add the pie crust and then adding it at the end, but we won't get into it). The crust is made from puff pastry, which is just like regular pie dough only it's flakier and, well . . . better.

Since these things are French, they seem fancier and more upscale. And the Uptown Girl loves things that are fancy and upscale. If you can just manage to pronounce all the words right, you might be hearing a little "Voulez-vous coucher avec moi?" later on, and we don't need to translate that, do we?

To Buy

10 Granny Smith (green) apples

1 bottle vanilla extract (1 teaspoon)

½ pound *haricots verts* if available—otherwise, green beans will do

1 baguette (long loaf of French bread)

1 sheet (½ package) frozen puff pastry (in the frozen section of most grocery stores)

4 strips bacon

10 pearl onions (fresh, not canned or frozen)

8 ounces button mushrooms (fresh)

2 pounds chicken pieces (breasts, legs, etc.)

1 jar Herbes de Provence (a spice) (1 teaspoon)

Staples

1 cup sugar

6 tablespoons butter, plus extra for the table

1 tablespoon balsamic vinegar

Salt (to taste)

Pepper (to taste)

1 tablespoon flour, plus a little extra for pastry preparation

2 cloves garlic

1 (8-ounce) can chicken broth

1 tablespoon olive oil

From the Liquor Store

2 to 3 bottles of very good-quality red wine—preferably Burgundy or Côtes du Rhône, but you can also use cabernet sauvignon or bordeaux

Good-quality Cognac or Armagnac (read the wine primer chapter in Part One for help)

Before she arrives:

5:00

1. Peel, core, and quarter 10 apples. Set aside.

5:30

2. In a 10-inch cast iron frying pan (or if you don't have one, a 9-inch square glass baking dish will do), on medium heat, add ½ cup sugar, stirring constantly until it melts into a dark caramel.

3. Remove the frying pan from the heat and stir in 2 tablespoons butter and mix well.

4. Line with the apple slices all the way around the skillet, round sides down and pointed sides up. Arrange them so that they overlap, as snugly as possible. Cram remaining apples (you can cut them smaller if you need to) into the center and into any air pockets so you've plugged up all the space. Sprinkle with ½ cup sugar and 1 teaspoon vanilla.

5. Set the frying pan on medium to high heat. Boil for about 45 minutes.

6:00

6. While the apples are cooking, get out a medium-size saucepan. Add the *haricots verts* and just enough water to cover them. Bring to a boil.

7. Then turn the heat down to low and simmer for 5 minutes. Drain in a colander and rinse under cold water. Transfer to a medium mixing bowl and set aside.

8. Slice the baguette and set aside—in a serving bowl or basket. Cover with a clean dish towel or cloth napkin.

9. Melt 2 tablespoons butter in the saucepan you cooked the *haricots verts* in. Add the *haricots verts* and 1 tablespoon balsamic vinegar, and a pinch each of salt and pepper, and stir. Cover and remove from heat.

6:15

10. Preheat the oven to 425 degrees.

11. Take the sheet of frozen puff pastry out of the freezer and leave it on the counter to defrost.

12. Cut the bacon into small strips.

13. Chop the ends off the pearl onions and peel off the outer skin.

14. Rinse the mushrooms and cut the bottoms of the stems off.

6:45

15. Take the frying pan of apples off the heat.

16. Take out a large cutting board and generously sprinkle some flour on it (or just do it on a clean countertop).

17. On the floured surface, use a rolling pin to roll out the puff pastry to a circle 2 inches larger in circumference than the pan of apples. Gently lift the pastry circle, and place it on top of the pan of apples, tucking the edges down into the sides of the pan. Use a butter knife to push the dough away from the sides of the pan. This will create air pockets to allow the steam to escape. Put it in the oven and set the timer to bake for 30 minutes.

7:00

18. Add 2 tablespoons butter and 1 tablespoon olive oil to a stockpot and put over medium heat. Add the bacon and cook for about 10 minutes.

19. Smash 2 garlic cloves and add them, along with the onions and mushrooms, to the stockpot with the bacon. Stir in 1 tablespoon flour. Cook, stirring occasionally, for about 5 minutes.

20. Add the chicken and cook until brown. Add ½ cup chicken broth and 1 cup red wine (or enough chicken broth and wine to cover the chicken pieces), 1 teaspoon Herbes de Provence, and salt and pepper to taste. Cover and bring to a boil. Then lower the heat and simmer for 30 to 40 minutes.

7:30

21. Take the tarte tatin out of the oven, and let it sit and cool. You need to let it cool for at least 30 minutes before you turn it out. Turn the oven down to 200 degrees.

22. Place the bowl of bread, a dish of butter, salt, and pepper on the table.

After she arrives:

8:00

23. By now you will have some outrageously fantastic smells wafting through the whole place. This will not go unnoticed. Pour her a glass of red wine.

24. When the chicken is done, transfer it to 2 oven-safe dinner plates. Set the stockpot on the stove. Top the chicken with the pearl onions, bacon, and mushrooms. Put some *haricots verts* next to the chicken on each plate. Stick the dinner plates in the 200-degree oven to keep them warm.

25. Turn up the heat under the stockpot and bring the remaining liquid to a boil. Simmer for 10 minutes, stirring occasionally, then cover and remove from heat until ready to serve.

26. Take the plates out of the oven and spoon the sauce over the chicken (but not on the *haricots verts*).

27. Here's how to turn out the tarte tatin: Take a butter knife and jam it down the side of the frying pan (or baking dish), then run it all around to loosen the edges. Then take

a large serving plate and cover the skillet or dish. Flip it and set it down hard on a counter. You might have to knock it kind of hard to get it to loosen. Lift the pan, and you should have your upside-down tarte tatin on the plate, now right side up. It's pretty to look at, so show it to your date before you cut her a slice. Serve with Cognac or Armagnac in brandy snifters.

Bonus Points

Actually rent a villa in Avignon and whip this up for her there. Oh, and forget about getting those coach tickets on Expedia. You mean you don't have your own private jet? Don't worry, she'll settle for first class. Business class if you're really cute. If you can't afford any of that, we suggest you get into a more lucrative line of work, like money laundering. In the meantime, get some vanilla ice cream for the tarte tatin and offer her decaf coffee.

The Gourmet Girl

First we eat, then we do everything else.

—M. F. K. Fisher

The Gourmet Girl is a Foodie with a capital *F.* All her activities seem to revolve around food, even when she's on vacation. She'd prefer to be mushroom hunting, sampling the wine country, or making a culinary tour of the South of France with the Michelin restaurant guide tucked under her arm. Or she might just rent a villa and spend the entire time in the kitchen, cooking elaborate dinners for friends and family.

Here's the key to the Gourmet Girl: She's a connoisseur. She appreciates the finer things, and she'll gladly pay more for them. She will shell out $1.59 for a blood orange instead of 69 cents for the navel variety, and it's not because they are fancier and more expensive. She doesn't care about status or prestige. For the Gourmet Girl, it's all about quality. She selects cars and clothes—anything she buys—based on how well they are made. While the Uptown Girl may sleep on high-thread-count, all-cotton sheets simply because she always has, the Gourmet Girl does it because, like *The Princess and the Pea,* she can feel the difference.

If you yourself are a foodie, then you probably met her in line at Williams-Sonoma. If you're not a foodie—then you are in for a challenge. This Girl's the toughest one in the book. Food is everything to her. With most Girls, if you mess up the appetizer, she'll let it slide. With the Gourmet Girl, choosing the wrong wine can spell disaster. One Gourmet Girl we know admits that she lost her attraction to a guy who made her a dinner of brown rice and vegetables. To make matters worse, he served her domestic beer in a can. In a can! While that would have been acceptable for a Granola or Athletic Girl, it was a big fat buzz kill for a Gourmet Girl. The Gourmet Girl sees every meal as an opportunity for ecstasy, and to lose even one is to lose a chance to experience the divine. Remember, the way to this girl's heart is not just through her stomach but across her taste buds.

Gourmet Girls are used to multiple courses and exotic ingredients. Fava beans instead of lima beans, quail instead of chicken, and fresh herbs instead of dried spices. Gourmet Girls are similar to Party Girls in the sense that they both enjoy entertaining. But a Gourmet Girl would rather drink a Kir than a Flaming Dr Pepper. The Party Girl likes food that's on fire or at least sizzling (like fajitas) whereas the Gourmet Girl prefers dishes you use a torch to prepare (such as crème brûlée).

Speaking of torches, we require you to invest in some special equipment when cooking for the Gourmet Girl. This will allow you to make extrafancy stuff—and it will also give you something to talk about. *Warning: Do not use or display gadgets or appliances you bought from an infomercial. This is an instant turnoff for the Gourmet Girl, equivalent to bad breath or air guitar for all other women.*

Lastly, if it looks like it might turn into an LTR (for you incurable bachelors, that's short for "long-term relationship"), consider investing in commercial-grade kitchen appliances, such as a Wolf range or subzero refrigerator.

She Might Be a Gourmet Girl If:

1. **She drives:** a practical car, often higher end. Japanese or European, but always highly rated (Gourmet Girls do their research). Volvo, Volkswagen, Honda, etc.

2. **She can talk for more than ten minutes about:** the difference between a California chardonnay and a French sauvignon blanc.

3. **She begins her sentences with:** "Jeffrey Steingarten says . . ."

4. **She'd never, *ever*:** drink wine out of a box.

5. **She owns any of the following:** a Kitchen Aid mixer, a complete set of All Clad pots and pans, Silpat baking mats, tins of foie gras she brought back from France.

Where You'll Find Her

At a four-star restaurant, sipping a glass of wine, languishing over the menu as though she were reading Proust. Shopping for a microplane lemon zester at Sur la Table, perusing the olive bar at a gourmet grocery store, wandering around the farmers' market on Sunday morning or in the cookbook aisle of the bookstore. She may run a restaurant or work as a caterer.

How to Spot Her

She'll be inspecting produce at the grocery store, sniffing the mushrooms and pinching the melons. At the checkout line, she'll have only fresh pasta, a bunch of raw ingredients (no prepared stuff), and weird produce like Jerusalem artichokes (sunchokes), kohlrabi, and other oddities such as black truffles, star anise, and quince paste.

Famous Gourmet Girls

Nigella Lawson, Sophia Loren, Martha Stewart, Jackie O, Monica on *Friends*.

Your Place

The first thing she'll notice is your kitchen and dining room. If she is at all interested in you, she will be trying to picture herself entertaining at your place. So make sure you spend some time in this department. Try to set the restaurant mood. A real tablecloth, cloth napkins, a kitchen that looks lived in and comfortable, with a pot rack, wine rack, butcher block island, that kind of thing. Oh, and if you have an herb garden, even if it's just pots on a windowsill, we guarantee you she will be impressed.

The Conversation

Talk about food. You don't necessarily have to exchange recipes with her, but of course, that wouldn't hurt. If you don't know anything about food, go out and buy books by any of the following food writers: Anthony Bourdain, MFK Fisher, Peter Mayle, Calvin Trillin, and the aforementioned Jeffrey Steingarten. (Note: Jeffrey Steingarten is the food editor for *Vogue* magazine. He has published two books of his essays—*The Man Who Ate Everything* and *It Must Have Been Something I Ate*—and he is considered a god among foodies. Dropping his name (especially if you have read any of his stuff) will win you big points with the Gourmet Girl.) Don't like reading? Get up to speed in a hurry by watching the Food Network. Catch a little Jamie Oliver, Molto Mario, even *The Iron Chef*.

The Coffee Table

Gourmet, Saveur, Cooks Illustrated, Bon Appétit, Wine Spectator, Food and Wine.

The Music

Think about what you hear in restaurants . . . jazz, classical, something pleasing (but still interesting—*not* Muzak) played quietly enough so it doesn't interfere with the food.

The Drinks

Most Gourmet Girls are wine connoisseurs. You need to know your wine. At the very least, learn the buzzwords ("oaky," "buttery," "hint of pear," etc.) and carefully read the chapter "For the Love of the Grape: A Basic Wine Primer" in Part One of this book. You will be serving different drinks for different courses—aperitifs before dinner, wine with the meal, digestifs and dessert wines after the meal. You can even do different wines with different courses—that is tremendously attractive to the Gourmet Girl. Even better, bring out the same wine but two different years, so she can taste the difference. Or a flight—a few different wines in different glasses, so she can taste multiple wines. That's crazy-hot to a Gourmet Girl. Lastly, most Gourmet Girls drink alcohol, but if by chance she doesn't, stick with fancy mineral water garnished with lemon or lime.

The Shoes

No, you don't have to wear clogs like the real chefs do. But it certainly wouldn't hurt. Boots with steel toes are also a good choice. Just don't wear anything from Payless. Remember, quality.

The Flowers

Heirloom roses, like heirloom tomatoes (see the Comfort Food Redux menu), are grown from seeds passed down from generation to generation. Unlike the factory-farmed roses that have no scent but last longer (so the growers can ship them around the world), heirloom roses smell like . . . well, roses. Imagine that! You can find heirloom roses at specialty nurseries. You could also go with any kind of flower you can eat: edible flowers or a flowering herb such as thyme. We actually know a Gourmet Guy who recently bought a house and is doing an entirely edible landscape. Instead of grass, he's planting rosemary, thyme, and mint, as well as twenty-four tomato plants and three fruit trees. Think he's getting lucky with Gourmet Girls? *Oh* yeah.

Comfort Food Redux: New American

FIRST COURSE:
AMERICAN HEIRLOOM TOMATOES
NAPA VALLEY CHARDONNAY OR SAUVIGNON BLANC

SECOND COURSE:
GRILLED BISON STEAKS
MASHED YUKON GOLD POTATOES WITH MAYTAG BLUE CHEESE
CORN COLESLAW WITH CHIPOTLE IN ADOBO SAUCE
CALIFORNIA RED ZINFANDEL

THIRD COURSE:
INDIVIDUAL BROWNIE BAKED ALASKAS WITH CHOCOLATE CHIP ICE CREAM
ALEXANDER VALLEY RIESLING OR KENTUCKY BOURBON

New American cuisine fuses European techniques and aesthetics with American ingredients. In other words, it's about making American comfort food "more fancy." In this menu we included only ingredients that are native to the New World. With the exception of cabbage, all the other foods—bison, Maytag blue cheese, chocolate chips, and brownies—were born in the USA, or at least North America. Corn, tomatoes, and chipotle peppers go back to the Aztecs, from the region that is now Mexico. Yukon Gold potatoes were invented in Canada in 1980. Even the drinks are from the New World: the wines from California and the bourbon from Kentucky. In fact, the word *bourbon* comes from the town, Bourbon, Kentucky, where it was invented.

While many people claim to have invented Baked Alaska, the name was coined by a chef at Delmonico's Restaurant in New York City in 1897. The dessert was created in honor of the United States' acquisition of Alaska. In case you don't know, Baked Alaska is ice cream on a layer of cake, encased in meringue and then baked, or fired with a torch.

You might be wondering what the heck "heirloom" tomatoes are. They are very ugly-looking tomatoes that come in lots of colors: red, yellow, purple, and green. Why buy heirloom? Because after the Industrial Revolution, farmers began to hybridize tomatoes to make them a uniform shape and color, and to make them more resistant to pests. These standardized tomatoes last longer once picked, so they can be shipped farther. What's wrong with that, you ask? Three words: *loss of flavor.* Heirloom tomatoes taste a billion times better than regular tomatoes, and, trust us, the Gourmet Girl knows the difference. You can find heirloom tomatoes at gourmet grocery stores and farmers' markets during the summer and fall.

Special equipment needed for this meal: a potato ricer. It's an inexpensive tool and the simplest way to make perfect, lump-free mashed potatoes. Also, for the individual Baked Alaskas, we suggest you pick up an ice-cream scoop, which is necessary in order to get the round scoops of ice cream you will need. If you want to make it easy on yourself (and go the extra mile to impress your Gourmet Girl), purchase a culinary torch (see description in the Some Like It Haute menu) to caramelize the meringue. If you don't have a torch, you can just brown them (as described in this recipe) in a very hot oven.

To Buy

1 box brownie mix

1 bottle vegetable or canola oil (for brownies)

2 bison (buffalo) steaks

3 Yukon Gold potatoes

3 ounces Maytag blue cheese

½ head red cabbage

24 ounces (3 cups) frozen yellow corn

1 jar chipotle peppers in adobo sauce (6 tablespoons of the sauce)

4 to 5 medium-size heirloom tomatoes (in varigated colors of red, orange, yellow, and green; if you can't find them, substitute good-quality organic tomatoes)

1 pint chocolate chip ice cream

Staples

2 tablespoons plus ½ tablespoon butter

2 eggs plus 3 egg whites

¼ cup balsamic vinegar

½ plus ⅓ cup olive oil

2 cloves garlic

2 teaspoons plus a pinch salt

Pepper (to taste)

⅓ cup milk

⅓ cup plus ¼ cup sugar

From the Liquor Store

1 bottle Napa Valley chardonnay or sauvignon blanc

1 bottle California red zinfandel

1 bottle good-quality Kentucky bourbon (such as Knob Creek) or Alexander Valley Riesling

Special Equipment

Potato ricer

Ice-cream scoop

Culinary torch (optional)

Before she arrives:

5:15

1. Chill the white wine.

2. Butter a 9x13-inch glass baking dish with ½ tablespoon butter.

3. Preheat the oven as directed on the box of brownie mix.

4. Make the brownies according to the directions on the box: mix all the ingredients (brownie mix, 2 eggs, vegetable or canola oil, and water), pour into buttered baking dish, and bake. Set the timer according to directions on box.

5:45

5. Put the bison steaks in a Ziplock bag with ¼ cup balsamic vinegar, ½ cup olive oil, 2 smashed cloves garlic, ½ teaspoon of salt, and pepper to taste. Seal the bag and mush the marinade around on the steaks with your hands, through the plastic. It's OK if the steaks are still frozen. Set aside.

6:00

6. Peel the potatoes with a vegetable peeler, quarter them with a chef's knife, put them in a medium-size saucepan, and cover with water. Bring to a boil, cover, and set the timer for 20 minutes. Once the water boils, turn the heat down slightly.

6:30

7. When the brownies are done, take them out of the oven and let them cool in the pan for 10 to 15 minutes.

8. When the potatoes are done (fork-tender), drain in a colander and put through the potato ricer.

6:45

9. While the brownies are still warm (but not hot), take a pint glass (or equivalent in terms of diameter) and, lip side down, cut out 2 circles of brownies. Use a metal spatula to lift the circles out and transfer them to a baking sheet. Cover with plastic wrap and put in the fridge.

10. In a medium mixing bowl, combine the mashed potatoes with 2 tablespoons butter, ⅓ cup milk, and 3 ounces Maytag blue cheese. Add ½ teaspoon salt, and pepper to taste. Stir with a wooden spoon until blended. Cover with plastic wrap or foil and set aside.

7:15

11. Take the ½ head of red cabbage, remove the outer leaves, and discard them. Chop up the remaining cabbage on a cutting board and throw into a large mixing bowl.

7:30

12. Add 3 cups frozen corn, ⅓ cup sugar, 1 teaspoon salt, ⅓ cup olive oil, and 6 tablespoons of the chipotle adobo sauce (don't use the peppers – just spoon out the sauce). Stir and add pepper to taste. Cover with foil or plastic wrap and put in the fridge.

13. Rinse and drain the heirloom tomatoes and set aside.

After she arrives:

8:00

First course:

14. Set the oven on broil. Uncork the white wine and pour. After you've chatted a bit, slice the heirloom tomatoes and arrange decoratively on salad plates—mixing the different colors in an attractive display. Sprinkle with a pinch of salt and pepper and serve.

Second course:

15. Pour her another glass of white wine and go into the kitchen. Uncork the red wine.

16. Take the mixing bowl full of potatoes and stick it in the oven to warm it. Put the marinated steaks in a 9-inch square glass baking dish and stick it in the broiler. Cook for 3 to 4 minutes on each side. They should still be red on the inside (but not bloody) when you take them out.

17. With a slotted spoon (or a fork if you don't have one), serve some of the coleslaw on dinner plates. When the potatoes and steak are done, arrange them next to the coleslaw and serve with the red zinfandel.

Third course:

18. Offer to pour her another glass of wine and ask her if she'd like to watch while you finish making the dessert. Set the oven to 475 degrees for the Baked Alaskas (or just fire up your culinary torch).

19. Now, make the meringue. First, separate the whites from the yolks of 3 eggs: Break each egg gently over a mixing bowl but capture the yolk in one of the halves of the shell. Gently pass the egg yolk back and forth between the shell halves, letting the white of the egg flow into the bowl. When nothing but yolk remains in the shells, throw the yolks and shells away.

20. Get out your electric hand mixer and beat the egg whites on high until stiff peaks form. Beat in ¼ cup sugar a little at a time. Set aside.

21. Take the chocolate chip ice cream out of the freezer. Get out your ice-cream scoop and hold it under hot water to make scooping the ice cream easier. Put one round scoop of ice cream on each brownie round.

22. With a rubber spatula or butter knife, as quickly as you can, cover the ice-cream scoops with meringue, being careful to completely enclose the ice cream with the meringue (it acts as insulation and will prevent the ice cream from melting). When you are done, they should look like tiny snow-covered mountains.

23. Immediately put them in the oven for 2 to 3 minutes, just to get the meringue slightly browned. You may also use your culinary torch (which will no doubt impress the Gourmet Girl).

24. With a metal spatula, transfer to serving plates and serve with either glasses of Riesling or bourbon (on the rocks or neat, which is the fancy word for "no ice").

Bonus Points

If you really want her interest to bloom, plant some heirloom tomatoes in your backyard. A man who raises his own heirloom tomatoes is to the Gourmet Girl what a Kennedy is to the Uptown Girl; what a Little League coach is to the Girl Next Door; what an Iron Man triathlete is to the Athletic Girl . . . well, you get the idea.

Some Like It Haute: Classic French

FIRST COURSE:
FRENCH ONION SOUP
APERITIF: KIR (PRONOUNCED "KEER")

SECOND COURSE:
DUCK CONFIT WITH CHERRY SAUCE ("CONE-FEE")
POTATOES DAPHINOISE ("DAHF-IN-WAHZ")
BRAISED CELERIAC ("SELL-LEER-EE-ACK")
WINE: CÔTES DU RHÔNE (OR PINOT NOIR)

THIRD COURSE:
CRÈME BRÛLÉE ("KREM BROO-LAY")
DIGESTIF: ARMAGNAC ("ARM-ING-YAK")

Haute cuisine means "high" or fancy food. It typically involves a lot of heavy sauces, cream, and butter, along with a ton of tedious preparation. Make no mistake, though, there's a reason classic French food is revered throughout the world. It's just that good. This meal may require some intense effort, but trust us, that effort will not be lost on the Gourmet Girl.

In case you were wondering, Duck Confit is duck preserved and cooked in its own fat. The dish originated as a way to preserve meat before refrigeration. You can keep the Duck Confit in your fridge for up to a month. However, it must be made at least a few days in advance, so if she's coming over tonight, skip over this menu.

Potatoes Daphinoise, also called potatoes au gratin, are essentially the same thing that Americans call scalloped potatoes. Celeriac is just celery root, and it has a delicious anise flavor that offsets the cherry in an interesting way.

The good news is, for this menu, you get to buy a gun. A gun that shoots fire. It's called a culinary torch, and it's used to caramelize stuff, which means to burn sugar. Crème brûlée actually means "burned cream," although it doesn't taste burned. It's the most popular French dessert of all time. You will also need two ramekins for the crème brûlée—these are little ceramic or glass dishes sturdy enough to put into a hot oven. If you really want to kick butt with the Gourmet Girl, you can also buy a mandoline to slice the potatoes, onion, and even the celeriac. You may also want to invest in a couple of brandy snifters for the Armagnac. All these items are available at stores like Sur La Table or can be ordered online.

To Buy

2 fresh duck legs (ask your butcher)

1 quart (32 ounces or 4 cups) rendered duck fat (available at gourmet grocery stores or online)

1 24-ounce or larger container heavy cream (3 cups)

1 small bottle pure (not imitation) vanilla extract (½ teaspoon)

8 ounces Gruyère cheese

1 pound russet potatoes

5 shallots

1 baguette (French bread)

1 (8-ounce) can cherries in light syrup

1 celeriac bulb (available at gourmet grocery stores)

Staples

½ cup plus ¾ teaspoon salt, plus more (to taste)

½ teaspoon pepper, plus more (to taste)

4 cloves garlic

4 egg yolks

3 tablespoons plus 3 teaspoons sugar

3½ tablespoons plus 1 teaspoon butter

12 ounces yellow onions (¾ pound)

2 tablespoons flour

4 (16-ounce) cans chicken broth

Balsamic vinegar

2 tablespoons olive oil

From the Liquor Store

1 bottle dry white wine (or French white table wine—for the kirs)

1 small bottle Crème de Cassis (blackcurrant liqueur)

1 bottle Côtes du Rhône, or you could go with a good pinot noir (see wine primer chapter in Part One)

1 bottle Armagnac (see aforementioned wine primer)

Special Equipment

Culinary torch

2 (10-ounce) ramekins

Mandoline (optional)

Five days before she arrives:

1. Lay the duck legs in a 9x13-inch glass baking dish. Cover with ½ cup salt and roll the legs around in the salt until covered on both sides. Sprinkle with freshly ground black pepper and 4 crushed cloves of garlic. Cover with plastic wrap or aluminum foil and stick in the fridge overnight.

Four days before she arrives:

2. In a large stockpot, melt 3 cups (24 ounces) of the duck fat over medium heat.

3. Take the legs out of the baking dish and rinse all the salt, garlic, and pepper off under cold water. Dry the legs and transfer to the stockpot with the melted duck fat. Cover, turn heat down to low, and cook until meat pulls away from drumsticks, about 1 to 1½ hours. Remove from heat and allow the duck legs to cool in the fat. Transfer to storage container, cover, and refrigerate for at least 36 hours.

The day before she arrives:

4. Preheat the oven to 325 degrees.

5. Separate the yolks from the whites of 4 eggs: Break each egg gently over a small bowl, but capture the yolk in one of the halves of the shell. Gently pass the egg yolk back and forth between the shell halves, letting the white of the egg flow into the bowl. When nothing but yolk remains in the shells, dump it into a medium mixing bowl and throw the egg whites away.

6. In the mixing bowl with the 4 egg yolks, add 3 tablespoons sugar and beat with an electric hand mixer until thick. Add 1 cup heavy cream and ½ teaspoon vanilla extract and mix until well blended.

7. Divide the mixture into 2 ramekins. Set the ramekins in a baking dish. Add hot water to the baking dish, being careful not to get any water in the ramekins. The water should come up about halfway up the sides of the ramekins. Bake until set, about 40 minutes.

8. When done baking, remove from oven. Let cool for at least 30 minutes, then cover ramekins with plastic wrap and put in the fridge to chill overnight.

The day of the date, before she arrives:

2:45

9. Chill the white wine and preheat the oven to 450 degrees.

10. Grate the Gruyère in the food processor, cover, and set aside.

3:00

11. Peel the potatoes using the vegetable peeler, then slice them as thinly as possible, using the mandoline if you've got one. Be sure to use the safety guard.

3:30

12. Butter a 9-inch square glass baking dish or cake tin with ½ tablespoon butter.

13. Mince 3 shallots and set aside.

3:45

14. Add 2 cups (16 ounces) heavy cream to a medium saucepan over medium heat. Add the minced shallots, ¾ teaspoon salt, and ½ teaspoon pepper. Bring to a boil, stirring occasionally. Remove from heat.

15. Pour a little bit of the cream mixture into the buttered baking dish, enough to coat the bottom. Layer with the potato slices, overlapping in concentric circles. Pour in a little more of the cream mixture, add another layer of potato slices. Continue adding cream and potato layers until you have filled the dish. Wash and dry the medium saucepan and set aside to use later.

16. Top last layer with ¾ cup of the grated Gruyere cheese. Set aside. Refrigerate the remaining ¼ cup cheese to use later for the soup.

4:15

17. To make the French onion soup, peel the onions, cut in half, and then slice thinly (using the mandoline if you've got it).

18. Mince 1 shallot and set aside.

4:45

19. Put the baking dish with potatoes into the oven and set the timer for 30 minutes. (Put some foil on the lower rack or bottom of the oven, just in case the cream boils over.)

20. In a stockpot, melt 1 tablespoon duck fat (scoop out of the container you stored your duck legs in) and 1 tablespoon butter. Add the sliced onions and brown on both sides.

21. Add the minced shallot and cook for about 15 minutes over low to medium heat, stirring occasionally.

22. Add 2 tablespoons flour and stir frequently, cooking for 5 more minutes.

5:15

23. Stir in 3 (16-ounce) cans of chicken broth, and salt and pepper to taste (take 1 of the chicken broth cans, rinse, and set aside—you'll be using it later). Turn up the heat and bring to a boil. Reduce heat to low and set the timer for 30 minutes.

24. Once the potatoes have baked for 30 minutes, turn the oven down to 350 and set the timer for another 15 to 20 minutes.

5:45

25. When the potatoes are ready, they should be brown and crispy on top and cooked in the middle. Remove from the oven, cover with foil, and set aside.

26. In a small saucepan on high heat, boil remaining chicken stock (16 ounces) until reduced to 8 ounces (in half). Remove from heat, pour into a small mixing bowl, and set aside. Wash and dry the small saucepan for use later.

27. When the timer for the soup goes off, remove the soup from heat, cover, and set aside.

6:15

28. Slice half of the baguette (stick the other half back in the wrapper and put aside— you'll be needing it later).

29. Stick the bread slices in the oven on a baking sheet until toasted, about 10 minutes. Remove from oven, cut up into bite-size pieces (or croutons), cover with foil, and set aside.

6:30

30. Mince 1 shallot and set aside.

31. Add 1 teaspoon duck fat and 1 teaspoon butter to a medium saucepan and stir until melted. Add the shallot and cook for 1 to 2 minutes or until shallot is softened.

32. Add the can of cherries and ¾ cup Armagnac, 1 teaspoon sugar, the reduced (8 ounces or 1 cup) broth, and 2 teaspoons balsamic vinegar. Boil until the cherry sauce has a syrupy consistency and has reduced by almost half.

33. Remove from heat and stir in 2 tablespoons butter, stirring until the butter is melted. Cover, and set aside.

7:15

34. Slice off the tough outer layer of the celeriac and then peel it until you are left with a white block. Using your mandoline (or a chef's knife), cut into matchsticks (julienne).

35. In a small saucepan over medium heat, add 2 tablespoons olive oil. Add the celeriac and let cook until the pieces are tender, about 20 minutes. Stir occasionally. Remove from heat, cover, and set aside.

After she arrives:

8:00

First course:

36. Set the oven on broil. Make her a glass of kir: Take out 2 wineglasses and add 1 tablespoon of crème de cassis to each glass. Then fill almost to the top with white wine. It should be a pretty rose color. (Maybe this is how they came up with that Edith Piaf song, *La Vie en Rose.*)

37. Pour the onion soup into 2 soup bowls, add several croutons to each bowl, and cover with enough grated Gruyère cheese to cover the croutons. Place the bowls in the oven for just a few minutes—until the cheese is melted and slightly brown. Using oven mitts, remove the soup bowls and turn the oven down to 200 degrees. Note: Some soup bowls can't withstand the heat of the broiler. If you have plastic or not-very-heat-resistant bowls, skip the oven.

38. Serve, making sure to tell her to be careful since her bowl will be very hot. Note: If she has finished her kir, uncork the red wine and offer her a glass to go with her soup.

Second course:

39. Stick the cherry sauce back on the stove on medium heat to warm it. Do the same thing with the celeriac.

40. Stick the baking dish of potatoes back into the 200-degree oven for a few minutes to warm them.

41. Slice up the rest of the baguette, and arrange in a basket or on a bread board (you can warm it if you like, but it's not necessary).

42. Wash and dry the stockpot you used to cook the soup. In the now clean stockpot, over medium heat, melt 1 teaspoon duck fat. Add the duck legs to the pan and cook for about 5 minutes, stirring frequently. Remove from heat, cover, and set aside.

43. Take the chicken broth can (the one you set aside at step 23) and use it to cut out 2 circles of potatoes. Dislodge with a metal spatula and transfer to dinner plates.

44. Arrange duck legs and celeriac next to the potatoes. Pour the cherry sauce over the duck, and serve with the Côtes du Rhône.

Third course:

45. After dinner, pour a couple of brandy snifters of Armagnac. Get out the chilled ramekins of crème brûlée and sprinkle the top of each with 1 teaspoon sugar. Caramelize them by running the flame over the sugar in a circular motion until hard and light brown. Hold the torch at least 3 to 5 inches away from the ramekins, so the custard doesn't burn. Serve immediately, with spoons.

Bonus Points

Serve the crème brûlée with fresh berries. You could also do a cheese course after the dessert. Overkill, you say? Not for the Gourmet Girl. Gourmet Girls know how to pace themselves—a well-prepared and well-served French meal can go five hours. Just pick a few very high-quality French cheeses and serve them on a tray with a knife. It is not necessary to serve bread. However, she will probably want to switch back to red wine to go with the cheese, so make sure you do your research on matching the wine with the cheese (either look online or ask at the gourmet store where you get the cheese).

R Is for Risotto, Radicchio, and Romance: Classic Italian

FIRST COURSE:
ROASTED RADICCHIO (PRONOUNCED "RAH-DICK-EE-OH") WITH SHAVED PEAR, FENNEL,
AND PECORINO ("PEC-OH-REE-NO") ON A BED OF ARUGULA ("AH-ROO-GUH-LAH")
PROSECCO ("PRO-SEC-OH")

SECOND COURSE:
LOBSTER RISOTTO ("RI-ZOH-TOH") WITH SHAVED WHITE TRUFFLES
ORVIETO ("OR-VAY-TO") OR PINOT GRIGIO ("PEE-NO GREE-GEE-OH")

THIRD COURSE:
SBRISOLONA ("SPREE-SA-LOH-NA")
VIN SANTO ("VIN SAHN-TO") OR GRAPPA ("GRAH-PA")

If Italian is the language of lovers (Casanova was Italian, after all), then Italian cuisine must be the food of love. This is a simple but very elegant meal, made from traditional Italian foods, such as radicchio, arugula, pecorino cheese, and of course, risotto.

Radicchio is a slightly bitter-tasting, beet-red-and-white-leafed chicory. The two most common varieties found in the United States are Verona and Treviso, named after the regions of Italy they are from. Verona radicchio is shaped like a small cabbage, whereas the Treviso radicchio is spear-shaped. You can use either one for this salad. Fennel, or finocchio, is a very flavorful vegetable commonly used in Italian meals. Arugula is a peppery salad green, while pecorino is a smooth, mild sheep's-milk cheese from Tuscany.

To accompany the salad, we've chosen Prosecco, an Italian sparkling wine, which is similar to Champagne and is the perfect aperitif. Unlike Champagne, you can get a good bottle of Prosecco for $10 to $20.

Risotto, a creamy and delicious specialty made from arborio rice, is one of the more difficult Italian dishes to make because it requires a lot of attention. Your mastery of it will not go unappreciated by the Gourmet Girl.

Lobster is often paired with white truffles. The white truffle is a mushroom from the Piedmont region of Italy. It grows underground and is very hard to find and thus expensive. Note: Fresh white truffles are only available between November and January; you may substitute with white truffle oil, which is available year-round.

Orvieto is a region in central Italy that produces a lot of dry white wines. You could also go with a pinot grigio, which comes from northern Italy. Sbrisalona, a very hard cake from Mantova in the Lombardy region, is made with cornmeal and almonds. The name comes from the word in the local dialect for "crumbly." To go with it, we've selected Vin Santo, one of the best Italian white wines, sweet enough to go with desserts. You may choose to serve grappa instead, which is an Italian brandy.

Special equipment required for this menu: the mandoline, the best slicing tool you can buy. It will enable you to shave the fennel and pecorino cheese paper thin for the salad. You can also use it later on to make julienne vegetables or waffle fries, and it comes in very handy when making Dauphinoise (or au gratin) potatoes (see Some Like It Haute menu). Note: Be very careful when using a mandoline, and be sure to use the safety guard. The blade is extremely sharp! You should also pick up some Champagne glasses for the Prosecco, and if you go with grappa, get some brandy snifters.

After you've eaten, the lights have been dimmed, and you're sipping your grappa or Vin Santo, you can whisper some Italian sweet nothings into her ear. Like, *Che bella*, which means "How beautiful you are," or *Cara mia, ti voglio bene*, translated as, "My darling, I love you." Or how about *Mi piace i calzini che tu indossi*, which means "I like those socks you are wearing." Of course, all this talk might be unnecessary because, after a meal like this, the Gourmet Girl will be crumbling like that sbrisolona you served for dessert.

To Buy

1 container cornmeal (6 ounces or ¾ cup)

8 ounces (1 cup) slivered almonds

1 fresh lobster tail

1 package arborio rice (1 cup)

1 head radicchio

1 pear

1 bag arugula

1 bulb fennel

4 ounces pecorino cheese

1 fresh white truffle (available November through January) or 3 tablespoons
   (1.5 ounces) white truffle oil (available at gourmet grocery stores or order online)

Staples

1⅓ cups flour

1 cup sugar

1½ teaspoons salt, plus more to taste

10 tablespoons (1¼ sticks) cold butter, plus a little more to butter the pan

2 egg yolks

24 ounces (3 cups) chicken broth

1 clove garlic

½ cup (4 ounces) plus 3 tablespoons olive oil

3 tablespoons milk

⅛ teaspoon pepper, plus more to taste

¼ cup balsamic vinegar

From the Liquor Store

1 bottle Prosecco

1 bottle Orvieto (or pinot grigio)

1 bottle Vin Santo or grappa

1 small bottle brandy (for the risotto—or you can use the grappa for this)

Special Equipment

Mandoline

Before she arrives:

4:45

1. Chill the Prosecco and Orvieto and preheat the oven to 400 degrees.

2. Butter a 9-inch square baking dish and set aside.

3. Put ¾ cup cornmeal into the food processor with a metal blade and run for a few minutes.

4. Add the 1 cup slivered almonds and roughly chop.

5. Transfer to a medium mixing bowl and add 1⅓ cups flour, 1 cup sugar, and ¼ teaspoon salt, and mix with your hands or a wooden spoon.

6. Slice the 10 tablespoons (1¼ sticks) cold butter and work it into the mixture (easiest done with your hands).

7. Separate the yolks from the whites of 2 eggs: Break each egg gently over a small serving bowl, but capture the yolk in one of the halves of the shell. Gently pass the egg yolk back and forth between the shell halves, letting the white of the egg flow into the bowl. When nothing but yolk remains in the shells, dump it into a small mixing bowl and set aside. Discard the egg whites.

8. Add the 2 egg yolks and mix well. Set aside or refrigerate (if your kitchen is warm) until ready to use.

5:30

9. Add the 3 cups chicken broth to a small saucepan and set the heat on low. (You will be leaving it on low the entire time you are cooking the risotto—and slowly adding the broth to the rice as you go along.)

10. Put the lobster tail in a stockpot, uncovered, on medium heat, and add enough water to cover the lobster. Add 1 teaspoon salt. Simmer for 8 to 10 minutes.

11. Transfer the lobster to a colander and run cold water over it to cool it, then drain.

12. Remove all the meat and then, using a chef's knife, cut into ½-inch cubes.

13. Back to the sbrisalona: Give the cake mixture one more stir and pour into the buttered cake dish. Put it in the oven and set the timer for 20 minutes.

6:00

14. Crush 1 clove garlic.

15. In a medium saucepan on medium heat, add 2 tablespoons olive oil.

16. Add the crushed garlic to the pan. Cook for a couple of minutes, stirring with a wooden spoon. Add 1 cup rice and stir for 2 minutes.

17. Add 2 tablespoons brandy or grappa. Reduce the heat to medium-low and cook for 2 minutes until the brandy is absorbed.

18. Add ½ cup of the hot chicken broth (you know, what you have on low heat on the other burner), and stir to incorporate.

6:15

19. For the next 20 minutes, or until the risotto is cooked through (taste it to see), stir and add broth (½ cup at a time) as it gets absorbed. (You might not use it all.) Stir constantly. (And we mean *constantly.* Risotto is one of those things you really can't walk away from. Not even for a minute.)

20. When the risotto is cooked, stir in the chopped lobster meat and 3 tablespoons milk. Remove from heat, cover, and set aside.

21. Remove the sbrisalona from the oven, but leave the oven on. Slice it before it cools too much, otherwise it will get too hard. Arrange the slices decoratively on a platter, cover with plastic wrap, and set aside.

6:45

22. Rinse the radicchio and cut into quarters. Transfer to a 9x13-inch glass baking dish. Drizzle with 1 tablespoon olive oil, and sprinkle with ¼ teaspoon salt and ⅛ teaspoon pepper. Bake in the 400-degree oven for about 15 minutes.

7:15

23. Rinse the pear and set aside.

24. Rinse the arugula and blot on paper towels or spin in a salad spinner.

25. Chop off the greens from the fennel so you are left with just the bulb. Using your mandoline, shave the fennel paper thin. Set aside.

7:45

26. To make the dressing, whisk (or use the food processor) ½ cup olive oil and ¼ cup balsamic vinegar in a bowl; add salt and pepper to taste. Cover and refrigerate.

After she arrives:

8:00

First course:

27. Pop open the Prosecco and pour into Champagne glasses.

28. On salad plates, lay a bed of arugula, then artfully (make it look pretty) arrange the quartered radicchio and some of the shaved fennel over it.

29. Use the mandoline to shave the pear and the pecorino cheese, and arrange on top of the fennel.

30. Drizzle with dressing and serve.

Second course:

31. To reheat the risotto, warm it up for a couple of minutes on a medium-heat burner. Be sure to stir, and don't burn it. Using a vegetable peeler, shave the white truffle

onto the risotto and spoon into serving bowls—or, if using truffle oil, stir 3 table-spoons of the white truffle oil into the risotto. Season with salt and pepper to taste. Serve with the Orvieto.

Third course:

32. Serve the sbrisolona with the Vin Santo or grappa. (Note: Use regular wineglasses for the Vin Santo. Serve the grappa in brandy snifters.)

Bonus Points

Add pine nuts (available at most grocery stores) to the salad. Sprinkle freshly chopped parsley on the risotto just before serving. Serve fresh berries and crème fraîche (available in the dairy section of gourmet grocery stores) or gelato (Italian ice cream) with the sbrisolona.

[hard]

It's a Small World After All: Pan-Asian Fusion

FIRST COURSE:

BEET, BLOOD ORANGE, AND ASIAN PEAR SALAD WITH A GINGER RICE
VINEGAR DRESSING

CHILLED *DAIGINJO* (PRONOUNCED "DIE-GIN-JOE"—WITH A HARD *G,* AS IN "GINZU
KNIFE") SAKE ("SAH-ᴋᴀʏ," NOT "SAH-ᴋᴇᴇ")

SECOND COURSE:

LEEK KIMCHEE ("KIM-CHEE") CREPES WITH KOBE ("KOH-BAY") BEEF IN A SHIITAKE
("SHIH-TAH-KAY") MUSHROOM CREAM SAUCE

BEET GREENS IN RICE VINEGAR

PINOT NOIR

THIRD COURSE:

GREEN TEA ICE CREAM

UMESHU ("OOH-MEH-SHOO"), OR PLUM WINE

Fusion cuisine refers to the blending of ingredients and cooking styles from different cultures. For example, you might use traditional French or Italian cooking methods with classic American ingredients. Chef Nobu Matsuhisa, owner of Nobu in New York City and Matsuhisa in Los Angeles, was trained to cook in Japan and in Peru. As a result, his cooking is based on the fusion between Japanese and South American foods.

This meal is a blend of pan-Asian foods, including Japanese, Chinese, and Korean. Kimchee pancakes are very common in Korea, although we've made them a bit thinner, more like French crepes. The sauce is also French, as it uses heavy cream, but the shiitake mushrooms are Asian. Kobe beef, the Rolls-Royce of meats, is a delicacy in Japan. It is an extremely tender cut of meat (like butter), rich with marbled fat, which comes from a Japanese breed of cattle called Wagyu. These cattle are fed the highest-quality grains, given beer to drink (to fatten them), and massaged by hand with sake, all to improve the flavor and consistency. You can find Kobe beef online and at a few select high-end grocery stores across the country. Beware, though, it's pricey. To get the real thing, raised in Japan and shipped over, it will cost you at least $100 a pound. Instead, we suggest buying American-raised Kobe beef, which you can get for half that price.

Sake is Japanese wine made from rice instead of grapes. The good stuff is generally served cold, while the less-impressive vintages are warmed to make them more fragrant. There are 55,000 different kinds of sake sold in Japan, so how do you know which one to buy? There are three basic categories: *junmai, hon-johzo,* and *ginjo* sake. For the Gourmet Girl, get the very best. That's *daiginjo* sake (the top echelon of *ginjo*). Don't worry about the brand or vintage or anything like that, as long as it says *daiginjo* on it. Second-best bet is *ginjo* sake. You can find it at Asian grocery stores or search for it online.

The plum wine, or *umeshu,* is a very sweet liqueur. You'll find lots of different kinds, including some made by Kikkoman, the same people who make the soy sauce. Do not, under any circumstances, buy that. If you whip out a bottle of Kikkoman wine, the Gourmet Girl will, guaranteed, run screaming to the hills and never speak to you again. To prevent a disaster like that, go with something like Hakutsuru.

There is some special equipment needed for this meal. First of all, you need some small metal fruit and vegetable cutters in the shapes of leaves, animals, and the like. It is an Asian tradition to use vegetable cutters to make attractive garnishes. You can find them at wok shops and Asian cooking specialty stores. We found ours at Sur La Table. Another thing we found at Sur La Table was the microplane ginger and spice grater for zesting the oranges and grating the ginger. Note: You do not need a special crepe pan—you can just use a regular frying pan (either 8- or 10-inch).

Lastly, and this is optional, consider buying a chilled sake serving set. It is essentially a glass pitcher that holds ice around a smaller compartment that holds the sake. It will also come with a couple of glasses. You can find them at upscale Asian cooking stores or online. Not a requirement for this meal—but it definitely will score major points with the Gourmet Girl.

To Buy

1 pint vanilla ice cream

1 tablespoon (½ ounce) matcha (powdered green tea, available at Asian food stores—if you can't find matcha, buy regular green tea and grind it into a powder with a mortar and pestle or with a food processor)

1 bunch fresh beets (with greens)

1 pound shiitake mushrooms

1 fresh ginger root (1 teaspoon)

1 bottle plain (not seasoned) rice vinegar (available at most supermarkets) (¼ cup plus 3 tablespoons)

4 blood oranges (available at some supermarkets and most upscale gourmet markets)

2 Asian pears

1 jar leek kimchee (available at Asian markets—if you can't find leek kimchee, you can substitute plain kimchee) (½ cup Kimchee, 2 tablespoons juice)

1 pound Kobe beef (available at select gourmet food stores, or order online and have it shipped; you can substitute a very good cut of filet mignon)

Staples

2 cloves garlic

¼ cup plus 2 tablespoons plus 1 teaspoon olive oil

½ cup chicken broth

1 cup milk, divided

1 tablespoon plus 2 teaspoons butter

½ cup flour, plus pinches for gravy

1 egg

From the Liquor Store

1 bottle *daiginjo* sake (see recipe introduction)

1 bottle good-quality pinot noir (see wine primer chapter in Part One)

1 bottle *umeshu,* or plum wine (see recipe introduction)

Special Equipment

2 very small cookie cutters (1 inch diameter) in the shape of stars, diamonds, leaves, or animals

1 microplane ginger and spice grater

Chilled sake serving set (optional, you can just use regular wineglasses instead)

Before she arrives:

3:15

1. Chill the sake and plum wine in the fridge and set the ice cream out on the counter to soften it.

2. In a small mixing bowl, mix 1 tablespoon lukewarm water with 1 tablespoon matcha (powdered green tea). Stir to form a paste.

3. Put the softened ice cream into a medium mixing bowl. Add the matcha paste and mix until it's completely incorporated. It should be a pale green color. Put into the freezer until ready to serve (for at least an hour). Wash and dry the small mixing bowl for use later.

3:45

4. Fill a stockpot halfway with water, cover, and set on high heat to boil.

5. Cut the greens off the beets. Rinse and chop the greens and set aside.

6. Peel the beets with a vegetable peeler, and then halve them with a chef's knife.

7. Put the beets in the boiling water for 15 to 20 minutes. When you can stab the beets through with a fork, they are done.

4:00

8. Rinse the shiitake mushrooms. Cut the ends off the mushrooms and slice them from top to bottom, no more than ¼ inch thick. Set aside.

9. Crush 1 clove of garlic and set aside.

10. In a medium saucepan, heat 1 tablespoon olive oil and add the garlic.

11. Once the garlic is soft, throw the mushrooms in. Cook 2 to 5 minutes on a low flame.

4:45

12. When the beets are done, put them into a colander and rinse with cold water.

13. Fill the stockpot they were cooked in with ice cubes and cold water. Put the beets back in and let them cool for 10 to 15 minutes.

14. Once the mushrooms are soft, add ½ cup chicken broth and ½ cup milk, stirring. Add 1 teaspoon butter. With a slotted spoon, take the mushrooms out and set them aside on a plate. Add pinches of flour, a little at a time, to the sauce, stirring frequently, until it is thick and gravy-like. Remove from heat, cover, and set aside to be used later.

5:15

15. Peel the ginger and grate it using the microplane grater. Grate ½ teaspoon ginger into the small mixing bowl.

16. Using the microplane grater, zest 2 of the blood oranges. Add ½ teaspoon worth of orange zest (or grated orange skin) to the bowl with the ginger.

5:30

17. Add ¼ cup rice vinegar to the bowl and beat with a wire whisk (or you can use the food processor). Add juice from the 2 oranges you just zested, ¼ cup olive oil, and a

little salt and fresh ground pepper to taste, and then beat some more. Put it in the refrigerator to chill.

5:45

18. Cut the cooled beets into ¼ -inch-thick slices and put them on a plate.

19. Peel the Asian pears and put them on a separate plate.

20. Peel the remaining 2 blood oranges and slice them into 1-inch cubes; put them on a separate plate.

6:15

21. Use the vegetable cutters to cut shapes out of the beets and Asian pears.

6:45

22. To make the crepes: Mince ½ cup of the kimchee using a chef's knife on a cutting board, or do it in the food processor. Set aside.

7:00

23. In a large mixing bowl, add ½ cup flour, 1 egg, and ½ cup milk, and mix together with a wooden spoon or wire whisk.

24. Melt 1 tablespoon butter in the microwave or in a small saucepan on the stovetop and add it to the mix, and then beat it some more.

25. Pour out some of the juice from the jar of kimchee (about 2 tablespoons) into the crepe mix. Add ¼ cup of the minced kimchee and mix together.

7:30

26. Melt 1 teaspoon butter in an 8- or 10-inch frying pan, let it get hot, and then pour on some crepe batter (use ¼ cup batter for an 8-inch pan, a little more for 10-inch).

27. Let it cook for a minute or two and, when it seems set, flip it with a spatula to cook the other side. Your first crepes may come out looking strange. That's OK, just keep trying until you get a couple of good ones. You can throw the early attempts away. Set the crepes on a plate and cover with another plate to keep them warm. Wash and dry the frying pan for use later.

After she arrives:

8:00

First course:

28. Arrange the salads on small plates. Arrange a row of beets, a row of blood oranges in the middle, and a row of Asian pears decoratively on each plate. Drizzle a little of the ginger dressing on top. Serve the salad with cold sake.

Second course:

29. After the salad course, put 1 teaspoon olive oil in the frying pan and set the stove on high. Once the pan is hot, salt and pepper the beef, then sear for 1 to 2 minutes on each side. Not too long—it should be rare or medium rare. If you cook it for too long, you will ruin it. Kobe beef is meant to be seared on the outside and rare on the inside, just like you would do with ahi tuna. Set the seared meat on a cutting board and let it rest for 5 to 10 minutes.

30. While the meat is resting, crush 1 clove of garlic and add it to a frying pan with 1 tablespoon olive oil. Add the beet greens and sauté for about 5 minutes, just until they are wilted and soft. Add a little salt, then douse with 3 tablespoons rice vinegar.

31. Put the plate of crepes in the oven for a minute, just to warm them up, and slice the beef into ½-inch slices.

32. Put the pan of gravy back on the stove on medium heat for a few minutes, just to warm it. Add the mushrooms, stirring occasionally.

33. Put a crepe on each plate. Arrange the meat on the crepes, pour a little of the mushroom sauce over the meat, and fold the crepes in thirds, like burritos.

34. Pour the rest of the mushroom sauce over the crepes, and sprinkle a little bit of the minced kimchee on top or on the side for a garnish. Add the beet greens on the side. Serve with the bottle of pinot noir.

Third course:

35. After dinner, serve the green tea ice cream in small bowls with glasses of cool plum wine (use regular wineglasses).

Bonus Points

Lightly sprinkle black sesame seeds on the Asian pears and white sesame seeds on the beets (you can buy the sesame seeds from the Asian grocery store). It's worth it to go the extra mile; the presentation is stunning. You can also add baby bok choy to the beet greens. Top the green tea ice cream with lychee nuts (available in jars) or pomegranate seeds.

There's No Taste like Foam: Spanish Surrealist

FIRST COURSE:
KIWI AND CUCUMBER GAZPACHO
CAVA

SECOND COURSE:
GRILLED QUAIL STUFFED WITH AN OLIVE STUFFED WITH AN ANCHOVY
AMANTILLADO OR FINO SHERRY

THIRD COURSE:
BACALAO WITH PIMIENTO ESPUMA (FOAM) AND GROUND MARCONA ALMONDS
ALBARINO

FOURTH COURSE:
MANCHEGO ICE CREAM AND QUINCE PASTE SANDWICHES
FUNDADOR BRANDY

When you bring up Spanish cuisine, most people think of tapas. Well, it ain't just tapas anymore. Spain is quietly leading a culinary revolution, and foodies all over the world are making the pilgrimage to Barcelona.

Essentially, the Spanish are reinventing nouvelle cuisine. French nouvelle cuisine was a trend that began in France in the 1970s. It focused on fresh ingredients, simpler sauces, and food emphasizing natural flavors and aromas. It was a reaction to the traditional heavy and rich French food—from the cassoulet to the crème brûlée—with its focus on butter, cheese, and cream sauces (see Some Like It Haute menu).

France, however, looks back on its short-lived affair with nouvelle cuisine with some shame. Due to the tiny, overpriced portions and overly artistic displays on the plate, it became a thing of great snobbery. But now Spain has adopted the bastard stepchild and made it something fresh and interesting. The enfants terribles who instigated the movement are a handful of three-star Michelin-rated chefs, the most controversial and famous of whom is Ferran Adrià of the restaurant El Bulli, just outside Barcelona.

One of the most celebrated chefs in the world, Adrià is known for his five-hour, thirty-course meals. Adrià says that if nouvelle cuisine was impressionism, then what he is cooking is cubism. But most people would describe his cooking as surrealist. In fact, he is known as the Salvador Dalí of the food world. "The mosaics of Gaudí are my inspiration and my reference," says Adrià.

Adrià and his pals have invented things like caramelized eggs, Spanish pizza with mango and sea cucumbers, and, the most famous creation, *espuma*—Spanish for "foam." That's right, foam. *Espuma* is the culinary art of taking something that is mostly liquid and forcing compressed air into it so that it becomes foam.

This may be the most difficult meal in the book, but for the Gourmet Girl, it is the most exciting. It is guaranteed to impress. And don't worry, you don't have to make thirty courses. We're not going to make you do anything ridiculously hard, like, say, construct a miniature replica of La Sagrada Familia out of mashed potatoes. (Speaking of La Sagrada Familia, Gaudí's famous cathedral in Barcelona . . . if things get serious with your Gourmet Girl, we can't think of a better honeymoon than a trip to gourmet mecca—El Bulli. Just make sure to get your reservations well in advance—like at least a year. Oh, and while in Barcelona, be sure to take her to El Mercado Boqueria, the giant food market—every Gourmet Girl's dream.)

Many of the items on the To Buy list are hard to find, but they can be procured either at gourmet grocery stores or online. To make the foam, you will need a whipped-cream gun (Yes! Another gun!), also called a siphon (1-pint size), available at Sur la Table or Williams Sonoma. You can also find them online. You will also need an ice-cream maker, which you can find just about anywhere, as well as a fine mesh strainer. Lastly, pick up a couple of cordial glasses for the sherry. Ask at the store—they'll know what they are.

In honor of those rebellious chefs in Spain, we thought it appropriate to stretch the rules ourselves a little. Therefore, the following recipe requires you to buy not ten but eleven ingredients. That's just the kind of badass rule-breakers we are.

To Buy

10 ounces Manchego cheese (aged at least 6 months; available at gourmet stores or online)

1 (14-ounce) package quince paste (available at gourmet stores or online)

½ pound *bacalao* (Spanish salted cod)

2 whole quails (available at specialty stores or online)

2 Spanish olives stuffed with anchovies (available at gourmet stores or online)

1 box Knox unsweetened powdered gelatin (½ ounce or 2 envelopes)

1 (7-ounce) jar pimientos (or roasted red peppers)

½ pint heavy cream (½ cup)

2 cucumbers

5 kiwifruits

4 ounces Marcona almonds (Spanish almonds; available at gourmet stores or online)

Staples

1 quart (4 cups) plus ½ cup milk

½ teaspoon salt, plus more to taste

10 egg yolks

1 cup plus 3 tablespoons sugar, plus more to taste

2 cloves garlic

¼ cup olive oil

Pepper (to taste)

From the Liquor Store

1 bottle Cava (Spanish sparkling wine; see wine primer chapter in Part One)

1 bottle amontillado or fino sherry (do *not* buy cream sherry—it must be real Spanish sherry from Spain, not from Teaneck, NJ)

1 bottle Albarino (supertrendy Spanish white)

1 bottle Fundador brandy

Special Equipment

Whipped-cream gun (1 pint size)

Electric ice-cream maker

Fine mesh strainer

Three days before she arrives:

1. Take the bowl part of the electric ice-cream mixer, wash it (if you just bought it), and stick it in the freezer. It needs to freeze for a minimum of 24 hours.

Two days before she arrives:

2. To make the ice cream: Cut the rind off of the Manchego cheese and discard. In the food processor with a steel blade, grate the cheese very finely.

3. In a medium saucepan, bring 1 quart (4 cups) milk to a boil over high heat. Add a pinch of salt. Remove from heat.

4. Separate the yolks from the whites of 10 eggs: Break each egg gently over a small bowl, but capture the yolk in one of the halves of the shell. Gently pass the egg yolk back and forth between the shell halves, letting the white of the egg flow into the bowl.

When nothing but yolk remains in the shells, dump it into a medium mixing bowl and throw the egg whites away.

5. With an electric hand mixer, beat the 10 egg yolks. Mix in 1 cup sugar and then ½ cup cold milk. Then slowly mix in the hot milk a little at a time until thoroughly incorporated.

6. Transfer mixture back to the medium saucepan and cook over low heat for 20 minutes, stirring constantly (do not let it come to a boil). Slowly add the grated Manchego cheese, continuing to stir constantly. When the mixture has thickened and the cheese has completely incorporated, strain through a fine mesh strainer.

7. Wash the medium mixing bowl and transfer the egg and Manchego mixture to the bowl. Cover with foil or plastic wrap, and let chill overnight in the fridge. (It will be used to make the ice cream.)

8. Cut the quince paste into ¼-inch slices. Cover with plastic wrap and put in the freezer overnight.

One day before she arrives:

9:00 A.M.

9. Soak the *bacalao* in cold water in a small mixing bowl or stockpot in the fridge, covered with plastic wrap. Soak it for at least 12 hours, changing the water every 4 hours. At the end of the 12 hours, change the water and leave to soak overnight.

9:15 A.M.

10. To prepare the quail: Crush 2 cloves of garlic. In a small bowl, mix together ¼ cup olive oil and the crushed garlic.

11. Lay the quails in a 9x13-inch glass baking dish and massage them thoroughly with the oil and garlic mixture. Lightly sprinkle with salt and pepper.

12. Stuff each quail with an anchovy-stuffed olive and set them in the baking dish.

13. Cover the dish of quails with plastic wrap and stick in the fridge to marinate overnight.

9:45 A.M.

14. Back to the ice cream: Take the frozen bowl of the ice-cream maker out of the freezer.

15. Insert the top part of the ice-cream maker and pour in the Manchego ice-cream mix, according to the ice-cream maker instructions.

16. Turn on and allow the ice-cream maker to run according to instructions (about 30 to 40 minutes).

10:45 A.M.

17. When it's done, transfer back to the medium mixing bowl (clean and dry the bowl first), cover with plastic wrap, and freeze overnight.

The day of the date, before she arrives:

4:45

18. Chill the Cava and Albarino.

19. Change the water out one last time on the *bacalao,* but use warm water instead of cold, which will really draw out the salt. Then pat it dry, transfer to a large mixing bowl, and refrigerate until ready to serve. Wash and dry the small mixing bowl.

5:00

20. Take the ice cream and the frozen quince paste slices out of the freezer.

21. Spread the ice cream on the quince paste slices and make "sandwiches." (You may need to let the ice cream soften a little in order to make it easier to work with.)

22. Put the ice-cream sandwiches on a plate, wrap in plastic wrap, and put in the freezer until ready to serve.

5:45

23. Wash and dry the medium mixing bowl and empty 2 envelopes (½ ounce) of unsweetened powdered gelatin into it. Add ½ cup cool water, stir, and let sit for 5 minutes.

24. In a food processor, puree 7 ounces pimientos until smooth. Strain through a fine mesh strainer into a small mixing bowl. It should look like very watery tomato soup.

25. Stir in the gelatin, ½ teaspoon salt, 3 tablespoons sugar, ½ cup water, and ½ cup heavy cream. Pour mixture into the whipped-cream gun. Transfer to the fridge to chill.

6:30

26. To prepare the gazpacho, peel the cucumbers with a vegetable peeler and then chop them in a food processor.

27. Peel the kiwis, add to the food processor, and pulse until blended. Add pinches of salt and sugar to taste, and then pulse a couple more times. Transfer to 2 soup bowls, cover with plastic wrap, and stick in the fridge to chill.

7:15

28. Preheat the oven to 400 degrees.

29. Spread the 4 ounces of Marcona almonds on a baking sheet and toast for 8 to 10 minutes at 400 degrees.

30. Remove the baking sheet from the oven and set aside to allow the almonds to cool. Leave the oven set at 400 degrees.

31. In the food processor, chop the toasted, cooled almonds finely with a steel blade. Set aside.

After she arrives:

8:00

First course:

32. Pop open the Cava and serve in Champagne glasses.

33. Serve the gazpacho. If you have crushed ice, add some to the gazpacho; otherwise, just add a few ice cubes to each bowl.

Second course:

34. Take the quail from the refrigerator and remove plastic wrap. Bake quail for about 15 minutes at 400 degrees. Check to see if it's done by poking it with a knife (make sure you test on your quail, not hers). If the meat looks raw inside, let it cook longer. While you're waiting, have another glass of Cava. Remove the quail from the oven and serve with the sherry in cordial glasses.

Third course:

35. Arrange slices of *bacalao* on dinner plates. Screw a charger canister into the whipped-cream gun. Hold the whipped cream gun upside down over the sink and let some of the foam shoot out into the sink. It won't be foam at first—it will look like an orangey-red liquid. Continue until you get the consistency of whipped cream (it may take a minute or so). Then decorate the *bacalao* with little peaks of the pimiento foam. Sprinkle the ground almonds lightly on top. Serve with the Albarino (in wineglasses).

Fourth course:

36. For the final course, pour the brandy into snifters and serve the ice-cream sandwiches on plates.

Bonus Points

Procure some extra funky dishes and serving utensils to push the artistic envelope on this meal. For example, Crate & Barrel has a great glass that would be perfect for the sherry. It's called the Roly Rocks and is designed to roll around without tipping (like that old toy, the Weeble). Look for wacky bowls in the shape of pumpkins, leaves, or what have you, or platters made out of wood or metal. Think outside the box and find creative, interesting ways to serve each course.

So You Got Lucky
Recipes for Breakfast

Morning, slugger.

Obviously, you did something right. You spent some time getting to know a lovely lady, began to understand her particular qualities, prepared a meal that was right up her alley, and managed to get through the evening without saying something hideous, thereby destroying the reputable yet intriguing image that you worked so hard to create. And now here she is, snuggled into your queen-size bed, clutching the sheet up under her sleeping chin, her head perched delicately on the one good pillowcase your mother gave you and looking for all the world like she belongs right there, doing just that. Poetry, isn't it?

If you think that you got points for the fabulous spread you laid out last night, however, wait until she shuffles out to the kitchen nook and sees what you've got planned this morning. Time to make the lady breakfast.

We're not going to complicate this situation unnecessarily. For one thing, if you stayed up late delving into deeper issues, you've probably got a few cobwebs drifting around in your brain right about now, especially if said conversation was fueled by that stop you made at the liquor store. So let's make this as straightforward as we can.

We've given you one breakfast for each type of Girl. Find your Girl. Make the breakfast. If you're an optimist, you already bought the necessary ingredients ahead of time and you're all set. If the whole thing was a little, um . . . unexpected, you're still not lost. Just tell her that you are going to get her a fresh latte and you will be right back. You can whip through the express lane, grab her latte (don't forget to ask her how she likes it), and be back before she knows it. Just in case, leave her *two* fresh towels and a new bar of soap at the foot of the bed, in case she wants to take a shower. You *did* clean the shower, right?

If you want to make the coffee at home, use a coffeemaker, a French press, or a vacuum coffeemaker. If you don't have any one of these three, find a good coffee shop. Stat. Don't try anything foolish, like filtering coffee through a paper towel. You aren't camping. You have *company*.

If you are doing a recipe that requires eggs to be made in one of several styles (Academic, Indie, or Girl Next Door), see our Guide to Eggs at the end of the chapter.

Academic Girl: Traditional British Breakfast

BACON

SAUSAGE

EGGS

GRILLED TOMATOES

TOAST

MUSHROOMS

BAKED BEANS

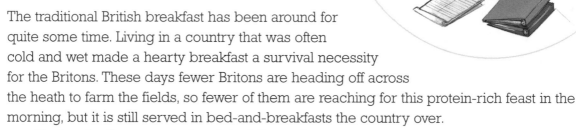

The traditional British breakfast has been around for quite some time. Living in a country that was often cold and wet made a hearty breakfast a survival necessity for the Britons. These days fewer Britons are heading off across the heath to farm the fields, so fewer of them are reaching for this protein-rich feast in the morning, but it is still served in bed-and-breakfasts the country over.

During the Saxon period and the Middle Ages, breakfast would have consisted of cold meat or preserved fish, bread, and a mug of ale or wine. It may seem questionable now to start the day with an alcoholic drink, but in those days it was safer than most well water, which could be sullied by animal droppings. In Scotland it wasn't uncommon to have a drop of whisky with breakfast, which makes sense if you have ever walked out of the house into a damp and dreary Scottish morning.

Queen Elizabeth I was said to enjoy beef and ale at the start of the day. However, more dairy produce was starting to enter the breakfast menu during the Tudor period, including butter and cheese. Surprisingly, tea and coffee were unknown in regional Britain before the seventeenth century, and then only as a beverage for the well-heeled. Even after the fashionable rich stopped drinking liquor with breakfast, the poorer folk still washed their eggs and sausage down with ale well into the eighteenth century.

The large country breakfast we know today—with eggs, poultry, meat, and cold cuts—began in the eighteenth century, partly out of necessity and partly as a social institution among the wealthy. With large groups heading out for a day of hunting among the hedgerows, breakfast became a huge event, complete with its own set of foods, traditions, and tableware.

To Buy

2 medium tomatoes

1 bunch fresh basil (¼ cup chopped)

1 package sausages (pick your favorite kind, either uncooked or precooked)

6 large or 8 medium mushrooms

1 (12-ounce) can baked beans

1 loaf of bread

Jam or jelly (look for a gourmet brand—it's worth a few extra dimes)

Tea (get black tea, such as English Breakfast or Earl Grey)

Staples

1 teaspoon olive oil

2 teaspoons butter

½ onion

1. Preheat the oven to 450 degrees.

2. Wash the tomatoes and cut them into eight wedges. Peel an onion and chop up half of it. Chop up enough basil to make ¼ cup. Mix the tomatoes, onions, 1 teaspoon olive oil, and the basil in a bowl until everything is covered in oil. Wrap the mixture up in foil and place in the oven for 15 to 20 minutes or until the onion is soft.

3. Put about a tablespoon of olive oil in a frying pan and add 2 sausages. If they were precooked, they will only need to be browned. If they are uncooked, you will need to cook them all the way through. Melt 2 teaspoons butter in a medium saucepan. Chop up the mushrooms and sauté them in the butter until soft. Meanwhile, heat the baked beans in a small saucepan. Ask her how she wants her eggs. Once the sausage is done, cook up the eggs in the same pan. Toast 4 slices of bread.

4. Serve the sausages, tomatoes, eggs, and mushrooms all together on one plate. Stack the toast on a plate and serve with butter, jam, and coffee or tea.

Athletic Girl: Power Smoothie

PROTEIN SMOOTHIE WITH STRAWBERRIES
AND BANANA

To Buy

1 small container protein powder
    (3 tablespoons)
1 banana
2 tablespoons Splenda, Sweet & Low,
    or Equal
1 package frozen strawberries (1 cup)
Almonds (optional)

Staples

Milk (2 cups)

Mix 3 tablespoons (or one scoop, if it comes with one) protein powder, 1 chopped-up banana, 2 tablespoons sweetener, 1 cup frozen strawberries, and 2 cups milk in a food processor. Blend and serve. Note: If she's on the Zone diet, add 6 almonds.

Career Girl: Wall Street Bagels

BAGELS WITH CREAM CHEESE AND LOX
ORANGE JUICE

To Buy

4 assorted bagels

1 tub low-fat cream cheese

1 package lox (smoked salmon)

1 Bermuda onion

1 tomato

1 small jar capers

1 bottle or carton orange juice

1. Ask her what kind of bagel she wants and if she wants it toasted.

2. Cut the Bermuda onion and the tomato into thin slices.

3. Spread the cream cheese on the bagel, then layer the lox, onion, and tomato on top. Sprinkle capers over the whole thing and serve with a glass of orange juice.

Girl Next Door: Country Kitchen Breakfast

PANCAKES

HASH BROWNS

SAUSAGE OR BACON

EGGS

ORANGE JUICE

To Buy

1 bell pepper

1 bag frozen hash browns

1 box pancake mix

1 can frozen or one bottle fresh orange juice

1 package sausage or bacon

Staples

1 onion

6 eggs

2 tablespoons butter

Salt (to taste)

Pepper (to taste)

1. Preheat the oven to 200 degrees.

2. Cut open the bell pepper and remove seeds. Chop up the onion and bell pepper. Heat 2 tablespoons butter in a medium saucepan over medium heat. Put the onion and peppers in the pan for about 2 minutes. Add the hash browns and cook for as long as the package directs. Once they are done, pour them into an oven-safe dish or bowl, cover it with foil, and place it in the oven to keep them warm.

3. While the hash browns are cooking, fry up the bacon or sausage in the frying pan, then transfer to a plate and keep warm in the oven.

4. Stir up the pancakes, following the directions on the package. Ask her how she wants her eggs. (See the guide to eggs at the end of the chapter.) If your frying pan is big enough, make the eggs and the pancakes side by side. Otherwise, make the pancakes first and keep them warm in the oven. Season the eggs with just a little salt and pepper.

5. Serve the pancakes, eggs, hash browns, and sausage or bacon all on one plate with coffee and orange juice.

Gourmet Girl: Hakuna Frittata

POTATO, PROSCIUTTO, AND GORGONZOLA
   FRITTATA
BROILED GRAPEFRUIT
FRESH-SQUEEZED ORANGE JUICE

A frittata is basically an omelet that you finish under the broiler. It's a little more work, but if you can get this one on the breakfast table, it's no worries for the rest of your days. Note that you will need a juice squeezer for this one.

To Buy

5 medium red potatoes

8 juice oranges

3 ounces prosciutto, cut into strips

1 bunch fresh rosemary

2 ounces Gorgonzola cheese

1 pink grapefruit

1 box or package brown sugar (2 tablespoons)

Staples

2 tablespoons olive oil

½ teaspoon salt

¼ teaspoon pepper

10 eggs

Special Equipment

Juicer

1. Fill the medium saucepan ⅔ of the way with water and add ½ teaspoon salt. Parboil the potatoes in salted water for about 10 minutes. ''Parboil'' means to cook them only partially, so don't worry if they are still firm when you take them out.

2. Using the juicer, squeeze the oranges to make two glasses of fresh orange juice. Chill in the fridge.

3. Drain the potatoes and rinse them under cold water until they are cool enough to handle. Cut them into ½-inch-thick slices, then chop them coarsely.

4. In an ovenproof frying pan, heat 2 tablespoons olive oil over medium heat. Add the potatoes, ½ teaspoon salt, and ¼ teaspoon pepper. Cook, turning the potatoes occasionally, until they are browned and tender, about 12 to 15 minutes. Spread them out to make an even layer in the bottom of the pan.

5. Preheat the broiler.

6. In a medium mixing bowl, beat the eggs with a little salt and pepper. If it isn't already, chop the prosciutto into long, thin slices. Chop enough rosemary to make 2 teaspoons. Add the prosciutto and the rosemary to the eggs and reduce the heat to medium-low. As with an omelet, you don't want to scramble or flip the eggs. Slip a metal spatula under the edge of the eggs and allow the liquid to flow down to the pan. Keep lifting each side of the eggs, letting the uncooked egg mixture flow down and cook underneath. Continue until the top is almost set, about 5 minutes. Crumble up the Gorgonzola and sprinkle on top.

7. Slice the grapefruit in half and put the halves peel-side-down in the 9-inch square glass baking dish. Sprinkle 1 tablespoon brown sugar on each half. Slide it under the broiler and let it broil until nicely browned—watch it, it shouldn't take more than a minute at most.

8. Stick the frittata about 6 inches from the broiler and cook until the top is set, about a minute.

9. Serve the frittata out of the pan, like a deep-dish pizza, with the chilled glasses of orange juice.

Granola Girl: Tofu Scramble

To Buy (organic whenever possible)

1 small red bell pepper

1 small green bell pepper

1 small tomato

1 small red onion

1 small red potato

1 (14-ounce) package firm tofu

1 small container sesame seeds

1 small package cheddar cheese (for Vegan Girl
   substitute soy cheese)

1 loaf whole-grain bread

1 small jar jam

Staples

2 tablespoons olive oil

Butter (to serve at table)

Salt and pepper

1. Slice the peppers in half and remove the seeds. Chop up half of the red pepper, half of the green pepper, the tomato, the potato, and about a quarter of the red onion, and toss them into a skillet with 2 tablespoons olive oil. Sauté them for 3 to 4 minutes over high heat.

2. Drain and rinse the tofu. Crumble it by squeezing it through your fingers. Add all the crumbled tofu to the skillet along with ¼ cup of the sesame seeds. Season with salt and pepper. Stir and cook for 2 to 3 minutes. If your Girl eats cheese, sprinkle ½ cup of cheese over the top just before you take it out. Stir long enough for the cheese to melt.

3. Serve the scramble with the whole-grain bread, butter, and jam.

Indie Girl: My Breakfast with Blassie

ORANGE JUICE
EGGS
HAM, BACON, OR SAUSAGE
PANCAKES
MAPLE SYRUP

High-art independent film meets breakfast kitsch with the film *My Breakfast with Blassie,* starring confrontational comedian Andy Kaufman and professional wrestler Freddie Blassie, famous for his novelty record "Pencil-Necked Geeks." Produced by Blassie's manager, Johnny Legend, the film is a parody of the famous independent film *My Dinner with Andre* and was filmed at the well known Los Angeles dive cafe Sambo's. Kaufman and Blassie improvised over breakfast for an hour, discussing such rarefied topics as wrestling (Kaufman's success with wrestling women is discussed at length), keeping your hands clean, why not to eat pancakes or waffles, giving autographs to fans, and other topics not nearly as intellectual as the ones discussed by actor Wallace Shawn and director Andre Gregory in the original.

Sambo's, a chain once numbering in the hundreds, is now down to a single location in Los Angeles. The menu features such items as "Papa Jumbo's Special: Choice of fruit juice, two fresh ranch eggs, ham, bacon, or sausage, six delicious Sambo's cakes, syrup and tiger butter, all for $1.35." The current owners are trying to restart the troubled chain, although the name is, predictably, a challenge.

Get a copy of the movie ahead of time if you can. It is still available on the Internet in VHS format. Serve breakfast in bed while watching the movie and speculating on the relative sanity of pseudo-celebrities.

To Buy

1 bottle or carton (1 pint or larger) orange, apple, or grapefruit juice

1 package ham, bacon, or sausage

1 box pancake mix

1 bottle maple syrup

Staples

6 eggs

Butter (per the instructions on the pancake mix)

Milk (per the instructions on the pancake mix)

1. Mix up the pancake mix, following the instructions on the box. Ask her how she wants her eggs. (Follow the instructions in the Guide to Eggs at the end of the chapter.)

2. If your frying pan is big enough, cook the meat and the pancakes side by side. If not, make the meat first, transfer to a plate, and keep warm in a 200-degree oven.

3. Once the pancakes and meat are done, make the eggs in the frying pan.

4. Serve it all with coffee and juice.

Party Girl: Hair of the Dog

HUEVOS RANCHEROS
BLOODY MARYS

If you've had a party night with a Party Girl, you might not be feeling your best when the sun peeps into your bedroom the next morning. The solution to overimbibing is pretty simple—imbibe some more. Party People call it the "hair of the dog."

Actually, taking a little of the "hair of the dog that bit you" has been popular advice since ancient times, based on the homeopathic principle of *Similia similibus curantur* (like cures like). In the beginning, it was literally a cure for dog bites, but as a cure for hangovers, it has many ardent supporters. Whether or not it has any medical value, having a little slug of vodka in the morning will definitely make it harder to feel your headache. Until the afternoon, at least.

Note that you can't buy alcohol on Sunday mornings in some locales, so we suggest picking up the booze the day before. Of course, if you are dating the Party Girl, stocking the liquor cabinet is never a bad idea.

Huevos rancheros is a Mexican classic, and going south of the border with the Party Girl is always a good idea, especially when the recipe is this easy.

To Buy

1 (16-ounce) can tomatoes

4 flour tortillas

1 small container chile powder (optional)

Chile peppers to taste (Serrano, habañero, jalapeño)

8 ounces Monterey Jack or Manchego cheese, shredded

1 (12-ounce) can black beans

1 bottle Bloody Mary mix

1 bottle vodka

Staples

4 eggs

¼ onion

3 cloves garlic

1 tablespoon olive oil

1. Start with the Bloody Marys. Fill 2 glasses with ice. Pour in 2 ounces vodka and fill to the top with Bloody Mary mix. You can make your own Bloody Mary mix, if you want (1 teaspoon horseradish, 3 dashes Tabasco sauce, 3 dashes Worcestershire, dash lime juice, 3 dashes celery salt, 3 dashes pepper, and 8 ounces tomato juice for each drink), but really, it's pretty early for that much effort, don't you think?

2. Chop up ¼ of an onion and the chile peppers. Chop 3 cloves garlic into tiny pieces or mash them with a garlic press.

3. Set a medium saucepan on high heat and add 1 tablespoon olive oil. Add the onion, chile peppers, garlic, the can of tomatoes, and a pinch of chile powder. Once the sauce boils, reduce the heat and simmer for about 10 minutes.

4. Warm up the beans in a small saucepan or in the microwave.

5. Put a little oil in a frying pan and fry two tortillas, about 30 seconds a side. Put the tortillas on a plate, then fry two eggs, sunny-side up, without cooking the yolk. Place one egg on top of each tortilla, then cover it with sauce. The hot sauce will cook the egg yolk. Sprinkle the shredded cheese on top.

6. Repeat the previous step for the other plate.

7. Ladle some beans onto each plate and serve.

Progressive Girl: Florentine Omelet

To Buy

1 package frozen spinach

6 large mushrooms

8 ounces Monterey Jack cheese

1 package hollandaise sauce mix

1 loaf whole-wheat bread

1 jar your favorite jam

Staples

2 tablespoons butter

¼ cup chopped onion

6 eggs

Salt and pepper (to taste)

1. The spinach needs to be defrosted, so defrost it in the microwave. Once it is unfrozen, put it in a clean dish towel and wring as much water out as possible. This might ruin the dish towel, so don't use the one your mom gave you. Use the one your ex-girlfriend gave you.

2. Follow the directions on the hollandaise sauce package and stir it up in a medium saucepan.

3. Preheat the oven to 200 degrees.

4. Grate up enough cheese to make 1 cup.

5. Chop up enough mushrooms to make 1 cup and enough onion to make ¼ cup. Sauté them both in 2 tablespoons butter until the onions are translucent. Add the spinach, stir, and turn the heat down low. Season with salt and pepper.

6. Mix up 6 eggs in a bowl. Pour half the mixture into a small saucepan (an omelet pan is ideal, of course) and let it cook for a minute. The key to an omelet is not to flip or scramble it. You slide the spatula under the edge of the cooked part and let the uncooked part swoosh around it, down to the surface of the pan. Keep sliding the spatula around the edge on all sides, letting the uncooked egg flow down, building up the fluffy, cooked omelet. It takes a little practice, but the eggs are pretty forgiving. When the eggs are almost entirely cooked (it can be a little runny on top), you are ready. Put half the spinach mixture on top, then sprinkle half the cheese on top of that. Fold the eggs in half over it. Place the omelet on an oven-safe plate and put in the oven to keep warm. Repeat with the other half of the eggs and filling.

7. When both omelets are done, spoon hollandaise sauce over both and serve with whole-wheat toast, butter, and jam.

Uptown Girl: Ladies Who Brunch

EGGS BENEDICT
FRESH-SQUEEZED ORANGE JUICE

To Buy

1 lemon

4 pieces Canadian-style bacon

2 English muffins

1 bunch chives (2 tablespoons chopped)

8 juice oranges or 1 bottle fresh-squeezed
  orange juice (not from concentrate)

Staples

7 eggs

½ cup butter

Salt and pepper

1. If you are squeezing the oranges yourself, do it now and put it in the refrigerator to chill.

2. Chop up enough chives to make about 2 tablespoons.

3. Unlike the Progressive Girl, you can't get away with prefab hollandaise this time. If you made "Dinner on the Yacht" last night, you might have some sauce left over that you can use. Otherwise, here's how to make it from scratch: Cut the lemon in half through the middle and fork out the seeds. Squeeze enough lemon juice to make 2 tablespoons. In a microwave-safe bowl, melt ½ cup butter in the microwave on high. Crack each egg over the sink and allow the white of the egg to fall into the drain as you pass the yolk back and forth between the eggshell halves. Put each yolk into a metal mixing bowl. With a wire whisk, mix in the fresh lemon juice. Put the bowl on top of a medium saucepan of boiling water (this is why you need a metal mixing bowl). Turn the heat down to medium. Slowly add the melted butter in a steady stream, whisking as you go. Salt and pepper to taste. Remove from heat and cover it to keep the heat in.

4. Turn the oven on to broil.

5. Now, the poached eggs. Refill the medium saucepan with 3 inches of water. Bring the water to a gentle simmer. Carefully break 4 eggs into the simmering water, and allow them to cook for 2½ to 3 minutes. The yolks should still be soft in the center. Remove eggs from water with a slotted spoon and set on a warm plate.

6. While the eggs are poaching, brown the bacon in a frying pan over medium-high heat. Split and toast the English muffins.

7. Spread butter over the English muffins, and put two muffin halves on each plate. Top each one with a piece of Canadian bacon and a poached egg. Cover with hollandaise sauce. Sprinkle with chopped chives and serve immediately.

Guide to Eggs

Scrambled. Crack the eggs into a small mixing bowl. Add a little salt and pepper. Scramble (beat) with a wire whisk or a fork until well blended. Drop a tablespoon of butter into a wide saucepan or frying pan on medium heat. Pour the eggs into the saucepan. Continue stirring eggs until they are fully cooked.

Sunny-side up. Drop a tablespoon of butter into a wide saucepan or frying pan on medium heat. Crack the eggs on the edge of the pan and drop directly into the saucepan. The yolk should remain uncooked, so keep an eye on the white. When it is fully set and the yolk is just starting to thicken, slide a metal spatula under the eggs and serve.

Over easy. Drop a tablespoon of butter into a wide saucepan or frying pan on medium heat. Crack the eggs on the edge of the pan and drop directly into the saucepan. When the white is fully set and the yolk is starting to thicken, slide a metal spatula under the eggs and gently flip them over. You want to yolk to be very runny, so leave them in the pan for only about 15 seconds longer. Slide the spatula under them and serve them onto a plate.

Over medium. Drop a tablespoon of butter into a wide saucepan or frying pan on medium heat. Crack the eggs on the edge of the pan and drop directly into the saucepan. When the white is fully set and the yolk is starting to thicken, slide a metal spatula under the eggs and gently flip them over. The yolk should be only a little bit runny, so leave them on the skillet for only about 30 seconds. Slide the spatula under them and serve them onto a plate.

Over hard. Drop a tablespoon of butter into a wide saucepan or frying pan on medium heat. Crack the eggs on the edge of the pan and drop directly into the saucepan. When the white is fully opaque and the yolk is starting to glaze over, slide a metal spatula under the eggs and gently flip them over. The yolk should be fully cooked, so leave them on the skillet for about a minute. Slide the spatula under them and serve them onto a plate.

Poached. Fill a medium saucepan with 3 inches of water. Bring the water to a gentle simmer. Carefully break 4 eggs into the simmering water, and allow them to cook for 2½ to 3 minutes. The yolks should still be soft in the center. Remove eggs from the water with a slotted spoon and set on a warm plate or in a shallow cup or bowl. Poaching eggs is much easier with an egg poaching pan—a good investment if you plan to be doing this a lot.

About the Authors

Ann Marie Michaels and **Drew Campbell** were married in 1997. Despite a shared fondness for vodka martinis and cutthroat Scrabble, they soon realized they were better writing partners than life partners. Their no-kids-no-foul marriage dissolved in 2003, and the fact that they didn't argue over a single CD should tell you something. With the marital storm safely weathered, however, they soon discovered something they did have in common: more than thirty-five years of combined dating experience. Writing a dating cookbook was the natural next step.

Ann Marie's passion for food and cooking came from her sister, a self-taught gourmet chef who refuses to acknowledge the existence of the *word* "margarine," let alone the substance. Drew learned to make Salisbury steak from his mother and held his first dinner party in the tenth grade—a casual affair that his father gleefully photographed, severely reducing Drew's chances of getting lucky that night, which, let's face it, were not that great to begin with. Ann Marie's recent culinary triumphs included a "Jew-au," a deli-style Hawaiian feast.

Drew, a Progressive Guy, has spent a lifetime in the theater world, gaining his BA in theater from Brown University and MFA in theatrical technology from the University of Illinois, Champaign-Urbana. He has worked as a technician, designer, high-school teacher, college professor, video editor, and professional musician. After a four-year stint at Universal Studios Hollywood, he has joined the faculty of the University of Texas at Austin, teaching theatrical technology. He has authored two guides to the backstage world of show business: *Technical Theater for Nontechnical People* and *Technical Film and TV for Nontechnical People.* He married the lovely and Progressive Valerie on July 23, 2004.

Ann Marie earned a BS in film from the University of Texas at Austin. Since then, she has worked for some of the top ad agencies and Internet consulting firms in the world. A Gourmet/Indie Girl hybrid, she now lives in Los Angeles with her dog, Maude, who is also a Gourmet Girl (evidenced by her love of foie gras and cassoulet). Ann Marie is an expert on pop culture, and is addicted to her TiVo and iPod. She freelances as an interactive producer and is working on a novel. This is her first book.